The English Village Church

The English Village Church

R.J. BROWN

ROBERT HALE · LONDON

Typeset by
Derek Doyle & Associates, Mold, Flintshire.
Printed in Great Britain by
St Edmundsbury Press, Bury St Edmunds, Suffolk
Bound by WBC Book Manufacturers Limited, Bridgend.

Contents

Illustrations

Note

Illustration references appear within parentheses throughout the text.

Acknowledgements

Although I have visited many hundreds of churches in the preparation of this book it has not been possible to visit all the churches described or mentioned. I am therefore greatly indebted to all the writers mentioned in the Bibliography and to all those other authors and in particular those writers of the guides produced by so many churches, who have assisted in some way with the production of *The English Village Church*. In particular I would like to acknowledge the help given by the works of Lawrence E. Jones, whose books *The Beauty of English Churches* and the *Observer's Old English Churches* have proved invaluable, to Alec Clifton-Taylor's book *The Pattern of English Building* for its help on materials, to F.H. Crossley, and F.E. Howard for their book *English Church Woodwork* and to Sir Nikolaus Pevsner's monumental series *The Buildings of England*, essential both in the field and for reference.

In addition I would like to thank my wife for her continuing assistance and encouragement throughout, and in particular for typing and correcting the draft.

Glossary

abacus	flat member on the top of the capital of a pier.
acanthus	decorative leaf-form sculpted on Corinthian capitals.
annulet	a narrow ring encircling a circular pier or detached shaft.
apse	semicircular or polygonal east end of a church, usually vaulted.
arabesque	surface decoration in fanciful, flowing lines interspersed with formal motifs.
arcade	series of arches, either open or blind, supported by columns or piers.
ashlar	masonry of large blocks wrought even on all faces with square edges.
ashlar piece	a short vertical timber member connecting rafter to inner wall plate.
aumbry	cupboard or recess to hold sacred vessels.
ballflower	form of fourteenth-century globular decoration with three incurved flower petals enclosing a small ball. Characteristic of the Decorated period.
baluster	small pillar, usually circular and swelling in middle or towards the bottom, used by Anglo-Saxon builders in window-openings.
base	lowest section of a pier or column.
battlement	a parapet with rectangular indentations at regular intervals, used for its decorative effect.
bay	space between two piers of an arcade.

beakhead	Norman motif formed of full-face bird or beast heads set in a row on a moulding, with beaks biting into moulding.
belfry	roof turret to hang bells in.
billet	motif on Norman hollow mouldings, which consists of square or cylindrical elements (alternately projecting and recessed) arranged in a chequerboard pattern.
boss	ornamental projection at the intersections of ceiling ribs.
brattishing	ornamental cresting found on late Gothic screens, usually formed of conventional leaves.
buttress	projection from a wall to resist outward thrust and provide additional strength.
cable moulding	Norman moulding shaped like twisted rope.
capital	the crowning member of a column or pier, giving support to superimposed arches or vaulting ribs.
caryatid	figure of a woman used as a pillar.
chancel	from *cancellus*, 'screen', because the eastern limb of a parish church was isolated by a screen.
chevron	Norman moulding in form of a zig-zag.
clerestory	the uppermost storey of the nave above the aisles pierced with windows.
column	a classical, upright structural member, round in section with shaft, capital and usually a base.
corbel	a stone projecting from a wall and supporting a roof vault or other feature, usually carved or moulded.
corbel table	row of corbels supporting a parapet or cornice.
crockets	in Gothic architecture, leaf-shaped projections placed equidistantly along the angles of spires, pinnacles, canopies, etc.
crossing	space at the intersection of nave, transepts, and chancel of a cruciform church.
cupola	small dome raised on pillars or a solid drum.
cusps	small pointed intersections between lobes or

	foils of tracery used to form trefoils, quatrefoils, etc.
diamond ornament	Norman decoration in the form of continuous band of diamond shapes.
diaper work	an all-over surface decoration of repeated square or lozenge shapes.
dog-tooth	Early English decoration in the form of four-pointed stars with raised centres set continuously along a hollow moulding.
dripstone	projecting moulding over doorways or windows to carry off water. Also known as a hood-mould and, when square, as a label.
embrasures	openings between two merlons of a battlemented parapet.
fan vault	late Gothic roof or ceiling in which the curvature of the ribs forms a series of fans.
fenestration	window arrangement.
fillet	narrow, flat band running down a pier or along a moulding.
finial	decorative termination to a pinnacle, canopy, etc.
flushwork	decorative use of knapped flints in surrounds of dressed stone to form tracery or lettering.
flying buttresses	buttress arched out from a wall to carry roof pressure.
foliated	carved with leaf shapes.
four-centred arch	depressed arch of a form struck from four centres.
freestone	stone of grain fine enough to be cut freely in any direction.
groin	plain edge at the intersection of two vaults.
herringbone	masonry or brickwork laid on the diagonal often alternating with opposing courses.
hood-mould	*see* dripstone.
impost	capital on top of pier from which the arch springs.
jamb	side of doorway or window.

label-stop	ornamental feature at the end of a dripstone.
lancet	slender pointed window in Early English churches.
long and short work	quoins consisting of stones placed with long sides alternating vertically and horizontally.
louvres	sloping boards fitted into belfry openings to allow the sound of the bells to come through.
lozenge	diamond shape.
lucarne	a vertical opening in a spire gabled and usually traceried but never glazed.
mensa	the stone slab of an altar.
merlons	the raised portion of a battlement.
moulding	the forming of continuous rounds and hollows to enrich walls, piers, arches, etc. into which they are cut.
mullion	vertical structural member sub-dividing a window.
nailhead	late Norman decoration in the form of square elements with raised centres, forming pyramid shapes.
narthex	a single-storey vestibule extending across the west end of a church.
niche	recess in a wall for a statue.
ogee	curve of double flexure, partly convex, partly concave.
parapet	part of the external wall of a building extending above the eaves of a roof.
parclose	a screen separating chapel or aisle from the main church.
pier	large masonry or brick support, often for an arch.
pillar	a free-standing upright member of any section but not conforming to one of the classical orders.
plinth	projecting base of pier, wall, etc.
poppyhead	*fleur-de-lis* finial on a bench-end.
quoins	dressed stones at the angles of buildings.

respond	half-pillar or corbelled termination to an arcade.
rib	a member, usually moulded, dividing the compartments of a vault or roof.
rood	a cross or crucifix.
rubble	masonry in which the stones are wholly or partially in a rough state; can be coursed or random (uncoursed stones in a random pattern).
rustication	treatment of joints of masonry to give an impression of strength; the joints usually recessed by v-section chamfering.
saddleback	tower roof shaped like a timber gable.
sanctuary	the part of the church in which the High Altar stands.
shaft	upright member of round section, especially the main part of a classical column.
truss	braced framework of timbers placed at intervals along the roof carrying the purlins which support the common rafters.
soffit	underside of an arch.
spandrel	spaces either side of the heads of arches, between the head of the arch and the bay that contains it, or the triangular-shaped blocking between the posts and beams of screens, roofs, etc. Sometimes decorated.
spirelight	*see* lucarne.
stair-turret	stone stairway giving access to the tower stages.
stiff-leaf	Early English decoration which resembles stiff stalks of curling leaves.
string course	horizontal band or moulding on the face of a wall, often projecting and usually continuous.
tabernacle work	ornamentally carved canopy-work over church stalls, fonts, niches etc.
tie-beam	beam forming the base of a roof-truss spanning the space from wall to wall.
tracery	curved patterns in stone or wood at the head of Gothic windows; also used in filling in panels

	in screens, doors, bench-ends etc.
transept	transverse (usually north or south) arm of a cruciform church.
triforium	an arcaded passage in a wall (or blank arcading) above the main arcade and below the clerestory.
tympanum	enclosed space between the lintel of a doorway and the head of the doorway arch in Norman and Gothic buildings; often filled with sculpture.
vault	arched ceiling or roof, either groined, as in Romanesque architecture, or ribbed as in all Gothic architecture.
voussoir	a wedge-shaped stone forming part of the inner curve of an arch.
wall plate	a continuous timber along the top of the wall which receives the ends of the rafters.
waterhold	hollow between two cylindrical or convex mouldings at the base of a pillar.
weatherboarding	external wall covering formed of timber boards, usually fixed horizontally and generally overlapping.
webbing	stone filling between the ribs of a vaulted ceiling or roof.
zig-zag	*see* chevron.

Architectural Periods

The styles in English architecture do not fall into any hard-and-fast periods, and it must be remembered that there is a considerable overlapping of styles between the various periods. Moreover, many different styles persisted simultaneously. The following will serve as a guide to the approximate dates of the principal phases.

Saxon	600 to 1066	} Romanesque	600 to 1200
Norman	1066 to 1190		
Transitional	1150 to 1200		
Early English	1200 to 1280	} Gothic	1200 to 1550
Decorated	1280 to 1380		
Perpendicular	1380 to 1550		
Early Tudor	1500 to 1550		
Late Tudor	1550 to 1600	} Renaissance	1550 to 1690
Stuart	1600 to 1690		
Hanoverian	1690 to 1830	Classical	1600 to 1830

*The English
Village Church*

1 The Setting

The village church seems to possess the ability to harmonize with the landscape in which it is set, often appearing to have been placed there with the assistance of the artist's eye. Although this is sometimes true of the estate churches of the eighteenth century, it is rarely so for the majority of village churches, which are often in their present location for a variety of reasons.

The range of settings is infinite, but village churches enjoying a central position are the most common. The typical English village scene, with its church dominating the landscape and the surrounding cottages, is to be found throughout the country. These days, although it is often no longer the religious and social centre of village life that it once was, the church building remains the focal point that over the centuries has given the village much of its character. In many of the 'postcard' villages of England it is the church that makes the picture.

These villages can be seen throughout the country, and countless examples can be cited. Perhaps the most famous, certainly one of the most photographed, is the church at Godshill in the Isle of Wight, (1) where the church is situated behind a group of thatched cottages. There are too many of these villages to mention them all, for most counties have at least one outstanding example. In Somerset there is Luccombe, where the tall tower dominates the village of thatched, cob cottages; Selworthy, with its view towards Dunkery Beacon and the colour-washed cottages of the village below, and Axbridge, set at the corner of the market square above the village and approached by stone steps. These are some of the most perfect.

1   Godshill, Isle of Wight

The Cotswolds boasts many fine villages but Stanton, Gloucestershire, (2) is usually, and probably quite rightly, considered the prettiest of them all. It has the charm of perfection, and the church adds to its enchantment. Castle Combe, Wiltshire, (3) often described as England's prettiest village, is well known with its old stone cottages, stream, bridge, market cross and church. However, there are others of almost equal charm to be found in the county – notable examples being Aldbourne, with the church standing high above the village green, and Steeple Ashton, a large church built at the height of the cloth-weaving prosperity of the fifteenth century.

In the south-east there is South Harting, West Sussex, a large farming village at the foot of the South Downs, whose demure collection of brick and chalk cottages winds up to the big cruciform church which dominates the village, and Shere, Surrey, a village noted for its quaint beauty. In Kent there is Chilham, with church

2 Stanton, Gloucestershire

3   Castle Combe, Wiltshire

and castle set around a large square of timber-framed buildings, Smarden, a village of weather boarded cottages, and Aylesford, with church and houses above the River Medway.

Essex has several notable villages, but none prettier than Finchingfield, where the church, with its large tower, dominates the cottages, village green, windmill and village pond. Cavendish, with its village green, cottages and church, and Kersey, its church high above the village looking down the village street of timber-framed and colour-washed cottages to the water-splash below, are two of the outstanding villages in Suffolk. Picturesque Westmill in Hertfordshire is renowned for its little green, with its pump backed by cottages and the church tower. Equally charming is nearby Braughing, where the cottages cluster around the church.

The Midlands too has many notable examples. At Bradenham in Buckinghamshire the church, big house, village green and the Chilterns behind make a perfect picture; in Oxfordshire there are Whitchurch, with its views from the Thames, and Westwell, with its ensemble of cottages, church, rectory, manor house and barns grouped

4   Chipping, Lancashire

around the duck pond. At Geddington, Northamptonshire, the church, Eleanor Cross and medieval bridge form another delightful group. One of the greatest pleasures of Lincolnshire is Folkingham, with its market square from which the church is approached up an alley at one corner. In Warwickshire there are the ancient village of Brailes, divided into two – Upper and Lower – and Tredington.

Although the landscape of the north is more rugged than in many more southerly parts, there are many fine villages, and there can be none better than Romaldkirk, County Durham, where the old houses, village green and church all blend to make this a memorable village. The same can be said of others, for instance West Tanfield, North Yorkshire, where the three arched bridge, church, chantry cottage and Marmion Tower make a most attractive picture, Bishop Burton, East Riding of Yorkshire, Thornton Dale, North Yorkshire, and Chipping, Lancashire (4).

One could continue almost indefinitely, for each village setting is unique, but it is not always the village that makes the scene; in some instances, particularly in the west and north, it is the scenery. In Cumbria there are, amongst others, the churches at Isel (5), Millom, Grasmere, Hawkshead, Matterdale (6), Ulpha and Waberthwaite; Northumberland can boast such gems as Bolam, set

5 Isel, Cumbria

6   Matterdale, Cumbria

in the midst of undulating parkland near the site of an abandoned
village, or Brinkburn Priory, set in wooded countryside near the
bank of the Coquet, or Bamburgh. In North Yorkshire there is
Arncliffe in its magnificent dales setting, Grinton in Swaledale,
and Husthwaite with its view of the Hambleton Hills.

Cornwall, too, has many of the most picturesque churches, and
none better than those near the sea or on a river estuary. The
finest perhaps is at St Just-in-Roseland (7), the heavily wooded
churchyard rising up steeply behind the church, the water almost
reaching the walls of the church at high tide. Those at Mylor and
St Anthony-in-Meneage are just as charming. Gunwalloe, built
next to the beach on a rolling coastline, with its thirteenth-
century detached bell tower built into the rocky headland, has
one of the loveliest situations of all Cornish churches. The
isolated church at Morwenstow sits high on the south side of a

combe exposed to the winds from the Atlantic. So does the church at Hartland in Devon (8), almost at the land's edge overlooking the Atlantic, its tower, 123 feet high, built as a landmark for mariners. Coastal sites are always memorable, and none more so than the church at Heysham, Lancashire (9), overlooking the bay towards Morecambe.

7   St Just-in-Roseland, Cornwall

8 Hartland, Devon

9   Heysham, Lancashire

Although the majority of churches are located within or close to a village, there are many in isolated settings far from any inhabitants. The reason for their isolation is not always clear and may reflect the fact that the villages that originally lay around them were deserted as a result of plague, war, economic necessity or repeated crop failure. There are many examples; Stoke Charity, Hampshire, now stands alone in a field but once had the manor house of the de la Charité family for company; the tiny church at Little Gidding, Cambridgeshire, survives the depopulated village and the hall; and all that remains of the old village of Goltho, Lincolnshire, is the church – the great house of the Grantham family and the dependent village that once stood nearby having long gone.

For whatever reason many of these isolated churches are the loveliest and often the least spoilt, but, as many of them no longer

10   Brentor, Devon

perform any useful function, they are often the most vulnerable. Many of these churches are now looked after by the Redundant Churches Fund.

Hill-top sites are most memorable, and none more so than the churches at Brentor in Devon (10), perched high on the summit of an extinct volcanic cone 1,100 feet above sea level with views across half of Devon and Cornwall, and Breedon on the Hill in Leicestershire, standing alone on top of its hill made steeper by the quarrying at the base.

These hill-top sites may be the most striking, but a great many churches stand alone, isolated in fields and often some way from the road. The church at Brougham, Cumbria, is approached by a rough track over three miles long; that at Walesby, Lincolnshire, standing high up on an isolated spur on the Lincolnshire Wolds, at one time had a tarred road leading to it, but now one has to climb on foot along a muddy track. There are many others with no road access. At Ford, West Sussex, a charming Norman church stands alone in fields almost hidden by yews and holm oaks; Tarrant Crawford, Dorset, is to be found down an often muddy farm track;

and at Low Ham, Somerset, a remarkable church was built in
1629–69 in a field below the terraces of a failed scheme for a great
house. At St Margarets in Herefordshire (11), the church is set in
fields in lovely countryside above the Golden Valley, and at
Ampney St Mary, Gloucestershire, a twelfth-century church is
isolated in a field with only a large cedar and Ampney Brook for
company. Another example is the church at Fairfield, Kent: a tiny
barn-like structure that stands isolated in a field on Romney
Marsh, surrounded by ditches and sheep but without a tree or
gravestone for company.

Many of these remote and isolated churches are surrounded, or
almost hidden, by trees. One such is at Broomfield, Somerset,
another is the small rustic church at Shocklach, Cheshire, while
Courteenhall, Northamptonshire, is engulfed in trees and well
away from any road. Norton Disney, Lincolnshire, is situated in a
romantic spot, lost in the willows of the River Witham and
surrounded by woods. Culbone church, Somerset (12) – claimed to
be the smallest medieval church in England still in use – is set in a

11   St Margarets, Herefordshire

12   Culbone, Somerset

wooded combe; there is no road, only winding tracks through woods and fields. In other instances the church has a backcloth of trees. Stocklinch Ottersey, Somerset, is pictorially perfect, standing as it does on a raised churchyard. Northorpe, Lincolnshire, also stands on a small eminence and is backed by large trees. North Cerney in Gloucestershire, Nynehead in Somerset and Farleigh in Surrey are just a few more of the many memorable examples.

Some churches are founded upon or near the sites of dolmens or stone circles, as at Stanton Drew, Somerset. The most spectacular monolith and certainly the largest standing stone in England is in the churchyard at Rudston, East Riding of Yorkshire. Some six feet wide and over twenty-five feet high with an unknown length below the ground, this black carboniferous sandstone weighs some twenty-six tons and in around 2000 BC was brought a distance of at least ten miles from the nearest outcrop of gritstone at Cayton Bay to a site of some religious importance. Other churches are built within prehistoric earthworks – such as Finchampstead, Berkshire, and Mawnan and Kilkhampton, Cornwall – or have ancient mounds or burrows nearby – as at Lilbourne, Northamptonshire, Brinklow, Warwickshire, and Ogbourne St Andrew, Wiltshire. Sometimes the church occupies the site of an Iron Age hill-fort: that at Cholesbury, Buckinghamshire, stands within the south-western perimeter of the Iron Age fort, while the one at St Dennis, Cornwall, occupies the inner circle of a hill-fort high up on the hills above St Austell.

In some instances two churches occupy a single churchyard. At Swaffham Prior, Cambridgeshire, and Antingham, Norfolk, pairs of churches originally served separate parishes, but, when these were amalgamated one of the pair was abandoned. The abandoned church at Antingham, became derelict, but that at Swaffham Prior has been repaired and is now used as the church hall. At Willingale, Essex, the two churches occupy the same churchyard but serve the adjoining parishes of Willingale Doe and Willingale Spain, and a similar situation occurs at Alvingham, Lincolnshire, where the churchyard is approached through a farm-yard. A slightly different arrangement is found at Trimley, Suffolk, where there are two churches side by side, each with its own churchyard.

There are many hundreds of churches that stand remote from the village but have a single house nearby. In medieval times the Lord of the Manor was usually responsible for building the church, and he frequently built it on his own land near his house. There are many examples of a small church situated close by a farmhouse that was once the manorial hall, often surrounded by farm buildings and approached along a private road or track. In some instances one may have to walk through a garden or farmyard, as at Coberley, Gloucestershire, and North Marden, West Sussex. In other cases – like Southrop, Gloucestershire, and Pixley, Herefordshire – the church is within the farmyard. At Up Waltham, West Sussex, the Norman church, farm and barns form a wonderful group, and at Wissington, Suffolk, the church is attractively grouped with farm and farm buildings within a moated site.

Another Norman church stands close by the farm at Kilpeck, Herefordshire, this time within the castle enclosure, with the large motte which bears the fragmentary remains of a keep standing to the west of it and the churchyard to the east. Here the site of the village, too, is within the castle enclosure. This close proximity of churches and mottes is to be found in many parts of the country, though particularly in Herefordshire, where Eardisley, Mansell Lacy and Staunton on Arrow may be mentioned. Elsewhere this association occurs at English Bicknor in Gloucestershire, which is on the site of a motte-and-bailey castle, East Lulworth in Dorset, Gilmorton in Leicestershire, and Rockingham in Northamptonshire. At Stokesay, Shropshire, the church is separated from the medieval castle only by a moat.

The relationship between manor house and church formed the origins of the estate church. As wealth increased, in some cases the old manor house was demolished and a new, larger house built to replace it. A decision then had to be made about the relationship between house and church. Some churches were either retained close to the house and perhaps assimilated the architecture, or else treated as an ancillary building to be grouped along with stables, dovecot or other subordinate buildings at a respectable distance from the mansion. Some were made the focal point within the park, or removed completely from the vicinity of the house and placed either at or beyond the boundary of the park.

At first the house and church kept close company, and in a few cases, as at Nevill Holt, Leicestershire and Wyke Champflower, Somerset, was actually attached to the house (at Ribston Hall, North Yorkshire, the church was completely absorbed into the main façade). A typical example of the close proximity of house and church can be seen at Great Chalfield, Wiltshire. During the 1450s the manor was acquired by Thomas Tropenell, who had either built or begun to build the present house before his death in 1488. He also made alterations to the present church, much of which dates from the thirteenth century. The intimacy between church and house makes this a classic manorial group. Another example is at Brympton D'Evercy, Somerset, where the small, mainly four-teenth- and fifteenth-century church, the medieval chantry-house and rambling Tudor manor house, all in golden Ham Hill stone, make a memorable scene set in their delightful gardens. Similar arrangements of house and church can be seen at Chastleton, Oxfordshire, and Westwood in Wiltshire (now owned by the National Trust). The church at Staunton Harold, Leicestershire, started in 1653 by Sir Robert Shirley, was built close to the

Jacobean mansion and overlooking the lake. The present façade, which faces the church, was begun in 1763 and incorporates the former Jacobean mansion.

At the end of the seventeenth century and throughout the eighteenth century emparking – removing entire communities and rehousing them away from the newly-built mansions of the new landed class and their landscaped parks – gained popularity in England. In many cases the existing church was retained as a focal point in the landscaped garden. Fawsley in Northamptonshire provides a prime example of this; the former village around the church was swept away, but the church (which had been a minster before the Conquest) was retained and occupies a solitary yet prominent position within the park, overlooking a pair of ornamental lakes but in view of the hall. In about 1729 Sir Robert Walpole retained the old church within his park but removed the village and built a new one, New Houghton, at the gates of his mansion Houghton Hall, Norfolk. In many instances a quite modest church was built to replace the earlier one; the little church at Babington, Somerset, (13) on the lawn of Babington House is a charming example.

After about 1725 Georgian men and women of sensibility began to embrace the Gothick taste (not to be confused with the later Gothic Revival). In such cases the old church was removed and a new church built. The first major Gothick church was at Werrington, Cornwall, built in 1742 about half a mile or so from the site of the original church, which was considered too close to the house. Another notable example is the church at Croome D'Abitot, Worcestershire. The present church was built in 1763 to replace an earlier one that had been sited a few hundred yards to the west and overlooking Croome Court, once the home of the Earls of Coventry. Other Gothick churches built as landscape ornaments include the little box-like structure (1756) standing in a field above the hall at Ravenfield, South Yorkshire, and the little octagonal church with its flanking towers at Hartwell, Buckinghamshire, built between 1753 and 1755. At Stapleford, Leicestershire, another remarkable Gothick church was built in the Earl of Harborough's park in 1783, after the removal of the village. It is approached by an avenue of beech trees and, unlike the other churches, is surrounded by trees, so it was not built as an eye-catcher.

13   Babington, Somerset

Emparking developed into the cult of the Picturesque in the eighteenth century. As early as 1716 the essayist and statesman Joseph Addison wrote, 'why may not the whole estate be thrown into a kind of garden by frequent plantations? A man might make a pretty landstrip of his own possessions'. This new approach was put into practice at Well, Lincolnshire. The village was rebuilt after emparking and, although the cottages were sited outside the gates, the church was placed inside and reconstructed in 1633 in the form of a neo-classical temple, to be viewed as a decorative ornament across the grass from the mansion's windows. The church at Gunton Hall in Norfolk, designed by Robert Adam and built between 1765 and 1767, looks for all the world like a small Greek temple – which is exactly what it is intended to do. In 1761 Lord Harcourt replaced the old village of Newnham Court, Oxfordshire, which stood behind his newly-built Palladian mansion, with a new village of cottages on either side of the road approaching the mansion and named it Newnham Courtenay. The church within the grounds was demolished and replaced in 1764 by one built in the Roman style to the design of the first Lord Harcourt. This church is a domed temple with a semi-circular portico and is lit by semi-circular mullioned lunettes in the Palladian style. At Ayot St Lawrence, Hertfordshire, (14), in 1778–9 Sir Lionel Lyde built a new church to the design of Nicholas Revett, to be viewed from his new home Ayot House. This certainly was an 'eye-catcher': a small Grecian temple with a spreading Palladian screen and pavilions facing the house, it is the first Grecian Revival church in Britain. Inside it is rectangular with a coffered ceiling, arched transepts and the altar at the west end in a coffered apse.

In some cases both village and church were swept away and rebuilt beyond the gates of the park. One such case was Milton Abbas in Dorset, where Joseph Damer, later Earl of Dorchester, razed a sizeable market town when Milton Abbey was extensively altered and the park laid out by Capability Brown. The village was rebuilt, together with its own little church, in a deep cleft in the downs which slopes gently down the valley. The village was begun in 1773 and not completed until 1786.

14   Ayot St Lawrence, Hertfordshire

2   The Churchyard

The church is usually set within a churchyard although a few, such as Fairfield in Kent, do not have one. In many cases the church-yards are considerably older than the church they contain, for, as we have seen, churches were often built on pagan sites and it was in fact on the advice of Pope Gregory 1 that these sites were used when available. Circular churchyards, such as those at Lavendon in Buckinghamshire, Ozleworth in Gloucestershire, East Hendred in Oxfordshire, Steeple Bumpstead in Essex, Rudston in East Riding of Yorkshire and St Buryan in Cornwall, are likely to be very old, and those that are both circular and on mounds, as at Edlesborough in Buckinghamshire and Winwick in Cambridgeshire, may well have been used in prehistoric times.

The origin of the churchyard in England is obscure, but its establishment is usually attributed to Archbishop Cuthbert of Canterbury, who in 752 obtained Papal permission to establish churchyards around city churches. At first the area was not enclosed; during the process of consecration the diocesan bishop marked its extent by means of four small wooden crosses, set at the cardinal points. It was not until the tenth century that the practice of enclosing the churchyard was introduced, and even then setting up a boundary could have been by no means general. In 1229 Bishop William de Bleys of Worcester specified that the church-yard should be properly enclosed by a wall, hedge or ditch, and no portion of it was to be built upon. In 1267 a Bishop Quivil stated the necessity for the enclosure of the consecrated land and that the grazing of animals should be prohibited. It is clear that parish priests continued to graze their livestock in the churchyard; in fact after the Reformation they regarded churchyard grazing as their right, and there are several instances of vicars being fined. This right of grazing animals within the churchyard persisted in some areas into Victorian times, when cattle are often depicted on engravings.

By the seventeenth century it is clear that most churchyards were enclosed and that it was the churchwardens' duty to ensure that they were kept in good repair. It became customary to make the parishioners responsible for the upkeep of the boundary, and in Sussex there are several churches with records allotting the responsibility for the upkeep according to the size of the farmer's holding. In 1636, the fence at Cowfold, West Sussex, was maintained by 81 individuals, whose initials were cut on their particular posts (these can still be seen). At Chiddingly in East Sussex, according to the records of 1722, 56 people were charged with the upkeep of the fence, the lengths for which they were responsible varying from three to forty-five feet. At Broomfield, Somerset, on the north wall of the churchyard are a number of small stone tablets bearing such letters and figures as 'ED 9 foot' 'SCT 18 foot' and 'HT 9 foot' stipulating who was responsible for the wall's upkeep.

In medieval times the churchyard, like the nave of the church itself, was put to various secular uses, for both were community property in which the interests of both God and man were invested. Before the advent of village greens, and later recreation grounds, the churchyard was the only convenient public meeting place, and a variety of activities took place there. This was not always to the liking of the authorities; in 1287 a synod in Exeter decreed that parish priests should forbid the use of churchyards for dances, combats or the performance of plays, especially on Saints' days. Whether this had much effect is doubtful, for there are many records of churchyards continuing to be put to secular uses. Until the thirteenth century various religious dramas and miracle plays were performed in the nave of the church, but their popularity was such that the nave was too small, and they were often transferred to the churchyard. Ritual performances by morris dancers in both church and churchyard continued well into the seventeenth century.

Various games and sports, including wrestling, ball games, fives, marbles and archery, were also enjoyed throughout the Middle Ages – and were indeed advocated as legitimate pastimes after Divine Service by James I in his *Book of Sports* of 1617. Cock-fighting, too, was regarded as a suitable churchyard pastime, and several churchyards had a cock-pit: for example, Alsop en le Dale, Derbyshire. Archery practice was encouraged by Parliament in medieval times, from the time of Edward I until Charles I. An Act of 1466 actually stated that every able-bodied Englishman should have a longbow and should practice on Sundays and feast days, and the churchyards or their vicinity seem to have been widely used to set up the butts. Grooves in church walls – as at Aston upon Trent, Derbyshire, and Barfreston, Kent – are commonly believed to have been made by archers sharpening their arrows. Contrary to popular belief it is doubtful whether medieval longbows came from the yew trees planted in village churchyards, for large quantities were imported from abroad.

Fairs and markets were also held in the churchyard, usually on feast days or Sundays – those held on Sundays often causing noise and tumult during the services. As early as 1285 the Statute of Winchester prohibited the use of churchyards for fairs and markets. The practice continued, however, and indeed for many village parishes the rent secured from stall-holders was a most acceptable source of income.

Another source of income was the so-called church-ale, held at Christmas, Easter, Whitsuntide or other festivals during the year either in the nave or in the churchyard. The ale was made in the parish brewhouse, the parishioners paid for the ale they consumed, and the profit went towards the repair of the church, alms for the poor or providing poor brides with dowries. By the end of the fifteenth century the brewhouse was in most places replaced by a church-house that was used for ales and other social activities. In Devon these often adjoined the churchyard, as at Walkhampton, South Tawton and Braunton.

Lych-gates

A great many churchyards are entered by means of a lych-gate, taking its name from the Anglo-Saxon word *lich* or *lic*, related to the modern German *leiche*, all meaning corpse. These gates mark the division between the consecrated and unconsecrated ground, where the funeral-bearers stopped with their load, resting it on a lych-stone, coffin-stool or trestle, while the priest conducted part of the funeral service before leading the procession to the church.

15   Lych-gate at Ashwell, Hertfordshire

In medieval times few churchyards would be without a lych-gate of some kind – at Troutbeck, Cumbria, there are three, and at Stoke Poges, Buckinghamshire, and Bockleton, Worcestershire, there are two. Lych-gates of great age – like those at Isleham in Cambridgeshire, Limpsfield in Surrey and Boughton Monchelsea in Kent, which date from the fifteenth century – are rare. Many were destroyed or damaged after the Reformation, and many of those that remained, being made of timber, decayed and were demolished in the eighteenth century, when the use of lych-gates declined. In Cheshire, for instance, lych-gates were frequently replaced by iron gates in the eighteenth-century, as at Bunbury, Malpas and Tilston. Although a few pre-Reformation lych-gates survive, no perfect examples remain; originally they would have incorporated seats along their length, a lych-cross, as well as a lych-stone or table. The seats were of the bench type, usually of timber, although in some areas stone or slate was used, as at St Just-in-Roseland, Cornwall. Occasionally one can still find a lych-stone or table; Bolney in West Sussex and Sheepstor, Atherington and Ashprington in Devon all possess one. Most lych-gates are single structures with one gate, but sometimes – as at Ashwell, Hertfordshire (15) – they are double structures, with two gates revolving on a central post. Most lych-gates to be found today are not of great age. Many were rebuilt, particularly during the Gothic Revival of the Victorian times, yet they still add charm to village churchyards.

In some cases lych-gates are not independent structures but are incorporated into another building, which gives access to the churchyard via a passage within or under the building. In the most common arrangement the lych-gate is formed between two cottages, with the upper floor of one of them being carried over it, as at Penshurst and Smarden, Kent. In Essex, at Finchingfield and Felsted, a similar arrangement is used, though the adjacent buildings are not cottages but former guildhalls. Another fine example is at Hartfield, East Sussex, (16) where the cottage, thought to have been built in 1520, has its upper jettied floor extended over the lych-gate. In some instances the lych-gate is an independent structure with a room or rooms above it which might have been used by a priest, as a schoolroom, a parish room or a library. This often occurs in Cornwall, at such places as Wendron, Feock, Kenwyn and St Clement (the last three are slate-hung). At Long Compton, Warwickshire, there is a thatched room over the gate, while at Bray, Berkshire, the lych-gate is incorporated into a fifteenth-century timber-framed gatehouse.

Churchyard Crosses

Before the Reformation all churchyards were dominated by free-standing crosses. These were erected to signify the sanctity of consecrated ground, and in the days before gravestones they were

16   Lych-gate at Hartfield, East Sussex

important, for they were the only memorial to all the departed. Remains of these crosses are common, particularly in those areas where good stone is abundant. Many were destroyed during the Civil War, when Puritan iconoclasts broke off and removed most of the heads, which bore sculptured images. The gabled head at Ampney Crucis, Gloucestershire, was removed and walled up inside the entrance to the rood loft; it was discovered and restored to the cross in around 1860.

The earliest crosses, which were carved monoliths, are to be found mainly in Cornwall and the north. There are some three hundred of these crosses, some of great antiquity, reaching back towards the days of the Celtic missionaries; they are difficult to date, for there is usually no inscription, but the one at Altarnun, Cornwall, is reputed to be sixth-century. The variety of design is enormous. Those in Cornwall are usually dumpy in appearance and of the wheel-headed Celtic type. The majority are of granite, and therefore not intricately carved: interlace or plait decoration with inscriptions in Roman, transitional or Hiberno-Saxon characters are a feature. Outstanding examples are at Mylor – the largest in the county, some 17 feet high overall – St Piran's and Mawgan-in-Fydar. Elsewhere these early crosses may be circular in section, as at Masham, North Yorkshire, and the eleventh century one at Brailsford, Derbyshire, but generally they are rectangular. Occasionally the shafts are constructed of both circular and rectangular sections: Ilam, Staffordshire, and Beckermet St Bridget, Cumbria, have examples of this. In many instances the shaft is tapered – well-known examples are to be found in the churchyards at Bewcastle and Gosforth in Cumbria (17), and Eyam in Derbyshire.

In the Middle Ages each churchyard would have had its cross, marking the true centre of the churchyard and used as a station on the processional path, particularly on Palm Sunday (which is why such crosses are sometimes referred to as 'Palm Crosses'). It was also where public announcements could be made. These later crosses were of the mounted shaft type and consisted of steps (between one and six), a plinth, a shaft that was usually square in plan, tapered and occasionally topped with a capital, and, on the top, the head or cross as the restored one at Halton, Lancashire (18). The heads themselves are either flat-topped or gabled. Gabled ones could be two or four-sided, those with two sides usually contain a crucifix or Crucifixion on one side and the figures of the Virgin and Child on the other. On the four-sided head at Ampney Crucis, Gloucestershire (19), the other two sides have St Lawrence with his gridiron and a man in armour of about 1415. Although a great many crosses have only part of the shaft remaining, there are many notable medieval crosses: that at Somersby in Lincolnshire, the fourteenth century one at Ashleworth in Gloucestershire, another at Bishops Lydeard in Somerset, and the one at Tyberton, Herefordshire, may be mentioned.

17   Churchyard cross at Gosforth, Cumbria

18   Churchyard cross at Halton, Lancashire

19   Churchyard cross at Ampney Crucis, Gloucestershire

Tombstones

Except for the very rich and important, most people throughout the
Middle Ages were interred in only a shroud tied at the head and
foot, with no headstone to mark the grave. Burials normally took
place on the south side of the church, beginning close to the walls

of the church and working out across the churchyard until the enclosure wall was reached, when the process started all over again. Consequently, in the course of time, people were buried one on top of the other – which is why the level of the churchyard is often above that of the floor of the church. Until the nineteenth century, it remained the belief among common people that the northern part of the churchyard was more suited for the burial of strangers, criminals, paupers, stillborn and unbaptized infants, those who had died a violent death and, in particular, those who committed suicide.

Before the Reformation headstones were not generally used; for those who could afford such luxuries had a monument within the church. For the majority, a timber cross would have been all that marked the grave, and this would soon have decayed and disappeared. Some use was made of both stone headstones and footstones in medieval graveyards, but these were small and, although sometimes carved, carried no inscriptions. After the end of the fourteenth-century they fell into disuse, and few now survive. During the latter half of the sixteenth century and throughout the seventeenth century, as wealth spread, there was an increasing desire by those who could afford it to buy plots and have their earthly resting place noted in some way. Local materials were used: stone and slate where they were available, but elsewhere, in areas with little freestone, timber was used, and iron in areas where iron-smelting had gone on for years, such as the Weald of Sussex and Kent. It was not until the nineteenth century – with the introduction of white marble from Italy, followed by polished black marble and multi-coloured chips – that the visual harmony of many village churchyards was spoilt.

After the Reformation headstones gained in popularity. At first there was little decoration; they were fairly small, thick and what decoration there was was boldly cut, sometimes on both front and back, with simple shaped heads, and often only a date, or a date and initials, was carved on them. Later headstones developed into slabs invariably decorated on one face only, with the top edge or head of the stone cut in various silhouettes to correspond with the accompanying symbolic imagery. The heads of the headstones were often flat, except perhaps for a scrolled shoulder, or flanked by winged angel-heads symbolic of the departing soul. These early seventeenth-century angel-heads had wings protruding from the heads in the place of ears. Later, by the middle of the century, the top of the stone was being shaped so that an angel-head could be provided in the hood, or else the shoulders were carved to curve around an angel at each corner. As classical influence grew, cherubs often replaced angels trumpeting their victory over death or extinguishing the torch of life. Skulls, crossbones, scythes, hour-glasses and wings also became popular features – all symbols of death and the fleeting days of life on this earth.

The finest headstones are Georgian. This period was the great age of the English tombstone, of good design with finely lettered inscriptions and, most important, the use of local stone (or, if there was none, stone from some accessible quarry). The Cotswolds is a specially notable area, but by no means the only one. Interesting collections of headstones occur in churchyards all over the country. The marshland churches at the head of the Wash have many fine examples, for instance, Upwell, Norfolk, and Lutton, Lincolnshire. Potton, Bedfordshire, has row upon row of delightful gravestones dating back to 1690, and Borden, Kent, has many dating from the eighteenth century. These are only a few of the many examples that could be given.

For those who could afford something grander than a headstone, a chest-tomb was a favourite form of churchyard memorial. Early chest-tombs were rectangular stone boxes with little or no decoration and with no inscriptions. In the fourteenth century the sides were decorated with tracery; the earliest example is at Loversall, South Yorkshire, where the tracery appears to be taken from some master-mason's pattern book. Not until the fifteenth and sixteenth centuries did this type of monument achieve its standard form of a thick moulded ledger and base, with the sides divided into either cusped quatrefoils or shields in tracery. At least forty pre-Reformation chest-tombs survive, those at Sutton Courtenay in Oxfordshire, Saxton in North Yorkshire and Teynham in Kent being good examples.

After the Reformation the chest-tomb preserved the essence of its medieval form, although often reduced to a massive moulded ledger and base with ashlar or brick sides. Because the usual construction was like that of a box, with four slabs or sides, it became natural to put pilasters at each corner to give the illusion of corner posts separating the side and end panels. There are few churchyards that do not possess at least one specimen of this type.

It is in the Cotswolds that chest-tombs are to be found in greatest number and the finest quality. In this area the wealth created by the wool industry was combined with a ready supply of the finest limestone. The earliest of these tombs, from the beginning of the seventeenth century, have heavy ledgers, sharply undercut, and bodies narrower than those of later tombs. Some have arched panels on the ends, or an arcade of them on the sides. Representative examples can be found at Snowshill, Evenlode, Oddington and Daylesford, all in Gloucestershire. Such chest-tombs have a simple dignity, but there are others which are lavishly ornamented. The older monuments at Painswick, Gloucestershire, (regarded as the finest churchyard in England) show the ends of the chest-tombs made into vigorous consoles, giving a lyre-shape that ends in a coil resembling the volute of an Ionic capital. Masons treated these ends in many delightful and elaborate ways: acanthus leaves on the sides of the consoles, portrait busts, cherub-heads, skulls, hour-glasses, fruit and flowers.

A variation of the Cotswold chest-tomb is the 'bale-tomb', with a large semi-cylindrical stone covering most of the ledger. Nearly half of these capping stones are carved with deep grooves running either along their length or diagonally across – hence the tradition that they represented corded bales of cloth and that they were connected with clothiers. However, this explanation cannot be correct, for such tombs are found to the east of the Cotswolds, away from the clothiers' stronghold in the west. Another theory is that they represented the corpse wrapped in a shroud of wool; the ends of the 'bales' usually took the form of a skull set in a shell or scallop. These tombs can be seen in many churchyards in Gloucestershire and Oxfordshire, centred around Burford; representative examples are to be found at Fulbrook, Swinbrook, Stow-on-the Wold, Little Barrington, Lower Slaughter and Asthall.

Yet another eighteenth-century Cotswold innovation is the so-called tea-caddy tomb. As the name implies these are upright, instead of the usual longitudinal shape, and they may be rectangular, circular or square in plan and are sometimes topped with a lid that often ends in some kind of finial. They seem to have originated at Painswick (20), which has several examples, but they also appear in many other Gloucestershire churchyards. Typical examples can be found at Leighterton, Minchinhampton, Owlpen, Pitchcombe, Siddington, Salperton and Withington.

20   Tea-caddy tomb at Painswick, Gloucestershire

In those areas which had little good local freestone, wood continued to be used, and this was particularly true of the Home
Counties. By the seventeenth century timber gravelboards, sometimes referred to as 'bedheads', became popular. These consisted of
two posts supporting a board for the requisite text, and were placed
along the length of the grave. It is clear that in many churchyards
this was the only form of memorial; John Aubrey noted in 1673
that in Surrey 'they use no tombstones in the churchyards but
rayles of wood over the grave on which are printed or engraved the
inscription'. This type of memorial persisted well into the nineteenth century. Gravelboards are becoming rarer each year as they
decay, but they are still to be found in many churchyards, mostly in
the Home Counties (in particular Surrey, Kent and Essex) and in
the area of the Chilterns.

Mausoleums

In some churchyards mausoleums are to be found: tomb-houses
built outside the church by important families when they could no
longer build an impressive vault or tomb within it. Often they are
imposing architectural achievements that dominate the churchyard. The style varies greatly; the late eighteenth-century
mausoleum at Little Ouseburn, North Yorkshire, (21) is built in the
neo-classical style, with a Palladian rotunda and a frieze supported
by Tuscan columns. Other notable churchyard mausoleums can be
seen at Chiddingstone in Kent (interesting because it leads directly
to a vault that is ventilated by a false tomb chest a few feet away,
which has a grating in the side), Lowther in Cumbria, Buckminster
in Leicestershire, Wroxham in Norfolk, Cobham in Surrey and
Fawley in Buckinghamshire (which has two).

Watchboxes

In the eighteenth and early part of the nineteenth century, when
surgical science was beginning to develop, 'resurrection men' (or
body-snatchers) would exhume the body of a newly buried person
under cover of darkness and remove it for anatomical study. To
prevent this, the church authorities erected in the churchyard a

21 Mausoleum at Little Ouseburn, North Yorkshire

small building called a watchbox, in which armed men were on guard at night to foil the body-snatchers. A few watchboxes still remain. In the north an early nineteenth-century example survives at Doddington, Northumberland, while Warblington, Hampshire, has two small brick-and-flint boxes: one at each end of the church-yard.

Other measures were occasionally employed to foil church-robbers. Some of the graves were built with brick walls, while others had iron railings around the gravestone; Henham, Essex

(22) has a grave with an iron cage around it. Another form of protection was by mortesafe: in its simplest form, a heavy stone slab buried on top of the corpse. This did not always deter the body-snatchers, and so a heavy, iron grille was placed over the grave with the headstone placed on top of the grille. Mortesafes were particularly common in Scotland.

When the Anatomy Act was passed in 1832, and the obtaining of bodies was legalised, all these methods of preventing the theft of bodies became redundant.

22   Cage at Henham, Essex

Schools, Priest's Houses, Almshouses, etc.

It is not uncommon to find buildings within the churchyard. When parish priests were the only literate members of the rural community, the church porch was often used as the village school, and, as demand for education increased, small schools were built close to the church – on occasion inside the churchyard itself. At Felkirk, West Yorkshire, the school dates from the sixteenth century and is believed to be the oldest church school in England; another, at Leyland in Lancashire, dates from the seventeenth century, and others, such as those at Wraxall in Somerset, Uppingham in Rutland and Wythall in Worcestershire, are of the eighteenth and nineteenth centuries. A schoolhouse at Old Cleeve, Somerset, was paid for by the vicar and opened as late as 1911; that at Bray in Berkshire, was a chantry chapel until the seventeenth century.

Sometimes a priest's house was erected within the churchyard. Elkstone, Gloucestershire, has in one corner a priest's house which dates from the fourteenth century, although it was remodelled in the sixteenth century. The timber-framed building at Itchingfield, West Sussex, is thought originally to have been a lodging for travelling priests, though it was later altered and used as an almshouse. Sometimes the house was attached to the church, as at Dale, Derbyshire. The siting of almshouses around the perimeter to the churchyard is also a feature in some places – for example Finchingfield in Essex and Mancetter in Warwickshire dated 1728. Guildhalls, too, are to be found close to the churchyard entrance, as at Clavering, Essex, and that at Finchingfield actually forms the entrance to the churchyard. Great Chart, Kent (23), has a small timber-framed building known as the Pest House, its origin being lost in time.

Sundials

Pillar sundials, found in so many of our village gardens, are also to be found in a few churchyards. In some cases they have been mounted on the broken shaft of the old churchyard cross – or, where good stone was not readily available, on an oak post, as at Aldbury, Hertfordshire. A few churchyards contain purpose-made sundials the most remarkable of which being the seventeenth-century example at Elmley Castle, Worcestershire. Another designed by Inigo Jones stands in the churchyard at Chilham, Kent.

Dole Tables

Graveside doles were at one time fairly common: the wealthy would bequeath a sum of money so that bread could be bought and distributed to the poor at their graveside on the anniversary of their death or some other appointed day. Often the tops of chest-tombs situated close to the south porch were used, but in a few instances dole tables were constructed to administer the charity. The one at Powerstock, Dorset, is said to date from the thirteenth century; others can be found at Shipley, West Sussex and Norton Malreward in Somerset; that at Saintbury in Gloucestershire has an octagonal top on an octagonal support.

23   Pest House at Great Chart, Kent

Mounting Steps

When it was common to go to church on horseback, mounting steps – usually in the form of a single block of stone – were often provided to help people to mount their horses. They are occasionally still to be found, either near the main entrance of the churchyard (as at Ightham, Kent) or close by the church porch. Steps close to the porch probably indicate that the churchyard was not enclosed at the time they were built. At Fairfield, Kent – a churchyard which is still not enclosed – the steps are of brick and were built when the church was encased in brick in 1913. Other examples can be found at Bockleton in Worcestershire, Altarnun and St Germans in Cornwall, Chollerton in Northumberland and Kirkland in Cumbria. At East Peckham in Kent there is a stable at the lych-gate in which the horses were fed and sheltered during the long services; it still contains the stalls, with the names of local gentry who used them painted above. Another stable and mounting platform stands at Wingfield, Suffolk.

Wells

Wells are sometimes found in churchyards, and they are particularly common in the West Country and in the upland parishes on the flanks of the Pennines where the distribution of springs is determined by geological factors. The one at Whitstone in Cornwall is especially fine. Another notable example is at Hinderwell, North Yorkshire. In Derbyshire the decking of wells with flowers – well dressing – is still practised in many places including Buxton, Hope, Tideswell, Tissington and Wilne. In the churchyard at Bisley, Gloucestershire, (24) is the only example of a 'poor souls' light. This thirteenth-century structure was originally built as a well-covering, but it was later used to stand lighted candles on during the Masses said for the poor.

Trees

Trees loom large in natural religion, and their beauty and antiquity in the village churchyard is well known. The oak, ash and yew were

24 Pour soul's light at Bisley, Gloucestershire

among the species held in special respect. Few native English are particularly long-lived, and a five-hundred-year-old oak would be very ancient indeed. No oak or ash in or beside a medieval church-yard is likely to be anywhere near the age of the church itself. This is not true of the yew, however, which in a few cases may be a thousand years old. It was Edward I who first ordered the planting of yew trees to provide some protection for the church against storms and high winds, but even before the conversion of England to Christianity in the seventh and eighth centuries the yew tree was considered sacred. Its main purpose in the church was to supply the evergreen foliage, a special symbol of immortality; twigs and boughs were used to decorate the church at Easter, and they were also used as a substitute for the palm on Palm Sunday.

Many yew trees were planted in the nineteenth century, but, as previously stated, there are a few of considerable age. The girths of these ancient specimens in a few cases exceeds thirty feet, as at Ulcombe in Kent, Linton in Herefordshire, Darley Dale in Derbyshire and Crowhurst in Surrey. Others of note are to be found at Breamore in Hampshire, Cusop in Herefordshire, Aldworth in Berkshire and Loose in Kent. Several are in a poor state; the one at Aldworth was largely blown down in a gale in January 1976, and all that remains is an unimpressive stump, but new branches are rising from it. At Ashbrittle, Somerset, a vast ruined yew stands on a mound close to the south porch. The tree was split apart by lightning in the 1970s and a new tree is growing within the hollow trunk of the old one. In a few cases the girths of such split trunks are so substantial that seats have been built inside them, as at Much Marcle, Herefordshire, and Crowhurst, Surrey, which can seat no less than twelve people.

At Painswick, Gloucestershire, it is not the age of the yews that is remarkable but the number; there are ninety-nine of them, all planted at the end of the eighteenth century. Legend has it that it was impossible to grow the hundredth, because the Devil took exception to a round hundred.

3   Materials

No church can be appreciated without recognizing the material used in its construction, for the building materials of our village churches play an important part in the visual impact these buildings have upon the landscape. The complex pattern of England's geology is reflected not simply in the infinite diversity of the country's landscape. It is reflected equally in its churches and other buildings, and in the wide range of materials and styles employed in their construction.

Before the Industrial Revolution it was virtually impossible to transport stone and other heavy materials except by water, and so most church-builders had to rely on whatever materials were available locally. As a result, somewhere or other, virtually every conceivable material has been used. It is largely the nature of these materials (and by this we really mean stone), and in many cases the limitations that they imposed on the builders, that gives village churches much of their character. This use of local materials is one of the most pleasing aspects of our medieval village churches, and it is the reason why they harmonize so well with the landscape, in a way which churches built from materials from afar seldom do. Imagine, for instance, a typical fifteenth-century church from Somerset nestling among Northumbrian Fells, or a Norfolk flint church set in the limestone belt of Gloucestershire. Think of a homely Sussex church placed in the Derbyshire landscape, a typical granite church from Cornwall in the Lincolnshire marshlands, or a church from Cumbria in Kent. How inappropriate all these buildings would be if removed from their own environment and the landscape from which they have grown.

25   Greensted-juxta-Ongar, Essex

Timber

Until well into the Middle Ages large parts of England were densely
forested, so timber, readily available, was the natural choice of build-

ing material. During the Anglo-Saxon period building in stone was rare, and bricks were not made, so the majority of churches would have been built of timber – and by this we mean oak. (The word for 'to build' in Old English was *timbrian*, which implies a timber structure.) The Venerable Bede testifies to the high-quality workmanship of Saxon timber-built churches, although most of them were later destroyed by fire or replaced after the Conquest. These would not have resembled the timber-framed structures of later centuries but were small buildings of stave construction. A unique survival of this form of construction is the nave at Greensted-juxta-Ongar, Essex (25), where split oak logs (staves) are set vertically and joined together by oak tongues. This was originally thought to date from around 839, but recent dendrochronological testing seems to date the building to between 1063 and 1100.

26   Lower Peover, Cheshire

27　Marton, Cheshire

Although stave construction may once have been a common form, it had no influence on later medieval timber-framed churches built with framed joints on exactly the same principles as the innumerable timber-framed houses to be found in many parts of the country. They were far more common than is evident today; many have been destroyed – partly, no doubt, as a result of decay and neglect, but also because of the desire to rebuild in a more fashionable material, such as brick. F.H. Crossley listed 27 timber-framed churches that once existed in Cheshire; today only two remain – Lower Peover (26) and Marton (27) – while six others, which have some timber work remaining, have been wholly or partly encased in brick. Other counties have fared even worse; only two remain in Shropshire (at Melverley and Halston), one in Worcestershire (Besford), and one in Hampshire (at Mattingley). The church at Fairfield in Kent, on Romney Marsh, was rebuilt in

28   Tower at Margaretting, Essex

1913 in brickwork but the timber interior was left untouched and unspoiled. Sadly, every one of these churches was drastically restored in the nineteenth century, with the possible exception of Fairfield, and today they offer only limited pleasure. The most exciting example of timber-framing in the church context is to be seen at Hartley Wespall in Hampshire. Here the timbers of the west wall – dating from the fourteenth century and the only original part of the church to survive – form one enormous, boldly cusped lozenge, divided by a cusped middle post and with smaller cusped timbers in the gable. No other church has anything to compare with this, and Hartley Wespall is worth a visit for this alone.

Far more interesting than the few much-altered timber-framed churches are the timber-framed towers and belfries attached to stone churches. These are to be found mainly in Essex and are characterised by stages of diminishing size. The finest example is Blackmore, with three stages, but there are many others (usually with two stages), for example at Margaretting (28), Bulphan and Stock, all of considerable charm. So varied are these structures that it is impossible to generalise; some have aisles on two or four sides, but most have aisles on three sides. At West Hanningfield the tower is unique in being built on a cruciform plan. A group of belfries closely related to those in Essex can be found, here and there, in Surrey, with the odd examples in Kent, Hampshire and Sussex. Similar structures, but built within the nave, are also to be found in a number of churches in Essex and the south-east and in the north-west Midlands. The construction of all these is of special interest.

There are also a few timber-framed towers to be found in north-west Midlands. However, unlike those in Essex and the south-east (which are clad mainly with weatherboarding), these have a completely different look, for all have the timbers exposed and blackened. Those at Pirton (29), Warndon and Dormston (30), all in Worcestershire, are the most notable but perhaps the most attractive is the close-studded tower at Upleadon, Gloucestershire (31).

Timber was also used in the construction of porches in all those areas where stone was not available. They are most plentiful in Essex but are not uncommon in the neighbouring counties, the south-east and, again, the north-west Midlands. The porches at Aldham in Essex, High Halden in Kent, Ewhurst in Surrey and Crowle in Worcestershire are all admirable examples of the many to be seen.

29   Tower at Pirton, Worcestershire

30 Tower at Dormston, Worcestershire

31   Upleadon, Gloucestershire

The importance of timber in the construction of our village churches lies not so much in these relatively few timber-framed churches, towers, belfries and porches as in its use elsewhere in the fabric of churches. More important is its use in the construction of roofs, where timber was almost universally used, and in the interiors of churches, where there is a vast amount of wood to be seen, in the construction of benches, pulpits, rood screens and other fittings.

Stone

Despite the immense strength and remarkable durability of oak, stone (where it was readily available) was generally employed in the construction of the village church from the Norman period onwards. Even when the available stone was of the poorest quality it was generally preferred to timber, and so many churches in the south-east and in the eastern counties were built with a 'hotch-potch' of materials, including chalk, flints, boulders, pebbles, pudding-stone and Roman bricks – all held together with large quantities of mortar. These walls – and other walls built of rough masonry, such as Silurian and Devonian stone, as well as flint – were, of course, never intended to be seen and would have been rendered and limewashed.

In some cases the walls were rendered to make them weather-proof, for, although the stone itself would be impervious, the mortar used for bedding and pointing seldom was. At Grasmere, Cumbria, (32) for instance, the entire church is thickly encrusted with roughcast, but in 1891 this was removed from the tower and its unhewn 'beck cobbles' exposed and pointed; they proved incapable of resisting the rain, and some twenty years later roughcast was reapplied. Today, either through neglect or desire, much of the rendering on most churches has been removed, leaving the rubble walls exposed. Older rendering can often look very acceptable, but much has been replaced with rendering that contains cement, and this is often aesthetically unattractive if left undecorated. In some instances, walls have been rendered in pebble-dash, and the coarse texture and colour is often disagreeable, spoiling the exterior.

The stones used to build England's village churches can be divided into three major groups – igneous, metamorphic and sedimentary – and each group includes many geological formations classified by their age, rather than the physical properties of the rocks they yield. Each geological classification, therefore, often covers a number of rocks that differ in texture, colour, durability and workability. It is this great variety of building stones that has had such a profound influence on the appearance of so many of our medieval churches.

Whatever the stone, its character plays an important part in the method of construction, and therefore in the visual impact of the church. The majority of village churches are built of rubblestone,

32   Grasmere, Cumbria

sometimes roughly coursed, invariably joined with plenty of mortar. It was only the freestones – those stones of sufficiently fine grain to enable them to be cut in any direction, and dressed and squared to give a perfectly smooth face with squared edges – that could be laid in level courses with the minimum of mortar. Known as ashlar, this type of masonry can be best observed on those churches built of oolitic limestone.

IGNEOUS

The principal igneous rock is granite, a stone of immense strength and durability. This intractable material can be seen at many churches in Cornwall and in the adjoining part of Devon, around Dartmoor; they all have a distinctive quality that seems to fit so well with the austere landscape. Before the seventeenth century most of the granite used would not have been quarried but would have been 'moorstone' – surface stones lying around the hills and moors – and laid as found; however, as the masons' method of dressing gradually improved, dressed quoins and jambs began to be incorporated. By the end of the Perpendicular period many notable churches were built of huge dressed blocks, though carving the detailing remained a problem.

A similar rock to granite is elvan, used at Probus, which has the finest church tower in Cornwall. On the Lizard peninsula another igneous rock can be found in a number of churches. This is serpentine, found nowhere else in the country: a dark green stone with red veins, which helps to give the churches on the peninsula their own distinctive appearance. It can be found at St Ruan Minor, the smallest of the little churches of the Lizard, where the walls of the nave are formed of six courses of large blocks. Sometimes serpentine is used with granite, as at Mullion and at Landewednack.

METAMORPHIC

Slate is the principal metamorphic rock used in English churches. In Devon and Cornwall this slate belongs to the Devonian rock formation, and in Cornwall the rock is actually more widespread than granite. In the north-west most slates come from the Ordovician series, and this was the principal building stone of the Lake District. It differs greatly from granite in that it is easy to split into slabs, but it is almost impossible to square the slabs, so most pieces tend to be irregular in size and shape and need a considerable amount of mortar to make a satisfactory wall. Compared with granite, the colours are more varied – browns, purples, greens, as well as greys, are all to be found. However, as can be seen at Creed, Cornwall, and at Chapel Stile, Cumbria, and other Lake District churches, the impression conveyed is, as Alec Clifton-Taylor puts it, 'by no means as monumental'.

SEDIMENTARY

By far the most important group, and the one to which most of the building stones of England belong, is the sedimentary rocks, which includes the limestones and sandstones. Both limestone and sandstone are general terms, and each covers a range of rocks of many geological ages, which differ greatly.

Limestone

The youngest of the limestones widely used for building is chalk. There are younger limestones, for instance Coralline Crag and the freshwater limestones, but their use was not widespread. Coralline Crag – only found in very small quantities close to the Suffolk coast near Orford, where it was mined – was used on the church towers at Chillesford and Wantisden. Freshwater limestones (generally known as Bembridge limestone), in the form of Quarr and Binstead stone, are found in the Hampshire Basin, their use being confined to the Isle of Wight, Hampshire and West Sussex.

Chalk is to be found mainly to the east of the limestone belt. It was used – for want of a better material – in many places from the Thames northwards. It can be found in Oxfordshire, for instance in the churches at Ashbury and Compton Beauchamp (33), as well as at Uffington (although here it has a coating of pebble-dash). It is found again in Buckinghamshire, for example at Boveney, where the chalk stone is galleted (the practice of inserting small pieces of stone into broad mortar joints) with flint. The most reliable and best-known chalk came from Totternhoe, Bedfordshire, and, like all the best building chalk, comes from the stratum known as the Lower Chalk. It was used in many of the village churches in Bedfordshire and Hertfordshire. Chalkstone, almost identical to Totternhoe, occurs in west Norfolk and again in the Lincolnshire Wolds near Louth, where many of the churches are built of it. Chalk was not always reliable; that at Legbourne, Lincolnshire, is so soft that pieces can be picked from the surface.

33   Compton Beauchamp, Oxfordshire

Because of its poor weathering qualities, chalk is seen to best effect internally, as at Edlesborough, Ivinghoe and Bierton in Buckinghamshire, for instance but nowhere more strikingly than at Eaton Bray, Bedfordshire, where the richness of the capitals, clustered piers and arch mouldings provide evidence of the ease with which chalk could be worked. In Surrey, too, it was frequently used for internal arcades at a number of old churches, including some, such as Stoke D'Abernon and Pyrford, which are some way from the chalk outcrop. Local clunch was used, again internally, in Cambridgeshire and nowhere better than in the flint-built church at Burwell. The only area to the west of the limestone belt where chalk was quarried was at Beer, Devon, where a shelly chalkstone was used at several churches in the district.

Another product of the same geological system as chalk is Kentish ragstone, a very different stone. Unlike chalk, which is soft and easy to cut, Kentish rag is hard, brittle and difficult to work. Many Kent churches are therefore of rubble construction, as at West Peckham, although at Hawkhurst the blocks have been squared. Mainly quarried around Maidstone, Kentish rag was much used in that area and, because of the lack of building stone in Essex, was also ferried across the Thames. It is, therefore, found in many old south Essex churches, particularly in towers, among them those at Fobbing, Rettendon and Canewdon.

Limestone from the Jurassic series is the most important of all the sedimentary rocks and the most widely used for church build-ing. The main area is the limestone belt which spreads northward in a great crescent from Dorset to North Yorkshire, comprising oolitic limestone (the more important of the two) to the east and liassic limestone to the west. Along its entire length were famous quarries – Portland, Purbeck, Bath, Chilmark, Painswick, Guiting, Campden, Taynton, Weldon, Ketton, Barnack, Clipsham and Ancaster, as well as many more. All these quarries yielded varieties of fine-quarried stone of different characteristics, colour and consistency, but all produced stone which was capable of being dressed and carved. From these quarries came the stones for the lovely Cotswold churches, for the great churches of southern Lincolnshire, Northamptonshire and Leicestershire and, with the aid of water transport, for the great marshland churches of Norfolk, Cambridgeshire and Lincolnshire.

Liassic limestone is a less reliable stone and often weathers badly, although it was widely used in the Midlands, Dorset and Somerset. The best of the stone was, and still is, obtained at Hamdon Hill, Somerset, which produced the famous Ham Hill stone: not only one of our most durable limestones but also one of the most attractive, with its rich, golden-brown surface often covered with lichen. This was used in many churches in southern Somerset – Norton sub Hamdon, Martock, Montacute – and the adjacent part of Dorset. Further north, in the midland region, the most attractive liassic building stone comes from the Middle Lias formation. Marlstone (as this rock is often called) is of various shades of brown, induced by the presence of iron within the stone. It was extensively used in north Oxfordshire, the Northamptonshire hills and the eastern half of Leicestershire, where the yellow, brown and orange stones produce a marked architectural change from the oolite areas to the south. In those areas where the oolite and liassic limestone meet, the yellowy-brown ironstone is sometimes banded with the grey limestone – as at Whiston and Woodford in Northamptonshire, and elsewhere in the Nene Valley.

A totally different liassic stone is Blue Lias, a whitish-grey stone obtainable only in relatively small pieces and difficult to dress. It is for this reason that this stone is one of our less attractive lime-stones, for it was seldom obtainable other than in small pieces and therefore tends to be 'over-coursed'. (Due to the nature of the stone the courses tended to be narrow.) It used to be quarried in the Lyme Regis district of Dorset as well as further north, where it was used in churches in the Bridgwater, Taunton and Glastonbury area of Somerset. A specially attractive feature is the mixing of Blue Lias with Ham Hill, Doulting or a similar oolitic limestone; famous examples are Isle Abbotts and North Petherton.

A number of much coarser Jurassic limestones, among them Coral Rag and Cornbash, are abundant in the counties of the south midlands. Of these Coral Rag is the most reliable, although only available as small rubble pieces. It was used in Oxfordshire, and along a line from Cumnor to Coleshill and into Wiltshire where many village churches are built of this material. Somerset has no Coral Rag, but it reappears in Dorset, where the quarries at Todber and Marnhull yielded a freestone that is to be seen in many of the medieval churches in the surrounding districts. Although mostly an indifferent building stone, Cornbash limestone was extensively employed from Cirencester through central Oxfordshire, the northern part of Buckinghamshire and the whole length of Northamptonshire on the Bedfordshire–Cambridgeshire border. Many of the churches around Buckingham are built of this inferior stone.

Yorkshire is endowed with many building stones. The most important is magnesian limestone, which is comparatively soft when quarried but hardens on exposure and is capable of being dressed and carved. It cannot withstand the chemicals in coal smoke, which attacks the stone below its surface, but in rural areas, where the air is relatively unpolluted, it retains the creamy-white colour it had when first quarried, as at Sprotbrough and Campsall in South Yorkshire, Womersley and Sherburn-in-Elmet in North Yorkshire and Darrington in West Yorkshire.

The other limestone of the north belongs to the Carboniferous series of rocks and is sometimes known as 'mountain limestone', for it is generally found in the sparsely populated mountainous regions of England. Grey in colour, this limestone is hard, rough-textured and intractable, completely resistant to the mason's chisel. It is found in the Peak District – where it is the principal building stone of the southern and central parts – and also in parts of the limestone plateau, where its greyish-white outcrops lighten the whole landscape. Outside the Peak District, carboniferous limestone is found in Cumbria, on the western side of the Pennines, across the border into North Yorkshire (where it forms much of the Yorkshire Dales), as well as further north in and around Richmond and into County Durham. In Northumberland, too, it was widely used, and here, as in Cumbria, North Yorkshire, and Durham it is a somewhat darker grey than in the Peak District. It was not uncommon for the little, lonely churches of these areas, particularly those of the northern Dales, to be whitewashed. Carboniferous limestone can be found again around the Mendips, where it was mainly used for humbler buildings, but also for churches, when no other material was at hand, as at Berrow.

Older than the Carboniferous are the Devonian limestones, which are hard and intractable, like the 'mountain limestones'. This stone is also grey (in various shades from almost black to nearly white) but can also be pink. Limestones from this geological formation were used along the southern fringe of Dartmoor.

One other limestone that must be mentioned is the rather unusual tufaceous limestone. This is formed by the action of spring water bubbling up through an existing limestone and precipitating upon it calcium carbonate, which hardens in time to produce a stone with a sponge-like appearance with many holes in its surface. This was used as a building stone by the Romans and also from Saxon times (for the tower stair-turret at Brixworth, Northamptonshire, probably added in the tenth century, and the Norman church at Moccas, Herefordshire) until the fourteenth century. It was used in a few churches in Worcestershire: at Shelsley Walsh, Eastham and the tower at Clifton upon Teme.

Plenty of tufa can also be seen at the church at Dursley, Gloucestershire. It was also used in association with other materials; in Kent, for instance, it was used with Kentish ragstone at West Farleigh, Leeds and East Malling.

The only other limestone to be found in our churches is Caen stone, imported from Normandy. Because Caen was readily accessible to south-eastern England, this material was widely used in Kent, as well as in Sussex, Surrey and Essex. Its principal use in churches was for quoins, doorways, window-frames and tracery, columns, corbels, pinnacles and other work requiring carving. At Barfreston, Kent, (34) the upper half of the church and all the dressings are of Caen ashlar.

Sandstone

The sandstones to be found in England are even more varied than the limestones and, like them, are classified according to their geological age. Nine systems yield sandstones for building, but the vast majority come from three: Cretaceous, which yields the Upper

34 Barfreston, Kent

and Lower Greensand stones and Wealden sandstone; Triassic, from which New Red Sandstones are obtained; and Carboniferous, which supplies the Coal Measure sandstones, the Millstone Grits, the Culm Measures and the Lower Carboniferous sandstones.

The Greensands from the Cretaceous system vary considerably in colour, and, while some are greenish-yellow or grey, the majority are stained with iron oxide and produce stones of every shade from the palest yellow to the darkest brown. These stones are often loosely referred to as 'ironstones'. Most are to be found in the south-east, and where they do occur there is a strong local variation. In parts of Surrey and Kent there occurs a dark brown 'ironstone' known as carstone. Perhaps the most important, certainly historically, is Reigate stone found at Gatton, Merstham, Bletchingley, and Brockham and several churches under the North Downs. Malmstone, another Greensand, is to be found in the Farnham area of Surrey and across the Hampshire border at Selborne. The most durable of these stones came from the Hythe beds (in Surrey); they were not a freestone but could be worked into large blocks, as at Witley, Surrey. Probably the most famous of these stones is Bargate, a greenish sandstone found in parts of Sussex and Surrey. The best of the Cretaceous sandstones is possibly the so-called Wealden stone from the Hastings beds, which, as the name implies, is found in and around the Weald of Sussex and Kent. This grey-brown-fawn stone weathers extremely well and can be dressed and ashlared.

Greensand is also found in a continuous, narrow band to the western side of the chalk escarpments from Hunstanton in the north to Abbotsbury in the south. In Dorset, Somerset and Wiltshire this soft grey and brown stone (rarely is it green) was easily squared and coursed, and even on occasions ashlared. In Wiltshire it was often used, to form the chequered pattern with flint so popular in parts of that county. It was also used in Bedfordshire, where the principal quarry was at Silsoe, and can be seen to good effect at Husborne Crawley. Here some of the walls are of the brown carstone (a stone of a coarse pebbly or gritty consistency), but those of the chancel, the north aisle of the nave and the tower have contrasting stones containing glauconite to give the stonework a partly yellow-green and partly blue-green colour. In other places (for instance at Northill) the brown carstone is used in combination with the Totternhoe chalk. It is also found in

Buckinghamshire, in that part of the county bordering upon Bedfordshire around Leighton Buzzard; at some medieval churches, such as Mursley and Soulbury, it may be seen mixed with limestone.

In Norfolk the greensand stone, known locally as 'gingerbread stone', appears again. The principal quarry was at Snettisham, which yielded a very dark brown, coarse, gritty stone which could only be obtained in relatively small pieces. It can be found in a number of churches, such as Ingoldisthorpe, Shernborne, South Wootton and Heacham, usually in the form of rubble often mixed with flint, and further south at West Dereham, where the Norman tower is built of large pieces of carstone topped by a brick Tudor belfry.

In the south-west, Greensand is to be found not only to the west of the chalk escarpment but also over a large area of south Somerset and west Dorset, from Chard to Lyme Regis, and into the adjoining parts of east Devon. It occurs again on the eastern side of the Lincolnshire Wolds, around Spilsby, often with much brickwork (as at Bratoft and Little Steeping). Although one of the most attractive of the Greensands, the Lincolnshire variety is especially vulnerable to the vagaries of our weather. It is a stone of infinite shades of greens, browns and greys, as can be seen on the Decorated porch at West Keal, but sadly, many churches – amongst them Irby in the Marsh, Haltham-on-Bain, Halton Holgate and Burgh le Marsh – show badly weathered areas as well as much patching, usually in brick.

From the Triassic, and to a lesser extent the slightly older Permian system, come the New Red Sandstones, the principal building stone of the western side of England from Devon northwards to Cumbria. They vary greatly, not only in colour (although known as red sandstone at Lapworth, Warwickshire, it has weathered to an attractive grey) but also in weathering qualities. Many quarries produced sandstone of excellent quality, but, regrettably, there were more that produced stone that blistered, spalled and crumbled once exposed to the English weather, and much architectural detailing has been lost. Despite this disadvantage the Red Sandstone was widely used. It was the favourite material of east Devon – from the coast around Paignton and Sidmouth up beyond Exeter, then to the west through the Vale of Crediton and northwards to Cullompton – and into west Somerset, towards Taunton.

Here some of the towers under the lee of the Quantocks are especially delightful, and that at Kingston St Mary is particularly grand. Sometimes, as at Kenton in Devon, the dressings are of white limestone from Beer, and the contrast between the red and white stone is very striking.

New Red Sandstones also cover much of the west midlands, from Warwickshire through Worcestershire, Shropshire and Staffordshire and into Cheshire, but it was most widely used in the Vale of Eden in Cumbria – especially in the coastal plain around St Bees (which, together with the quarry at Hollington, Staffordshire, produced the most durable of these sandstones). In Shropshire the finest stone was quarried at Grinshill and used in many of the mellow village churches in the northern half of the county.

The Jurassic series is composed mostly of limestone, but there are two areas of England where it has sufficient silica to rank as sandstone. One such area is in Northamptonshire, where, from the base of the oolite beds, a stone varying in colour from buff to deep reddish-brown was produced. It was widely used in the villages around Northampton; the churches at Naseby, and Duston are of this stone. A stone of a similar nature is to be found in North Yorkshire; here, however, it yields a yellow-grey sandstone from which most of the buildings of the North Yorkshire Moors and surrounding districts are built.

For strength and durability no sandstones can compare with those belonging to the Carboniferous system. They are found in the south-western counties, but it is in the north that they are of paramount importance. These rocks from the Coal Measures – the Millstone Grit and the sandstone from the Carboniferous series (known as the Lower Carboniferous sandstones) – have much in common. Quartz, the principal material from which they are all formed, and some feldspar are cemented together with silica, an extremely hard and virtually indestructible substance. This produces a stone which is hard, intractable and difficult to work, but which adds much to the rugged simplicity associated with the buildings of the north. As if to match the architecture, the colours are also sombre, usually brown, buff or various shades of grey – only the Lower Carboniferous sandstones of Northumberland produce the more pleasing yellows. Of the three, Millstone Grit, generally known as gritstone, is the most important. (The sandstones from the Coal Measures are usually associated with industrial regions of the North, whereas gritstone is more characteristic of rural areas.) It is the principal stone of the southern Pennines, extending east and west of the limestone plateau in Derbyshire, Lancashire and into North Yorkshire as far north as Richmond. It appears again to the west of the Carboniferous limestone in north Lancashire.

The Culm Measures, also of the Carboniferous period, cover much of central Devon and extend over north Cornwall to the coast. Sandstone from these deposits was widely used in central and western Devon, for instance at Bampton, Chulmleigh, King's Nympton, Monkleigh and Tawstock. These churches (and many others) have hard, rubbly walls, mainly dark reddish-brown in colour, which are fortunately spotted with plenty of silver-green lichen which helps in their appearance.

Apart from the Cretaceous, Triassic and Carboniferous systems, several other systems produce sandstone used in churches. From the Tertiary system comes sarsen – the youngest of all our sandstones. This is found just below the surface of the ground in the form of boulders of indeterminate size: the firmly cemented remains of what was once a more continuous layer which has largely eroded away. Sarsen is to be found mainly in Wiltshire, Berkshire and Surrey, where it is scattered about the heaths and downs. Predominately grey in colour it is very difficult to work, but it is found to good effect in a few churches in Surrey; the towers at Ash, Worplesdon, Chobham and Pirbright all contain sarsen, that at Pirbright having the blocks roughly squared and laid in courses.

At the other end of the time scale are the Old Red Sandstones, formed some 345 to 395 million years ago. Like the New Red Sandstones, they yield rocks of many colours – pinks, purples, browns, greys of various shades, as well as dark reds – which often change from block to block, even sometimes within the same block. Also like the New Red Sandstones they are only moderately satisfactory for building, being liable to spall and crumble when exposed to weather. An important rock in parts of Wales and Scotland, in England they are encountered only west of the River Severn in north Shropshire, Gloucestershire and Herefordshire. Unlike the friable New Red Sandstones of the west midlands, some of the Herefordshire stone is extremely hard, as can be witnessed at Kilpeck.

The Devonian rocks, formed during the same geological period as the Old Red Sandstones, differ considerably. Most are of slate with some limestone and here and there some sandstone. These rocks cover much of north Devon and west Somerset, including the whole of Exmoor, as well as most of Devon to the south of Dartmoor, and they also spread over a large area of Cornwall. Where found, sandstone from this series was an important building material.

Even older sandstones belong to the Silurian and Ordovician systems and are perhaps up to 575 million years old. Silurian stones – hard stones, normally used as rubble, which contain particles of grey shale – span a colour range of rather sombre greys, browns and blacks. They are found only in the Lake District, around Ulverston, Windermere, Hawkshead and spreading down the coast to Grange-over-Sands and Ireleth. In this area it was at one time common to cover the walls with roughcast and whitewash, but in many cases this has been removed, as at Hawkshead. The Ordovician series, which produces the slates of the Lake District, also produces an uncompromising building stone, often dark and sombre in colour.

Flint

One material that was used extensively when found, is flint. The Romans made great use of it, and during the Saxon and Norman periods it was a building material of paramount importance, and continued to be so in many areas throughout the Medieval period. Flints are irregularly shaped nodules of silica and, although extremely hard, are brittle and easily fractured. They are found in the upper layers of the chalk formation and, when first dug, are practically black, often with a white 'rind' over the surface.

Flint is much the most common material for churches in Norfolk and Suffolk and the adjoining parts of Essex, Hertfordshire and Cambridgeshire, as well as elsewhere in the southern and south-eastern counties, where chalk is to be found: in Berkshire, Surrey, Kent, Sussex and Hampshire and parts of Dorset and Wiltshire. The flints could be mined, for instance around Brandon in Suffolk, in which case they were larger and more irregular and used for the best work, but often they were picked from the fields or, in coastal areas, sea-washed and collected from the beach. Because of their small size and often irregular shape, plenty of mortar was generally necessary – which, unless the work has been done with care, can look disagreeable. Flints are best seen when they are knapped – that is to say broken across – to expose the dark interior. When employed in combination with a dressed white or nearly white limestone they can look striking. This technique is known as flushwork and is an East Anglian (and principally Suffolk) speciality, and in nearly all cases belongs to late fifteenth or early sixteenth centuries. The decoration was achieved by forming a sunken pattern in a slab of freestone which was filled with split flints with their black interior exposed, which contrasted with good effect with the freestone. The freestone was cut into a variety of patterns and was frequently applied to buttresses, parapets, plinths and clerestories, as well as porches and towers. The designs included heraldic shields, saints' emblems, monograms and single letters, crowns, stars, trefoil-headed panels and many other devices (35). Typical flushwork can be seen at Long Melford, Coddenham, Cavendish, Kersey, Framsden and Laxfield in Suffolk and at

RJBROWN.

35   Flushwork at Dedham, Essex

Redenhall in Norfolk. All along the base of the north aisle at Stratford St Mary, Suffolk, runs an inscription, partly in English and partly in Latin, in boldly-cut Gothic lettering; above the buttresses is more lettering, and higher still a complete alphabet.

Because of the nature of flints it was normal to provide stone or brick for the dressings to quoins, windows and the like, but in some areas these other materials were used to create a much more striking effect on the appearance of the church, the two favourite patterns being horizontal bands and chequers. Although its effect was decorative this technique also produced a stronger wall than one built entirely of flints. Another popular form of decoration in most areas where flint is to be found combined flints, usually knapped, and squared stone to form a chequer pattern. In Wiltshire and Dorset, banding appears as well; one of the finest places to see this is at Affpuddle, Dorset, where the banding can be compared with the chequer work of the tower. Similar banding can be seen at Toller Porcorum, Dorset, as well as at Cliffe in Kent. At Fingringhoe in Essex both banded and chequer work are to be found on the tower.

There are no flint buildings on the chalk wolds of Lincolnshire and Yorkshire, but in the alluvial plain of Holderness 'boulder stones' or cobbles, either collected from the boulder clay or gathered from the beach, were at one time used quite extensively for cottages and farmhouses and even occasionally for churches around Spurn Head and northwards along the coast. The churches of Skeffling, Roos, Burton Pidsea and Tunstall all show these large stones (sometimes nearly a foot long and five to six inches thick) interspersed with rubble and a great deal of mortar. At Easington the large cobbles are to be seen laid in a herringbone pattern.

Conglomerates

The only other building stones so far not mentioned are the conglomerates and concretions, of which only puddingstone and septaria were used in churches. Puddingstone is an unworkable material and so was used in undressed form. It consists of natural cement – iron oxide or some siliceous material – which binds together flinty pebbles or small pieces of sandstone. Dark brown in colour it is a product of the pebble beds of the London Basin and the gravelly regions of north-west Surrey and for lack of anything better it was used in all the Home Counties with the exception of

Kent. It can be found at Ripley, Cranleigh (used with carstone) and Pyrford in Surrey, as it can in a group of churches around Wokingham, Berkshire: for example Binfield, Warfield and Winkfield. It provided a valuable foundation for many churches in Hertfordshire, but it is in Essex, a county devoid of good building stone, that it is most often seen. In the north-east of the county it was widely used, often in combination with rubble, flint and Roman bricks; churches at Ardleigh and Boxted are characteristic examples.

The other material in this group is septaria – found in the Thames estuary, north-east Essex and along the Suffolk coast as far north as Orford – which looks like petrified clay of various shades of ochre and brown. It was freely used, together with rubble, flint and bricks, in churches in north-east Essex between the Rivers Stour and Colne and down towards the River Blackwater, for example those at Lawford, Great Bentley and Goldhanger. It can also be seen in Suffolk, where it is to be found along the banks of the River Stour, at Erwarton and on the tower at Harkstead. In Kent it can be seen at the church at Herne.

Brick

The Romans used brick extensively, and today their flat, tile-like bricks are to be found in many of our village churches, taken from ruined buildings and reused by medieval builders. There are Roman bricks in over seventy churches in Essex, sometimes incorporated with flint and rubble, and the seventh-century church at Brixworth, Northamptonshire, was largely built with Roman bricks.

There is little evidence of brick-making following the withdrawal of the Romans until the earliest known English bricks appeared in the eastern counties (the arcade arches at Polstead in Suffolk) in the twelfth century. It was not until the Tudor period that bricks became an acceptable material for church building, and then they were only used where stone was not available. The finest Tudor brickwork is to be found in Essex; entire churches (East Horndon, Layer Marney, Woodham Walter and Chignall Smealy) show what could be achieved in brick. To these must be added many towers, porches and even the occasional clerestory and arcades, all built of delightfully coloured red brickwork, which has mellowed over the centuries, often enriched with the usual Tudor diapers of dark blue. Tudor brickwork can also be found elsewhere. In Norfolk, for instance, there is the church at Shelton which, apart from its small flint tower from an earlier church, was built around 1485–90. The quality of the building is exquisite, and the clerestory is even faced with limestone. Of about the same date is Lutton, Lincolnshire, which is almost all of brick, except for the tower and spire. Slightly later is the church at Smallhythe, Kent, built in 1516–17 after the destruction of the village by fire.

The years between 1540 and 1660 were not a good time for church-building, and brick churches from this period are by no means common. That at Fulmer in Buckinghamshire, its north

36   Willen, Buckinghamshire

porch and tower still surviving, is one dating from 1610. Another charming example is the little church at Hoveton St Peter, Norfolk, with the date 1624 above the porch door. The crow-stepped gables are original, but the bell-cote and the thatched roof replaced a wood bell-turret and tiled roof during the nineteenth century, when the buttresses, too, were added.

After the Restoration churches designed in the Classical style began to appear, and the popularity of brick increased in many parts of the country. The brickwork was often plain, any decoration depending largely upon stone dressings. Willen in Buckinghamshire, (36) built in 1676–80, is an admirable example, and Farley, on the Wiltshire–Hampshire border, is another. It is interesting to note that the brickwork at Farley was still laid in English bond – such a late use of English bond, which by then had generally been abandoned for Flemish bond, probably indicates that the church was built by local workmen. As the eighteenth century advanced, brick was employed more and more, for now in many areas it was for the first time substantially cheaper than stone.

Roof Coverings

The materials used for the roof were just as important aesthetically as those used for the walls. Here, too, the range has been extremely wide; thatch, lead, slate, stone slates, shingles, plain tiles and pantiles are all to be found adding great charm to many of our village churches.

In early times, thatch would have been one of the materials most widely used, and it is first reported, on a church at Lindisfarne in Northumberland, about the middle of the seventh century. Its use was not restricted to small village churches. Churches of some importance were often roofed in this material, and Sherborne Abbey, Dorset, was thatched in the fifteenth century. At one time a great number of small church roofs were thatched with straw in the southern counties, especially in Hampshire and Berkshire, but today I know of none. In parts of East Anglia, Cambridgeshire and Lincolnshire thatch would have been almost universally used, something which is easily understood when one thinks of the availability of reeds and sedges from the Broads and the marshes that covered such a large proportion of the area, especially Norfolk.

37　　Thornham Parva, Suffolk

Even today many church roofs are thatched: in Norfolk over fifty churches are still wholly or partly roofed with this material, and nearly twenty in Suffolk.

No matter to what extent the thatch survives, these roofs give great pleasure. The ridges are frequently decorated with scallops and zigzags, and an especially ornamental roof is the one at Thurton, Norfolk, which has three tiers of decorative patterning. In some cases even the underside is decorated; at Burlingham St Edmund and Irstead, Norfolk, the underside is treated with a sort of plaiting. Only one thatched church remains in Lincolnshire, that at Markby, and in Cambridgeshire the impressive nave roof at Longstanton survives.

Lead was also used as a roofing material for centuries before the Conquest – the thatch on the timber-framed church at Lindisfarne was replaced by lead plates at the end of the seventh century. Its widespread use in medieval times was restricted, firstly by the cost (especially that of transporting it from Cornwall and Derbyshire), secondly by the difficulty of casting it into sheets, and thirdly by the difficulty in finding skilled labour locally to lay it. In the late Middle Ages lead from the mines in Derbyshire, the Mendips and Wendale was in great demand all over the country and was widely used on the steeply pitched roofs so common in the early part of the fifteenth century. The silvery hue of lead produces a roof of considerable charm, but on steeply pitched roofs it has one main disadvantage: it is impossible to stop the lead from creeping and slipping, so repairs are constantly needed. Towards the end of the fifteenth century almost flat roofs were introduced, and lead was the only material which could be used. Spires were also frequently roofed with lead, because, once again, despite its disadvantages, it was one of the few materials which could be used on a very steep pitch.

Slates are another of the oldest roof coverings – not the Welsh slates introduced to so many areas in Victorian times but the lovely stone slates that can be found in many parts of the country. These are made of a fissile stone that could be split after quarrying to produce stone slates. Both limestones and sandstones were suited to this, but limestone, as associated with the Cotswolds, was perhaps the better of the two, because it could be split into thinner slates to produce a lighter roof. Even so the weight was considerable: a roof weighed almost a ton per square (100 square feet). These slates are rarely flat and almost always have a slight camber, so a steep pitch (usually between 45° and 55°) was required. (Due to the camber and the fact that the tiles were laid breaking joint, the slates were positioned on a steep pitch so that rain could not be driven under the slates). Because limestone slates could be easily split and cut into relatively small sizes, a delicate, intricate roof could be achieved. In contrast, sandstone slates – or flags, as they are often called – are thick and heavy and can be as big as four feet wide and three inches or so thick. Because of this they are rarely laid at a pitch in excess of 30°, and their size and weight gives such roofs tremendous presence. The appearance of both limestone and sandstone slates is greatly enhanced when they are laid in diminishing courses – the largest at the eaves and the smallest at the ridge.

The best limestone roofs can be found in the Cotswolds, but comparable stone slates can be found in Northamptonshire (from the quarry at Collyweston) and spreading out into the neighbouring counties of Leicestershire, Cambridgeshire, Lincolnshire and Bedfordshire. Sandstone slates are much more widely used for church roofs and, although less pleasing than limestone, are nonetheless an appropriate roofing material for churches in northern England as well as those in the Welsh border counties. In the north they come from a variety of rock formations – the Coal Measures and Millstone Grit – while in the Welsh marches they are from the older rock formations, the Old Red Sandstones and the Ordovician and Silurian rocks. Sandstone slates are generally restricted to the highland zone, although in Sussex Horsham slates add a distinctive character to many of the churches, the roofs often being carried over nave and aisles in a single span and in some cases descending to within a few feet of the ground.

Most of the slate found on village churches today is Welsh slate: a blue-grey slate that can be split into thin slabs of uniform size and thickness to produce a roof which is smooth and precise – and also uninteresting. English slate, on the other hand, is full of interest and colour and, (unlike Welsh slate, which was always laid in regular courses) was graded, with the largest slates at the eaves and the smallest at the ridge. English slate is only to be found in the south-west, Leicestershire and Cumbria. In Cornwall it is almost the universal roofing material for churches, as it is in parts of Devon – South Hams and north-west Devon. Whereas slates in the south-west are dark grey, in Cumbria they are found in a variety of colours – greys, greens and blues – and numerous shades. The only other place in England where slate was quarried was at Swithland in the Charnwood Forest.

Plain roof tiles can be found on churches in many areas – in particular the south-east and eastern England, where, because of their quality, they have been used for many centuries. In Kent, parts of Sussex and Essex they are almost universally used, and handmade peg-tiles, each one varying slightly in size, shape and colour, give an aesthetic appearance that few other roofs can match. In Sussex these plain tiled roofs often sweep down low in a great single roof, like those of Horsham slates.

Pantiles – S-shaped tiles – were imported from Holland in the seventeenth century and soon became popular in eastern England, being supplemented in the early part of the eighteenth century by the first English-made pantiles. Although widely used on domestic buildings they are seldom to be found on church roofs. However, they were used to good effect on a number of churches in Norfolk, as at Bawburgh and South Pickenham, as well as a few in

Lincolnshire – for instance the little eighteenth-century church at Hannah (38) – and even into Nottinghamshire at Holme. The only other place in the country where pantiles were traditionally used is in Somerset around Bridgwater, for example at Thurloxton. Their main advantage was that they were a single-lap tile, each tile overlapping the one beneath, with the S-shape making it possible for each tile to form a sideways lap and so produce a relatively light, economical roof. They were probably used to replace thatch on many churches in eastern England.

Another material used as a roof covering was shingles, traditionally made from split oak (but now largely replaced with Canadian cedar, which, although not a traditional material, weathers to a pleasant silver-grey). Today shingles are mainly used in the roofing or cladding of the small timber spires found on many churches in the south-east and Essex.

38   Hannah, Lincolnshire

4   The Plan

The visual appearance of a church is affected not only by the material it is built of but also by its plan. The evolution of the medieval village church, from the simple, severe, one- or two-cell building of the Saxon and Norman periods to the fully developed, beautiful structure of the fifteenth century can be traced in many churches today. While some early churches have remained virtually unaltered since they were built, the majority owe their present appearance to the continuing adaptation of the original plan. It was generally not until the Perpendicular period that earlier churches were swept away and churches of one style erected in their place in any great numbers.

The medieval church was planned on an east-west axial, with the sanctuary placed at the east end. The reason for this orientation is not clear; it is often suggested that it was the custom of the congregation to face eastwards towards the Holy Land, but it is equally likely that it derived from primitive man's worship of the rising sun.

The early churches built in Saxon England are of two distinct types: the south-eastern, or Augustinian (of Roman origin) and the Northumbrian (of Celtic origin). Those in the south-east, consisted of a rectangular nave with a triple arcade carried on tall columns separating it from a chancel terminating in an apse at the eastern end. From each side of the building projected a square chamber (known as a porticus) which served as a sacristy, and at the west end of the nave stood the vestibule. The church at Bradwell-on-Sea in Essex, which was built of Roman materials around 656, was of this type; the chancel, portici and vestibule have all gone, but the nave remains, and in the blocked eastern end one of the springings of the three arches that opened into the chancel can still be seen. The church at Reculver in Kent, founded in 669, was similar, although with later additions – and remained virtually intact until it was wantonly destroyed by the vicar in 1809. This early Kentish plan reappears in the tenth century at Worth, West Sussex (39), with the important differences that the portici were moved to the west, away from the chancel, and used as chapels, and the triple chancel arch was replaced by a single arch.

A much more ambitious church, built to an aisled basilica plan on the Italian model was built at Brixworth, Northamptonshire. Although it is often claimed to have been built in around 680, when a monastery was founded there, this is far from certain. It originally had a nave with side aisles, a chancel separated from the nave by a triple arch, an apsed sanctuary with a crypt below it and a two-storey porch at the west end. It was altered in the late Saxon period,

39   Worth, West Sussex

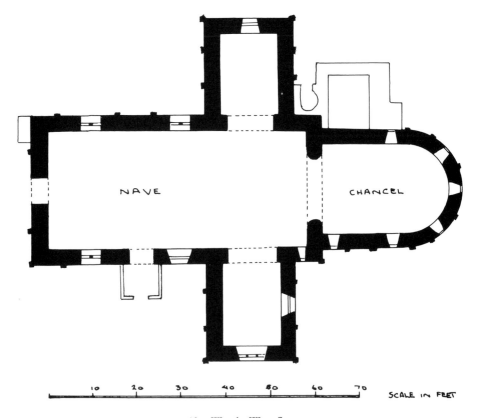

NAVE

CHANCEL

SCALE IN FEET

40　Worth, West Sussex

and again in post-Saxon times. The aisles have been destroyed, perhaps after the Norman conquest, but Sir Alfred Clapham nevertheless claims that the church is 'perhaps the most imposing architectural memorial of the seventh century north of the Alps'. The Brixworth plan is unusual in the early churches of Saxon England and does not reappear until the tenth century – at Wing, Buckinghamshire, where the main variation is that the apse is seven-sided instead of round.

The Northumbrian church differed from the Augustinian in the exceptional height and extreme narrowness of the nave and chancel as can be seen at Escomb (42) which contrast with the proportions of the Kentish group of churches. This relationship between height and width is a characteristic of northern churches and can again be seen at Whittingham in Northumberland (43), an important Saxon church largely rebuilt in 1840 in the Gothic style and at

Monkwearmouth, Sunderland. Only the western porch (later raised as a tower) and the west wall of the nave still stand at Monkwearmouth, but the remaining walls of the nave are probably built on the original foundations.

41   Escomb, County Durham

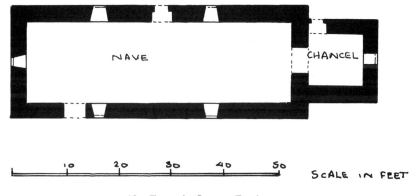

42   Escomb, County Durham

43 Whittingham, Northumberland

One of the most interesting and important early Saxon churches is at Deerhurst, Gloucestershire, (44) where the present nave and a chancel was built in the seventh or eighth century to replace an earlier timber church on the site. The new church was built to the Northumbrian plan (60 feet long by 20 feet wide, with walls some 40 feet high); later a two-storey west porch was added, together with a two-storey north and south portici. A little later the porch was raised another storey and portici extended westward to flank the nave. In the tenth century the earlier chancel was replaced by an apsidal chancel, now in ruins, and the porch was further raised to form a tower. The original Northumbrian plan was thus developed into an Augustinian church.

44   Deerhurst, Gloucestershire

The majority of pre-Conquest churches would have been of the simple two-cell type, as at Boarhunt, Hampshire – Saxon churches with arcades, like Brixworth, Wing and Great Paxton, Cambridgeshire, and the remains at Lydd in Kent, were exceptional. The cruciform plan with a central tower carried by four arches was rarely employed, for building wide, lofty arches was generally beyond the skill of the pre-Conquest masons. The only church approaching this form is at Breamore, Hampshire, but here the flanking chapels or transepts, of which only the southern one remains, are narrower than the tower.

After the Conquest the Normans were apparently content to accept and adopt the Saxon plan of nave and chancel. The simplest form involved a single cell with no structural division between nave and chancel, as at Little Braxted and Little Tey in Essex (45), North Marden in West Sussex, Nateley Scures in Hampshire (46) and Winterborne Tomson in Dorset. The greater number of these Norman churches, however, were two-cell buildings consisting of a nave and a narrower chancel. The square, or almost square, chancel of the Saxon period gave way to one of greater length in proportion to its width, terminating in either a square or apsidal east end. The apsidal end derived from the Roman basilica church, whereas the Celtic tradition had always favoured the square east end. Eventually the square end ousted the apse in England, though apses were more common in those counties nearest to Normandy. The entrance to such churches was by a doorway to the south-west of the nave. Simple churches, for example, at Heath Chapel in Shropshire and Stoke Orchard in Gloucestershire (48) and later and more ornate ones, like those at Barfreston in Kent, Hales in Norfolk and Adel in West Yorkshire, are all of this simple nave-and-chancel type.

A slightly larger type of Norman church had another cell between the nave and chancel, known as the choir, with each of the three compartments being defined by arches. In this plan the chancel (or sanctuary) could be either square, as at Elkstone in Gloucestershire, or apsidal, as at Kilpeck in Herefordshire (49), Wissington in Suffolk (50), Steetley in Derbyshire (51) and Birkin in North Yorkshire. Where the chancel or sanctuary was square-ended a tower was sometimes raised above the choir space, as at Studland in Dorset (52), Stewkley in Buckinghamshire, and Cassington and Iffley in Oxfordshire.

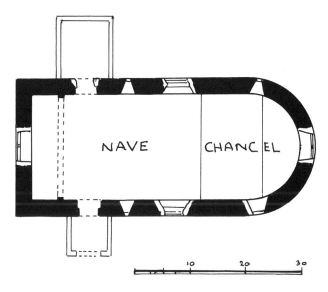

45   Little Tey, Essex

46   Nateley Scures, Hampshire

47   Up Waltham, West Sussex

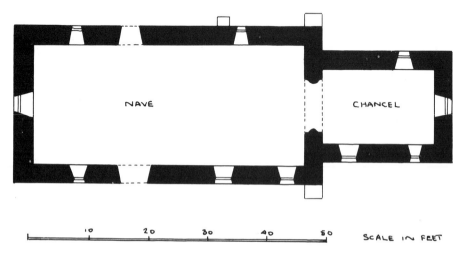

48   Stoke Orchard, Gloucestershire

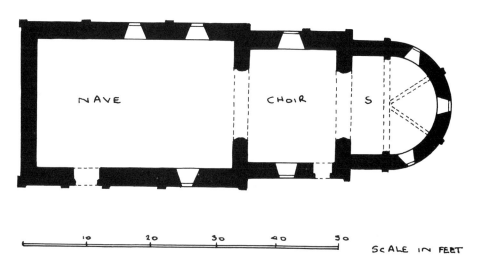

NAVE CHOIR S

SCALE IN FEET

49 Kilpeck, Herefordshire

50 Wissington, Suffolk

51   Steetley, Derbyshire

52   Studland, Dorset

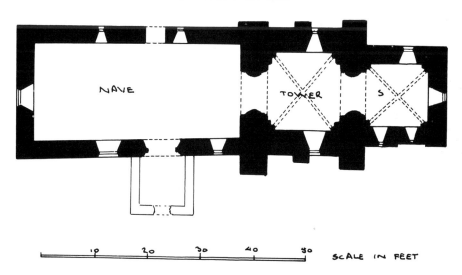

53   Studland, Dorset

Transepts were added to the body of the church to create a plan
in the form of a Latin cross. This type of plan increased in popularity during the Norman period, and the essential feature of such
churches was a central tower supported only at its corners. This
had obvious disadvantages, for the massive piers indispensable to
supporting a central tower obstructed the view of the chancel from
the main body of the church, and in the aisleless examples it also
cut off the transepts from the rest of the church.

A feature known in Normandy was a two-storied chancel, and
one twelfth-century example survives in this country at Compton,
Surrey. Here an upper chamber was built into the original
eleventh-century chancel around 1180, with a guard-rail on the
side overlooking the nave; it is thought to have been built to house
pilgrims who travelled to Canterbury along the Pilgrims' Way on
which Compton stands.

It was not long before the Normans realized the advantages to be
gained by having aisles; not only could they provide additional
accommodation, they were also convenient for the ever-increasing
popularity of processions. Altars could be, and often were, placed
against the eastern walls of the nave – which in unaisled churches
flanked each side of the chancel arch, as at Castle Rising, Norfolk.
The most common plan was an adaptation of the simple two-cell
nave-and-chancel plan that involved an aisled nave and an unaisled
chancel. The churches at Castle Hedingham, Essex, and Walsoken,
Norfolk, are typical examples.

Some churches are called round churches, though it is only the
nave that is actually round. These were built by the Knights
Templar and the Knights Hospitaller after the plan of the church
of the Holy Sepulchre in Jerusalem. There are four: in London
(Inner Temple), Cambridge, Northampton and Little Maplestead,
Essex (54).

During the next three-and-a-half centuries the development of
the village church occurred principally through the alteration and
expansion of existing buildings: at first in response to the growth
of the population, and later in response to the increase in church
ritual. Although the nave-and-chancel plan continued to be used
for many smaller village churches, across the country the aisled
nave and unaisled chancel established itself as the standard church
plan throughout the Middle Ages. It dates principally from the
thirteenth century, but, although many new churches were built at

54 Little Maplestead, Essex

this time, it would have been exceptional for them to reach such a relatively sophisticated point of development in a single initial building campaign. Saxon and Norman chancels were always small, and many (especially those with apsidal ends) were extended and built square. Very occasionally the chancel was widened, but, as it entailed rebuilding the walls, this was seldom undertaken. Naves, too, were often extended westwards, but from the end of the thirteenth century the provision of aisles, either to the north of the nave or the south, or both, became the commonest method of increasing the size of the church.

The church at Walkern, Hertfordshire, illustrates the development of a typical village church over the centuries. Built in the eleventh century to the usual nave-and-chancel plan, a south aisle was added in the twelfth century, followed in the thirteenth century by a north aisle and the rebuilding of the chancel. The tower was added in the fourteenth century and the south porch in the fifteenth century – when many of the windows were enlarged and buttresses added. In the nineteenth century a north chapel was constructed and a vestry added. Hundreds of similar examples can be found throughout the country. Another can be seen at Withington, Gloucestershire (55). Here a church existed in Saxon times but was completely rebuilt in the twelfth century to the Norman plan of nave, central tower and chancel; the chancel was lengthened in the thirteenth century, the south transept added in the fourteenth century, and in the fifteenth the clerestory was added to the nave and the tower raised.

When only one aisle was added, it was generally built on the north side for the cemetery normally lay to the south. At first these aisles were no more than narrow passages – often no more than six feet wide, as at Ayston, Rutland – but in the fourteenth century they were often twelve or fourteen feet wide, and in some cases as wide as the nave. The provision of aisles accommodated not only larger congregations but also the increasing number of processions.

55   Withington, Gloucestershire

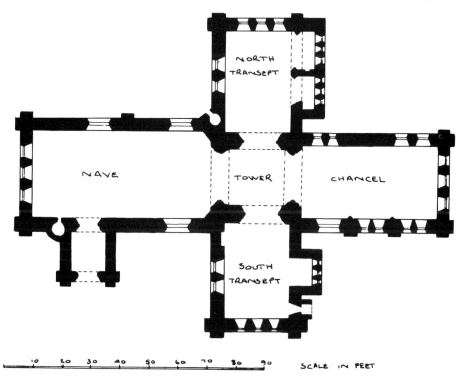

56   Uffington, Oxfordshire (thirteenth century)

The nave itself was generally not widened, because widening an aisled nave would virtually amount to a complete rebuilding. This was carried out occasionally, however, as the evidence of continuous weather moulds on the east wall of the tower at Skidbrooke, Lincolnshire, indicates.

In some cases aisles were provided in both chancel and nave, and this was favoured during the Perpendicular period. In many churches of this type the nave and aisles ran uninterrupted from one end to the other, unbroken by a chancel arch. This is most marked in Cornwall and Devon, where there is hardly a fifteenth-century church that had a chancel arch; it is also a feature of many churches in Kent and also in East Anglia, where some of the larger village churches have the aisles stopping short to allow good lighting to the sanctuary.

The cruciform plan, with or without aisles, continued to be built throughout the thirteenth century; there are impressive examples at Bampton and Uffington in Oxfordshire (56) and

Potterne in Wiltshire. Other churches were sometimes built with transepts but without a central tower, as at Achurch in Northamptonshire, and Acton Burnell in Shropshire. The cruciform plan continued well into the fourteenth century (one can cite Poynings, West Sussex, built about 1370) and into the fifteenth century: the church at Minster Lovell, Oxfordshire (57), built in 1430, is regarded as one of the finest examples of a cruciform church. The construction of aisles for transepts, fairly common in cathedrals and minsters, also occurred in a few of the larger parish churches. Perhaps the finest example is the fourteenth-century church at Patrington, East Riding of Yorkshire, where the transepts have aisles on the east and west, with those on the east being divided into three chapels. Cruciform churches without a central tower can occasionally be found, as at Heckington, Frampton and Weston, all in Lincolnshire.

It might be appropriate here to discuss the term weeping chancel: one which is angled from the line of the nave to one side or the other. This is often said to symbolize the inclination of Christ's head on the Cross. If this was the case, it would imply that early

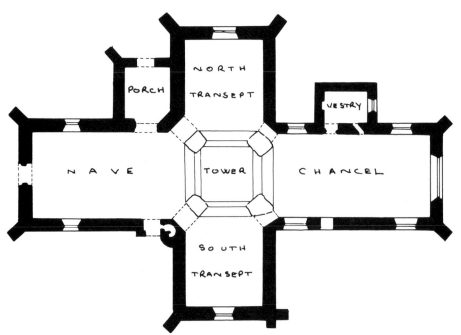

57   Minster Lovell, Oxfordshire (fifteenth century)

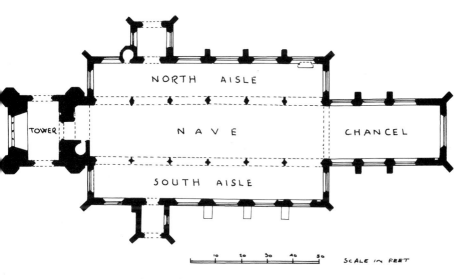

58   Dedham, Essex (sixteenth century)

medieval builders could work to a degree of accuracy of which we
know they were incapable. In fact, up to the beginning of the fourteenth century it is rare to find an exact right angle, or walls built
parallel to one another, or the tower, nave and chancel built on a
common axis. In fact it was not until the fourteenth and fifteenth
century, when many churches were rebuilt, that the setting-out
became more accurate. Furthermore, if the inclination is supposed
to represent that of Christ's head on the Cross then they would all
'weep' one way – in medieval times Christ's head was always shown
inclined to the right, and this must have been known to all
builders, for crucifixes were displayed in all churches. Yet one finds
some chancels which weep to the south and others which weep to
the north.

Today one normally steps up to the chancel. However, during
nineteenth-century restorations chancels were almost universally
either levelled to, or raised above, the floor of the nave. Before that,
it seems that many chancels were in fact below the level of the nave.
Although this is not common as a surviving feature, it is by no
means rare, and it can be found at, among others, Cavendish in
Suffolk and Ashwellthorpe and Wickhampton in Norfolk. At
Myton-on-Swale, North Yorkshire, the ground slopes from west to
east, and a flight of three steps leads down to the chancel. In many
cases the former change in floor level can still be detected by

observing the height of the piscinas, sedilia, aumbries and string courses in relation to the floor level. It appears that the medieval builder cared nothing about levels, and if the site sloped he would follow that slope. It is not uncommon to find the nave sloping in this way; that at Badingham, Suffolk, rises as much as 25 inches over the length of a comparatively short nave.

Towers

The tower, though ritually not essential to the church, is usually its most striking feature. No two towers are alike; they differ considerably not only in ornamental detail and materials used but also in proportions and form. Occasionally towers are detached from the church; usually, though, they form part of the main structure, and they can be found in almost any position except at the east end. The most common position is at the west end, but south towers – the lower storey serving as a porch – are by no means rare as at Bulford, Wiltshire (59), nor are those placed centrally (towers to the north of the nave are less common, however).

59 Bulford, Wiltshire

Very occasionally a village church has two towers. At Purton, Wiltshire, there is a spired central tower and a Perpendicular one at the west end. Great Yeldham, Essex, also has two towers built at different times, though only one was completed. In around 1400 the lower stages of a tower were built at the south-west of the unaisled nave, only to be abandoned, and a century or so later another tower was built at the west end of the nave. The ground floor of the earlier tower was converted into a porch and a brick chamber built over it.

Belfries were, in the main, reached by means of a stair-turret, or by stairs built within the thickness of the tower wall. Towers without these facilities had wooden steps or ladders to give access to the belfry. An original example of the wooden steps, rudely constructed out of huge oak timbers, can be found in the Norman tower of Brabourne, Kent. There is another example at Old Romney, Kent, and a similar structure is to be found at Piddinghoe, East Sussex. Most steps were fixtures, but in some early cases they were no more than a ladder which would be drawn into the belfry in times of attack.

Today the sole purpose of a tower is to house the bells – to call the people to worship and spread tidings, both joyful and sad – but it seems probable that at first many towers were for defensive purposes. It is known that, even as late as the thirteenth century, towers were provided for protection on the turbulent borders of Scotland and Wales. The western tower at Great Salkeld, Cumbria, is a good example, with its doorway at the west end of the nave being barred and iron-clad on the inside. At Bedale, North Yorkshire, the stairway in the tower has a groove for a portcullis that could be lowered to isolate the tower from the rest of the church. Other typical examples are those at Bosbury in Herefordshire and Ormside in Cumbria.

It is claimed that many of the round towers, particularly those of Suffolk and Norfolk built in the period of the Danish invasions, were also built for defensive reasons – either as look-outs or as temporary refuges for villagers during an attack. There are over 160 round towers remaining in England, of which over 150 are in Norfolk and Suffolk – the others being in Essex, Sussex (61), Cambridgeshire and Berkshire. Many built near the sea or on a river are Saxon in origin and, when unaltered, show signs which point to a defensive purpose. Originally they were detached – or at any rate had no permanent building abutting them – and were

60   Cranwick, Norfolk

61   Tower at Southease, East Sussex

certainly never intended to house bells. None were provided with staircases (although in a few cases these have been added), and they appear never to have had any openings near the ground, except for the occasional narrow window. None have a doorway at the western end, but high up on the eastern face all have a narrow, arched opening through which it was possible to gain access to the upper part, hauling a ladder up afterwards. Many still retain their circular double-splayed openings and triangular-headed windows divided by a baluster-shaft: clear indications of their Saxon or possibly very early Norman date. The later insertion of Norman doorways – and even the addition of a tower arch at ground level on the eastern side, when a stone church was built on, as at Little Saxham, Suffolk – all adds confusion to the subject. Many round towers in Suffolk and Norfolk have had octagonal upper storeys added in the thirteenth, fourteenth and fifteenth centuries, even with some flushwork, as at Theberton, Suffolk. Occasionally typical Norman arcading has been added to the top of the tower, as at Little Saxham, Suffolk. These round towers are generally built of flint – Bessingham and West Dereham in Norfolk, are built mainly of brown carstone – and it has been suggested that they were constructed to a round plan so as to obviate the necessity of importing stone for corner dressings from a great distance at great expense. This seems, unlikely, though, for the Saxons could build towers of flint without any stone dressings, as at Little Bardfield, Essex.

Indeed, the majority of the Saxon towers that survive are square, and usually of lofty and slender proportions, their height accentuated by the absence of buttresses. The earliest ones are probably those at Monkwearmouth and Corbridge, which were raised above their porches in around 900. These porches, and those at Brixworth, Northamptonshire, and Ledsham, West Yorkshire, were already two-storeyed, so it was easy enough to raise them. The characteristics of the period – the long and short work, the general absence of ornamentation apart from the pilaster-strips, belfry windows that were never recessed and usually consisted of round-headed openings divided by a baluster-shaped shaft – are to be found in most towers of the Saxon period. All are present in the most famous of all Saxon towers, that at Earls Barton, Northamptonshire. Lincolnshire has more towers from the Saxon period than any other county; those at Bracebridge, Glentworth and Rothwell all have examples of baluster-shaft belfry windows. One of the finest arrangements of these

62   Kirk Hammerton, North Yorkshire

belfry windows can be seen at Appleton-le-Street, North Yorkshire, which has two tiers. Other towers of note in that county, are at Kirk Hammerton (62) and Wharram-le-Street (63).

Northumberland, too, has notable Saxon towers at Bywell St Andrews (64) and Bolam. The square towers were capped with low pyramidal roofs of timber, many of them probably thatched. The Saxon tower at Sompting, West Sussex (65), retains its unique Rhenish helm-gabled roof of the early twelfth century, a form of roof derived from the Romanesque churches of the Rhineland, where they are still to be seen in abundance. Stone staircases were exceptional in Saxon towers, access to the upper floor being gained by means of a wooden ladder. At Brigstock and Brixworth in Northamptonshire, and Broughton and Hough-on-the-Hill in Lincolnshire, a later round stair-turret has been attached to the western face of the tower. There is some evidence that on occasions the towers were used as naves. The churches at Earls Barton in Northamptonshire and Barnack in Cambridgeshire are two examples; in each case the overall plan of the tower is larger than would otherwise be necessary.

63   Tower at Wharram-le-Street, North Yorkshire

64   Saxon tower at Bywell St Andrews, Northumberland

65   Saxon tower at Sompting, West Sussex

66 Norman tower at South Lopham, Norfolk

67   Early Norman tower at Weaverthorpe, North Yorkshire

The majority of Norman churches had no towers, and their bells were hung in small openings at the apex of the ridge or, more rarely, on the gable above it. When a tower was provided it was often built over the choir, and most of the better Norman towers are in this position – for example, those at South Lopham, Norfolk (66), and Iffley, Oxfordshire. Many others were built at the west end of the nave and, in contrast to the slender towers of the Saxons, were frequently large, square, squat structures. Occasionally these Norman towers were not built on the main axis of the church, and one finds towers attached to the church in most unusual positions. In Cornwall there are several instances of early towers over a transept. Others are found to the south of the south transept (Climping, West Sussex) on the north side of the chancel (Chedgrave, Norfolk), on the south side of the chancel (Barford St Michael, Oxfordshire), south of the nave (Patrixbourne, Kent, and Claverley, Shropshire) or south of the east end of the nave (Alberbury, Shropshire). The belfry windows generally consist of two round-headed arches divided by a shaft or column, the whole recessed and encompassed within a larger round-headed arch. Circular openings are also to be found, as at East Meon, Hampshire. In many cases Norman towers are very plain, like that of Weaverthorpe, North Yorkshire (67), but others are very decorative. Blind arcading as a means of decorating central towers – as at South Lopham in Norfolk and Stewkley in Buckinghamshire – is a characteristic, and a small turret containing a vice, or stairway, is another marked feature of Norman tower design.

The towers of Norman village churches generally had either a saddleback roof resting on the gable-ends of the tower wall (a fair number of these remain, as at Duntisbourne Rouse in Gloucestershire, Sarratt in Hertfordshire (68), Wadenhoe in Northamptonshire and Begbroke in Oxfordshire, for example) or a

68   Sarratt, Hertfordshire

low pyramidal roof covered with thatch, shingles or tiles. Instances of the latter occur at Climping and many other churches in Sussex, Sarnesfield in Herefordshire, Eastleach Martin in Gloucestershire and Godmersham in Kent. At Fingest in Buckinghamshire the massive Norman tower, 27 feet square, is roofed with a double saddleback, believed to be an eighteenth-century renewal of an original Norman roof.

In the thirteenth century towers were still relatively uncommon in village churches, a bell-cote generally being provided to house the bells. However, where they did occur, there was a much greater variety of design and proportion. Central and western towers remained popular, but the towers in asymmetrical positions began to fall out of favour unless there was a strong reason for them. The prevalent tower plan was square, but some examples are octagonal (Stanwick, Northamptonshire) or square with an octagonal upper part (Uffington, Oxfordshire). The belfry windows are often large and deeply recessed, with numerous bold mouldings to the jambs, and sometimes appear to have been left quite open, as at Middleton Stoney, Oxfordshire. For the first time towers were often finished with pinnacles at the corner. A corbel-table was sometimes provided beneath the eaves of towers, particularly when a spire was provided. The finest Early English towers are at West Walton in Norfolk, Bury in Cambridgeshire and Haddenham in Buckinghamshire; the finest Early English towers often have stone broach spires.

In the Decorated period towers grew richer; those at Whissendine in Rutland and Heckington in Lincolnshire (with a stone spire) are two of the finest. Their tabernacle work now incorporated the favourite ogee motif with crocketed and ballflower ornamentation. The angle buttress imparted greater structural stability than in previous periods. Sometimes two buttresses were built at each corner, one at right angles to each face of the tower; in others a single angle buttress supported each of the corners.

The Perpendicular period was the supreme building period, so far as towers were concerned. Throughout the country church towers were built or rebuilt, larger, grander and more magnificent than ever before. Yet, compared with those of previous periods, they were often plain and meagre in their ornamentation, relying for their effect on proportion and outline. The fifteenth-century desire for large windows of many lights can also be seen, often inserted at each stage in addition to the belfry openings. The tower was finished with a battlement: straight or stepped, occasionally panelled, and sometimes pierced and adorned with pinnacles. Generally pinnacles were placed at each corner, but intermediate pinnacles, one to each side, were sometimes provided – at Winterton in Norfolk there are eight intermediate pinnacles in the form of figures. Octagonal angle buttresses were used on the tower at West Walton, Norfolk, in the thirteenth century, but it was not until the fifteenth century that these were used to any great extent, always terminating in a pinnacle. They occur in many parts of the country, particularly in the south – for instance on some towers in Wiltshire at Mere and Cricklade, in Dorset at Cerne Abbas and Bradford Abbas, along the Thames and in the Waveney Valley (for instance Laxfield, Suffolk, and Redenhall, Norfolk) and the Stour valley (at Stoke-by-Nayland, Suffolk, and Dedham, Essex).

There was an infinite variety of tower design in the Perpendicular period, but the finest towers to be seen in England are in Somerset. They may not be as large and imposing as many in East Anglia, but for composition and exquisite detail no other area can match them. Many attempts have been made to classify Somerset towers into groups according to local variations. There are those in the west Mendip group which have three windows abreast, with only the centre one penetrating the wall (a local feature, for elsewhere louvre-boards are usual), the other windows being blank arcading; the parapet is straight and pierced with a beautiful pattern. The towers at Banwell, Bleadon, Brent Knoll, Mark, Weare and Winscombe are all of this type. The finest towers of the east Mendip group are those at Bruton, Leigh upon Mendip and Mells, each with three belfry windows abreast, all penetrating the wall, and each with battlemented parapets. Churches of the south Somerset group have only a single belfry window, extending through the two upper stages and divided by a heavy ornamental transom, with a large area without windows below; the towers often have an octagonal stair turret with pinnacles. Worthy examples include Hinton St George, Norton sub Hamdon and Dundry. The Vale of Taunton has perhaps the most outstanding towers; called the Quantock group these are characterized by two belfry windows abreast and by their harmony of proportion and a wealth of detail including many niches (that at Isle Abbotts still retains its original statues) and pinnacles that sometimes have slender 'flying' pinnacles attached. There are many fine examples, like those at Chewton

Mendip, North Petherton and Huish Episcopi: the three which A.K. Wickham in his *Churches of Somerset* describes as 'among the greatest masterpieces of English architecture'.

Some Dorset church towers are influenced by those in Somerset; Marnhull, Charminster and Piddletrenthide are among the finest and have three pinnacles at each corner. Elsewhere in the south-west there are only two towers that can compete with those of Somerset and Dorset: Probus, Cornwall, with its traceried panels, and Chittlehampton, Devon – both obviously influenced by those in Somerset.

Elsewhere in Devon and Cornwall there are some notable towers, if usually austere in form. In west Devon as well as much of Cornwall there are some tall fifteenth-century towers, often constructed of granite, crudely fashioned and carrying large octagonal pinnacles with plain spirelets finished with a ball (Gulval) or a cross (St Just-in-Penwith). Others have crocketed spirelets, as at St Cleer, Breage and Poughill, Cornwall, and Widecombe in the Moor, Devon. Towednack, in the Land's End peninsula, and Landewednack, near the Lizard point, have simple, massive granite towers only two stages high to withstand the winter gales. A feature of some south Devon church towers is a prominent stair-turret placed in the middle of one side wall, instead of the more usual place in the corner; the tower at Ipplepen is an example.

Along the western side of Wiltshire some of the church towers show signs of Somerset influence. Perhaps the finest is Westwood, built in the middle of the sixteenth century and said to have been modelled on the central tower of Wells Cathedral. Another attractive Somerset-type tower can be seen at Yatton Keynell.

In East Anglia many of the Perpendicular towers are lofty and of stately proportions, with over twenty of them exceeding a hundred feet. On the coast they are very tall and were used as landmarks for mariners – for example those at Walberswick, Covehithe and Kessingland in Suffolk and Winterton (130 feet high), Happisburgh and Blakeney in Norfolk. The church at Blakeney also has a slender, lofty tower known as 'the lantern', rising from the north-east corner of the chancel – open on each face, it was undoubtedly used as a beacon for those entering the harbour.

Although they are robust and admirable, the towers of East Anglia lack the decorative beauties of those of the West. This is because of the shortage of good stone in the region. Flint was almost the univer-

sal building material, and flushwork, mostly in the form of thin tracery patterns, is a feature of many churches. The buttresses rarely
extend the full height of the tower, often stopping at the bottom of
the belfry stage, and the middle stage of the tower frequently has a
square aperture filled with elaborate tracery, known as a Norfolk 'air
hole'. Parapets are neither straight, as at Trunch, or battlemented, as
at Walcott and Filby and when there are pinnacles they quite often
take the form of figures or animals, as at Filby, Honingham and
Blofield. In Norfolk stairways are, in the main, internal, and even
when a turret is provided it is rarely prominent and nearly always
ends below the top. In few areas can church towers compare in either
height or appearance with those of Norfolk and, to a lesser extent,
Suffolk (there being over a thousand old church towers in the two
counties). Great towers can be seen at Cawston, Salle and Redenhall
in Norfolk and at Stoke-by-Nayland in Suffolk, and yet the innumerable small, unassuming towers are equally charming.

There are plenty of notable Perpendicular towers outside the
West Country and East Anglia, many of them to be found in the
east midlands; in Northamptonshire one can cite Fotheringhay,
Lowick, Warkton and Titchmarsh (said to be the finest parish
church tower outside the Somerset group). Stockerston and Belton
are two of the finest in Leicestershire, and in Cambridgeshire there
are notable examples at Haslingfield, Conington, Great Staughton
and Hamerton. Lincolnshire is more famous for its spires than for
its towers, but it does also have some distinctive fifteenth-century
towers. In the villages around Stamford there are several churches
which have prominent parapets, pinnacles and belfry windows
with the curious local feature of the central mullion of the windows
continuing upwards to the head of arch; Great Ponton, built by a
wealthy wool merchant in 1519, is an example.

Yorkshire has some splendid church towers, often with characteristic lace-like open work parapets; the best example can be seen
at Beeford, East Riding of Yorkshire. Another Yorkshire characteristic is the use of very lofty, almost disproportionately large, belfry
windows – as at Howden. Other notable Yorkshire towers are at
Skirlaugh and Holme-on-Spalding-Moor, in East Yorkshire. Two
towers, those at Sancton, East Riding of Yorkshire and Coxwold,
North Yorkshire, are octagonal from the base upwards; the one at
Sancton is regarded by many as the finest of all octagonal towers.

Further west in Gloucestershire there are a number of fine

Perpendicular towers, as one would expect: Bitton, Chipping Campden, Tortworth, Upton St Leonards, Wickwar and Yate are some of the best. Rather unexpectedly, one finds a most attractive timber-framed tower at Upleadon, built about 1500 with an abundance of close vertical studs and brick nogging between. The sandstone counties to the north of Gloucestershire do not possess many towers of the highest quality, but in Worcestershire there are a few attractive black-and-white half-timbered towers attached to stone churches. These are to be found at Pirton, Dormston and Warndon, all ascribed to the fifteenth century and all with a singularly domestic appearance in the western school of carpentry. A similarly constructed tower stands on a stone ground floor that forms the porch at Kington. The oldest is the one at Cotheridge: the lower part dates from around 1300 and is formed of solid timbering in wide oak boards some four inches thick.

Because of its proximity to Suffolk, Essex has a number of fine towers, especially in the villages along the Stour Valley. The one at Dedham is outstanding. Built between 1500 and 1520, it has openings at ground level in the north and south walls to enable the Sunday procession to pass round the church. However it is not the stone towers that make an impact in Essex but the late medieval mellow brick towers – thirty or so which are as fine as any to be found in any part of the country. Pride of place must go to Ingatestone, but those at Gestingthorpe, Great Holland, Wickham St Paul, Layer Marney, Castle Hedingham, Sandon and Fryerning are all delightful. Suffolk, too, has a couple from the same period: Hemley and Waldringfield.

In the south-east, Kent has many delightful Perpendicular towers, often with a distinctive type of prominent stair-turret extending above the parapet. Those at Seal, Ivychurch and Charing are good examples. Pinnacles are rare, but a feature of Kent towers is the belfry windows, which are usually square-headed. In Sussex, Surrey and Hampshire there is a noticeable lack of good Perpendicular towers; that at Worplesdon, Surrey, with its prominent stair-turret, is one of the best.

In some villages which could not afford to rebuild the whole tower, yet wanted the latest Perpendicular style, a belfry storey was often raised off an earlier tower; Little Houghton in Northamptonshire and Gedney in Lincolnshire are fine examples. At Elton, Cambridgeshire, and Moulton, Northamptonshire, the extended tower is in a different stone.

In some churches the tower is surmounted by a tall octagonal lantern with windows, battlements and pinnacles, as at Fotheringhay, Northamptonshire; at Lowick, also in Northamptonshire, the octagon also has pinnacles supported by flying buttresses.

In the seventeenth and eighteenth centuries, some church towers were built in the Perpendicular style (sometimes with Classical detailing, as at Frampton, Dorset, built in 1695), but most are built in the Classical style, with large round-headed windows (often with projecting keystones), a classical balustrade with urns instead of pinnacles, and possibly a cupola. Gayhurst and Willen in Buckinghamshire, Wimborne St Giles in Dorset and Avington in Hampshire are all notable examples of the period.

The towers mentioned here are some of the grandest and most famous, but it must be stressed that there are innumerable small, simple, unassuming towers of all periods that are the real charm of the English village church.

Detached Towers and Belfries

As we have seen, some towers are detached from the church they serve, but there was always a sound reason for this. In several parts of the country it was because of the poor bearing of the land. For instance, on marshland there was a fear that the settlement of a heavy tower attached to the main church would cause disruption to the church itself. A number of detached towers can be found in the marshland villages at the head of the Wash – the most famous being that at West Walton, which was mainly built around 1240 and sited some sixty feet away across the churchyard. Other examples include the fine Perpendicular tower which stands north-west of the nave at Terrington St Clement, Norfolk, and the ones at Fleet in Lincolnshire and Tydd St Giles in Cambridgeshire. The tower at Terrington St John, Norfolk, which now stands at the west end of the south aisle, was originally detached from the church, but was connected to it in the sixteenth century, when a two-storey building incorporating part of the tower and aisle was built to house the chantry priest. On Romney Marsh there stands the well-known timber-framed belfry belonging to the church at Brookland, Kent (70), and here the evidence of settlement can be seen within the church, with the arcades between the nave and aisles leaning outwards.

69   Fifteenth-century tower at Michelmersh, Hampshire

70   Belfry at Brookland, Kent

In other parts of the country there are other reasons for these detached towers; at Lapworth, Warwickshire, there was no room for a tower at the west end of the nave, so a detached tower was built at the north-east of the nave. Other such towers were probably built as places of refuge from hostile attacks; we have seen that many of the round towers of East Anglia were built for defensive purposes and not attached to any permanent building, and the one at Bramfield in Suffolk, remains like that today. The solidly built detached tower at Garway, Herefordshire, close to the Welsh Borders, also seems to have been built for defensive purposes.

In Herefordshire there are a number of detached timber-framed belfries, most notably the fourteenth-century one at Pembridge (71). At Gunwalloe, Cornwall, the detached tower stands on the beach and is built into the rocky headland, while at Marston Moretaine, Bedfordshire, the tower is sited some seventy feet from the north wall of the chancel.

Porches

We have seen that in Saxon times porches were sometimes provided at the west end of the nave. Generally, though, they were one of the last additions to the floor plan, and almost all examples are later than the end of the twelfth century. There are several porches that have Norman outer doorways, but it is usually found that the porch itself is a later addition, and the original doorway of the nave has been re-used. This was done at Forest Hill, Oxfordshire. Even in the thirteenth century porches were not regarded as a necessity. It was not until around 1300 they began to increase in popularity; it was no doubt felt that some sort of shelter should be provided for those parts of church ceremonies conducted at the church door – such as the preliminary parts of the baptism and marriage services.

In medieval times porches were of greater importance than they are today. It was in the porch that penitents received absolution before entering the church, those breaking vows did penance and those breaking marriage vows stood in a white sheet on three consecutive Sundays asking for the prayers of those who entered. It was there that women knelt to be 'churched' (purified and blessed) after the birth of a child, and that the part of the marriage

71   Belfry at Pembridge, Herefordshire

ceremony involving the placing of the ring on the finger took place. Often it was there that the first village schools were held, with the priest as schoolmaster. Civil business was also conducted in the porch, most legal matters were also conducted there, executors of wills paid out legacies, and sometimes coroners held their courts here. A reminder of the former importance of the church porch is in fact that, by law, certain public notices must still be posted there.

Where a porch was provided, it was most likely to be on the south side – or on the north side, if the manor house or village lay on that side. A west porch, however, is not as rare as sometimes stated; Woodstock in Oxfordshire, Cley next the Sea in Norfolk, Yapton in West Sussex, and Otford and Boxley in Kent may be cited as a few instances. In many churches one finds porches to both north and south, and some (like King's Sutton, Northamptonshire) have one on the west as well. Most porches are of different periods, but one does sometimes find those to the north and south built apparently at the same period. It is not uncommon to find that one has to step up or down from the porch into the church, and when this occurs it indicates that the porch was not the original entrance. At Boxford, Suffolk, the wonderful timbered fourteenth-century north porch (described by many as the finest timber porch in the country) has a level entrance into the church, whilst the fifteenth-century stone south porch has several steps down.

As we have seen, porches from the Early English period are rare. They occur in Gloucestershire, Oxfordshire and Northamptonshire, and some are vaulted (as at Enstone) or have upper storeys. Some fine examples with arcaded sides survive, for example at West Walton in Norfolk and Polebrook and Warmington, both in Northamptonshire. The gables are generally to a steep pitch and some porch roofs are made entirely of stone slabs supported on transverse arches, as at Barnack, Cambridgeshire. In the Cotswolds and the surrounding district they are much plainer.

By the fourteenth century a porch began to be regarded as a necessity, even for the village church. Where stone was scarce, single-storey timber porches began to appear – on some the side walls were solid, on others the upper part was open and filled with tracery. These early timber-framed porches are generally confined to southern and eastern sides of England. One of the earliest, at Aldham in Essex, is said to date from around 1325. The one at Boxford in Suffolk is outstanding, and other notable examples are at High Halden in Kent, Warblington in Hampshire and West Challow in Oxfordshire. Where stone was plentiful the porch was constructed of stone, often with an upper storey reached by a winding stair in an octagonal turret. The architectural treatment of most porches was restrained, as at Patrington in East Riding of Yorkshire, although the south porch at Heckington, Lincolnshire, is a work of 'full-flowered luxuriance'. Those at Bampton, Oxfordshire, and Little Addington, Northamptonshire, also show this intensification of ornament, with the ogee arch, the cusp, the crocket and the ballflower all used to good effect.

As with towers, however, it is in the fifteenth and early sixteenth centuries – the Perpendicular period – that the porch reached perfection. Porches were now often of two, or sometimes (as at Bruton, Somerset) even three storeys, enriched with pinnacles, battlements and pierced parapets with niches and canopies for statues, together with heraldic badges and much traceried panelling. The porch at Northleach, Gloucestershire, beautifully adorned with turrets, pinnacles and niches, is regarded as the finest of them all, but the one at Woolpit, Suffolk, is often held to be its equal in proportions and detail. At Addlethorpe, Lincolnshire, the original gable cross survives, carved with the Crucifixion and the Virgin and Child. The porches at Pulham St Mary the Virgin in Norfolk and Framsden and Fressingfield in Suffolk can be chosen almost at random from the many other admirable examples.

Timber porches continued to be used throughout the Perpendicular period, but they are not to be compared with their stone counterparts. They differed little from those of preceding periods, except that the upper parts of the sides are almost always open; notable examples exist at Aconbury, Herefordshire, Crowle and Huddington, Worcestershire, and Ewhurst, Surrey, to name but a few.

In the fifteenth century brick porches began to make their appearance. There are many examples in Essex, a county noted for its early use of brick, and those at Feering, Sandon and Pebmarsh are all notable examples. The use of brick was not, of course, restricted to Essex, and many such porches are to be found elsewhere – three of note in Suffolk, for instance, are at Stoke-by-Nayland, Great Ashfield and Winston.

Many porches retain their original roof structures, which are generally of the open type and reflect in miniature those of the main structure. One of the most remarkable is at Kersey, Suffolk. It measures only 13 feet by 11 feet and is divided into sixteen panels

72   Porch at Radwinter, Essex

of heavily moulded timbers with brattishing surrounding each panel; each panel is divided into four and filled with elaborate tracery. For many years this beautiful roof was plastered over, and it was only rediscovered when the plaster was being renewed.

Many porches built in the fifteenth century have a chamber

above, often (though wrongly) described as a parvis. In a few cases there is a piscina – as at Salle, Norfolk, and Fotheringhay, Northamptonshire – showing that the chamber once contained an altar and was used as an occasional chapel. Sometimes there is a squint, giving a view not only of the high altar but the entire church.

In medieval times, however, the church was used not only for religious purposes but also for the secular requirements of the parishioners. Since in most cases the church would have been the only substantial building in the village, it was no doubt used as the safest repository for articles of value. It seems probable that valuables were kept in these upper chambers, for it is not uncommon for the door to be completely iron-clad. It is known also that these chambers were used as the village armoury (Mendlesham, Suffolk), as well as school rooms (Colyton, Devon, and Berkeley, Gloucestershire), treasury rooms (Hawkhurst, Kent), muniment rooms and libraries. At Titchmarsh, Northamptonshire, in the seventeenth century the upper chamber of the porch was fitted out as a family pew.

Two-storey porches made of timber are rare; at Radwinter, Essex, (72) there is a fine example, jettied on all three sides and thought to date from around 1350. Another porch of black-and-white half-timber construction is at Berkswell, Warwickshire (73).

Vestries

On the north side of the chancel – or even occasionally at the east end – there is often a rectangular room: the vestry or sacristy, for the keeping of vestments and vessels and for the robing of the priest. In medieval churches the priest would robe in the space beneath the west tower or some specially screened annex, but from the fourteenth century it became popular to construct an additional room for this purpose. Access from it to the church was by means of a door in the chancel wall, near the High Altar, and where there is no external door it probably indicates that the vestry also served as a treasury. Good examples occur at Islip, Northamptonshire, and at Worstead and Hingham, Norfolk. Now and again (as at Hawton, Nottinghamshire) the vestry contains a piscina, and occasionally it may have two storeys (as at Roos, East Riding of Yorkshire), the upper storey being provided with a window looking into the chancel – though more often there is a squint overlooking the High Altar. In a few cases the upper room contains a latrine, as at Warmington, Warwickshire. A great number of vestries were added during the last century.

73   Porch at Berkswell, Warwickshire

Crypts

Crypts are rarely found in village churches. Pre-Conquest examples survive at Brixworth, Northamptonshire, and Wing, Buckinghamshire, both of which date from the tenth century. There are a few vaulted Norman crypts, notably the well-known ones at Lastingham, North Yorkshire, (74) and Berkswell, Warwickshire, and that under the chancel of the little church at Duntisbourne Rouse, Gloucestershire, (75) where the steep slope of the ground necessitated some kind of undercroft. Another crypt occasioned by a sloping site is the thirteenth-century vaulted example at Shillington, Bedfordshire, and a fourteenth-century example is to be found at Madley, Herefordshire. The construction of crypts practically died out in the late Middle Ages, but where the church was enlarged into the graveyard, a bone- or charnel-hole was sometimes provided for the storage of the disturbed remains; this also took place when the churchyard became full, the uncoffined bodies being dug up so that part of the churchyard could be reused. A good example is the bone-hole at Hythe, Kent, which was constructed in the thirteenth century when the chancel was lengthened. It is still filled with skulls and bones.

Chantry Chapels

In pre-Reformation times it was the custom of every God-fearing man to have masses said for his soul after his death. For the rich there was the prospect of having prayers and masses said for ever by establishing a chantry – an endowment for maintaining a priest – to pay for the repose of the souls of the founder, his family and others named by him, either at set periods or on the anniversary of his death. Medieval wills abound with this form of bequest, and in some cases the number of masses to be recited within a certain period was fantastic. For the important and wealthy, chapels were sometimes provided for the use of the chantry – either within the church and surrounded by a screen (known as a parclose) or built as an extension to the main structure which in some cases significantly affected the development of the church plan. The chantry cult was a popular form of endowment from the close of the thirteenth century until the Dissolution in the sixteenth century.

74   Crypt at Lastingham, North Yorkshire

75   Duntisbourne Rouse, Gloucestershire

It was not only the great and wealthy who manifested their piety in the construction of chantry chapels. Although personal chantry endowments were beyond the means of most people, humble parishioners formed religious guilds to provide for their mutual benefit during their lifetime – but above all to secure the repose of their souls after death. From the middle of the fifteenth century trade and craft guilds also began to establish their own chapels and pay the stipends of the chantry priests. Consequently, there are thousands of these chapels all over England – many in towns (where often more than one chapel was provided). There are, however, many to be found in village churches, usually related to local trades.

In some instances the bequest required the priest to live on the premises, and a room was sometimes provided. This might be above the porch. In the case of Cavendish, Suffolk, the room was in the tower, complete with fireplace, shuttered windows (with the original shutters remaining) and window seats; this room is now the ringing chamber. On occasions a priest's house was built near the church, probably for the same purpose.

In 1529 an Act was passed forbidding anyone to accept a stipend for singing masses to the dead, and this signalled the end of the chantry cult. In 1547 another Act was passed (which gave the Crown all property rents and annuities which had furnished stipends for chantry priests) and in 1549, when the monasteries were suppressed, many of the chapels were destroyed.

The chantry chapels that remain today, particularly those in cathedrals and larger town churches, often contain some of the finest carvings and works of art to be found in England. Besides the altar, they would often contain the tombs of the founder and members of his family.

Anchorites' Cells

Anchorites and anchoresses were people who sought to live solitary and pious lives, and they were almost regarded as saints by the common people. They were inducted to their cell by the Bishop in a ritual procession. This cell usually took the form of a lean-to annex built on to the outside of the cold, north wall of the sanctuary of the church. Here they would spend the remainder of their lives, for once they were inside, the entrance was permanently blocked up. Their only contact with the outside world was through a small opening in the inside wall, giving a permanent view of the High Altar, so that the occupant could observe the priest celebrating mass – and a small barred and shuttered window in the outer wall that admitted some light and enabled food and drink to be passed to the occupant. Bequests were made for the support of the anchorite, who in return would pray for the souls of his benefactors.

Few of these cells remain today. Most have disappeared without trace, and, with one or two exceptions, most of the structures claimed to have been anchorite's cells are of doubtful authenticity. One exception is at Shere, Surrey: a diminutive chamber, some six feet square, which was the dwelling of Christine Carpenter, who was granted a licence to occupy it in the fourteenth century. Another two-storied anchorite's cell dating from 1160–80 is at Compton, also in Surrey. The cell is now occupied by a staircase leading to a unique Norman upper chancel, thought to have been used by pilgrims on the Pilgrims' Way. Anchorites' cells also existed at other places, for instance Cliffe and Staplehurst, both in Kent, but only the foundations are to be seen today; that at Staplehurst was excavated in 1936.

5   External Features

Externally, the outstanding feature of many churches is the tower, which often dominates not only the village but the surrounding countryside. Towers and porches have been dealt with in the previous chapter, but there are other features which influence the external appearance of the church.

Walls

The methods employed in the construction of walls depended not only on the type of stone available but also in styles which varied throughout the centuries. In Saxon times walls were generally no more than 2' or 2'3" thick, and any so-called pre-conquest work with walls thicker than 2'6" should be looked upon with some suspicion. Saxon walls were built either of rag or rubble, sometimes partly of herringbone work (as at Diddlebury, Shropshire, Wigmore, Herefordshire, Elsted, West Sussex, and Burghwallis, South Yorkshire), without buttresses and in many cases were plastered both inside and out. Considerable use was made of old Roman or British materials, where they were available (as at Escomb, Durham), and the reuse of Roman bricks and tiles was common in stoneless areas.

Generally Saxon work is of better quality than Norman work, more care being taken with bonding. Large stones were much sought after for quoins and were usually placed alternatively flat and on end: a kind of construction known as 'long and short work', which is an infallible indication of a late Saxon date. The stages of the building were sometimes marked by courses of wrought stone that projected slightly from the face of the wall, corresponding with the storey courses, as can be seen beneath windows at Worth, West Sussex. Narrow vertical strips of ashlar, also projecting an inch or two from the face of the wall, are known as pilaster-strips. These, too, were commonly employed where freestone was available, as at Breamore in Hampshire, Stanton Lacy in Shropshire and on the towers at Earls Barton in Northamptonshire and Sompting in West Sussex; they have no structural purpose and are purely decorative.

The style of building changed with the coming of the Normans. In contrast with the large stones and relatively thin walls which the Saxons loved so much, their building method used small stones, each of which could be easily handled, and thick walls were at least 2'6" thick, and it is not uncommon for them to be 4' thick in some of the larger churches. A string course is sometimes provided both internally and externally beneath the window sills, as at Steetley in Derbyshire, Birkin in North Yorkshire and Barfreston in Kent. In freestone areas a characteristic Norman feature was the corbel-table: a continuous projecting band of masonry, usually just underneath the roof, supported at intervals along its length by small corbels. The corbels were generally elaborately carved – grotesque heads and monsters were commonly employed – and often linked by a range of small arches. At Kilpeck, Herefordshire, there are some eighty corbels encircling the outside; others can be observed at Elkstone in Gloucestershire, Barfreston in Kent, Steeple Langford in Wiltshire, Bossall in North Yorkshire and Berkswell in Warwickshire. Although it was a decorative feature, the corbel-table had a practical use, for it gave the eaves a greater overhang, allowing the roof to project further and throw rainwater clear of the wall.

In the thirteenth century Early English walls generally became thinner and better built, although still often of rubble. When ashlar was used, the blocks were usually larger and longer. In areas where freestone was available a plinth began to be provided; in Lincolnshire, for example, it was by this time often fully developed. There was often a simple string course beneath the windows, as on the chancel at Little Faringdon in Oxfordshire, but the corbel-table, such a feature in Norman times, is rarely found in the period except in early work; when it is used, the arches between the corbels are commonly trefoils, as at Stanwick, Northamptonshire.

A hundred years later the walls of the Decorated church were in the main better constructed than ever before. They were thinner, and if ashlar was used the blocks were large, well squared and coursed. The plinth became general, although in some areas it may take the form of a simple splayed offset; in Lincolnshire, it became fully developed, of considerable height with a bold projection, as at Heckington. A string course was provided beneath the windows of some of the larger churches, for example Chinnor, Oxfordshire. Parapets, hitherto almost unknown in village churches, began to appear, generally low with a deep moulded course and coping. In Northamptonshire and the surrounding counties battlemented parapets were a feature, as at Whissendine in Rutland, but elsewhere they were rare. The parapet was sometimes decorated with sunken tracery, as at Heckington, and in late examples with open tracery (although this is rare). It was not until later that the use of parapets spread into the west.

With the arrival of the Perpendicular period the quality of workmanship improved immensely. When ashlar was used, the blocks were large and finely jointed, often faced both externally and internally; in stoneless districts brick began to be used. Plinth courses were almost universal, except for some churches in the west. In Norfolk and Suffolk they were richly decorated with sunken tracery or with flushwork. The majority of walls finished with a parapet; many were embattled, others enriched with sunken tracery or pierced, as at Batcombe, Somerset. Pinnacles were also employed, sometimes being extensions of the buttresses. External string courses below the parapets were sometimes relieved by gargoyles.

Clerestories

When aisles were provided, medieval builders were faced with the problem of lighting the body of the church. The simplest way to roof a newly formed aisle was to continue the slope of the nave roof, as is often seen in Sussex churches, but this made the interior of the church dark. The most effective solution was to raise the nave wall above the arcade and pierce it with a row of windows above a lean-to aisle roof.

Clerestories date mostly from the Perpendicular period, though they can, of course, date from any period. Those few Norman churches which were built with aisles all seem to have had clerestories, the finest surviving examples of which are in the late Norman churches of St Margaret's at Cliffe, Kent, and Compton Martin, Somerset. Clerestories were still rare in the thirteenth century, but they appear on some larger Early English churches, such as those at West Walton in Norfolk, and Elm in Cambridgeshire, and even on a few smaller churches, as at Downham in Cambridgeshire and Aymestrey in Herefordshire.

It was not until the fourteenth century, as flatter roofs became more popular, that clerestories began to make an impact, and then only in some parts of the country.

At first they were most common in Northamptonshire, but they soon spread into Lincolnshire, East Anglia and the south midland counties. Very often they were low with small openings, as at Chinnor, Oxfordshire, (76) but in Northamptonshire and Lincolnshire the windows were often of considerable height and divided into lights. In Norfolk the openings were often circular, as at Snettisham, and in some cases alternated with two-light arched windows, as at Cley next the Sea.

76 Chinnor, Oxfordshire

As we have said, the great majority of clerestories are of the Perpendicular period, corresponding with the widespread introduction of flat lead-covered roofs. They are a feature of many churches in East Anglia, where aisled churches tended to have clerestories with large windows – so large, in fact, that the upper nave wall became a continuous series of windows. At Blythburgh, Suffolk, there are no less than eighteen two-light windows on each side, while in the same county the clerestories at Long Melford – which has eighteen three-light windows per side – Lavenham, Coddenham and Stonham Aspal, are of outstanding beauty. Norfolk, too, has many notable examples; the church at Terrington St Clement, which not only has clerestory windows in the nave but also around the transept and chancel as well, is uncommonly attractive. The finest clerestory outside East Anglia – perhaps the finest anywhere – is at Gedney, Lincolnshire, where the twelve three-light windows on each side almost completely cover the entire wall.

Occasionally, clerestories are found in aisleless churches, when they form a second tier of windows to the nave, as at Halford and Ilmington in Warwickshire and Sandiacre and Wilne in Derbyshire. In these instances it seems probable that an aisle or aisles were contemplated but never built. An unusual arrangement in which a second tier of windows is provided in the aisle walls is at Broughton, Oxfordshire.

At the time that many fifteenth-century clerestories were being built it was not uncommon to provide a window over the chancel arch. Its purpose must have been to flood the church with extra light, rather than to provide additional light to the rood, for the glare from such a window would have been a serious distraction.

Not all areas are rich in clerestories; in west Devon and Cornwall they are extremely rare, and the nave and aisles usually have long unbroken parallel roofs ending in three gables. Rather curiously, this roof arrangement can also be found in Kent, the other side of the country. Likewise clerestories are rather rare in the extreme south of England.

Buttresses

An external feature of many medieval churches is the use of stone buttresses to support the external wall. The weight of the roof tends to thrust the walls outwards, so it was necessary either to build thicker walls or to strengthen thinner ones with buttresses placed at the point of greatest thrust – usually corresponding to the positions of the roof trusses. As buttresses give support in proportion to their weight, the heavier the buttress, the thinner the wall needs to be.

As we have seen, Norman walls were of considerable thickness, and so the buttresses provided were generally little more than pilasters with very little projection. These added little to the substance of the wall; in fact at Heath Chapel, Shropshire, (77) it was possible to pierce them with windows without causing any structural damage, and it may be assumed that they served more as a decorative feature, breaking up the large plain wall surface, than providing support to the wall against the thrust of the roof. They are generally not divided into stages, but continue the same width and thickness from ground to the top, where they die into the wall with a slope immediately below the roof line.

77   Heath Chapel, Shropshire

From the thirteenth century onwards, as masonry techniques improved, walls became slimmer, but they were weakened by the introduction of larger windows. Consequently, the buttresses, although narrower, projected further from the walls than those of the Norman period. In early English buttresses the projection was generally reduced in stages, the tops of each set back sloping at an acute angle dividing the stages. The buttresses terminated at the top either with a plain slope dying into the wall or with a triangular head. The angles of Early English buttresses are very often chamfered or occasionally moulded. At the corners two buttresses set at right angles to each other, known as rectangular buttresses, were used.

Like the Early English buttresses, those of the Decorated period are also invariably worked in stages, and often incorporate niches with crocketed canopies. Sometimes (though this applies generally to larger churches) they terminate in pinnacles, which can be of openwork, forming niches or canopies for statues. The diagonally set angle buttress was introduced, and the V-shaped buttress – as at Raydon, Suffolk – made its appearance in the fourteenth century.

Perpendicular-period buttresses differed little in general form or arrangement from those of the Decorated period, but they did take on the prevailing character of Perpendicular architecture. Consequently, the face of buttresses was frequently decorated with traceried heads, and in East Anglia the panels were generally filled with flushwork.

When the nave walls were raised above the level of the aisle roof, so as to take clerestory windows, they were occasionally strengthened by flying buttresses – arched stone supports between the nave wall and the buttress of the aisle wall. These first appeared in the grand churches of the Early English period, but they did not become common until later.

Buttresses were not used in Classical architecture, the projections being formed into pilasters, thus disguising or destroying the appearance of strength.

Gargoyles

In the days before lead downpipes, introduced only in the Tudor period, rainwater which collected in the gutters was thrown clear of the church walls by means of projecting spouts, known as gargoyles. These are to be found on many of our ancient village churches, particularly on towers and parapet walls. As so often in the Middle Ages, craftsmen seized the opportunity to turn something purely practical into an interesting and decorative form, giving rise to a wide and uninhibited range of subjects.

The finest gargoyles are to be found in those areas with good-quality freestone; notable examples can be found at Evercreech and Monksilver in Somerset, Winchcombe and Coates in Gloucestershire, Patrington in East Riding of Yorkshire, East Markham in Nottinghamshire and Denford and Welford in Northamptonshire (where two figures hold the projecting spout between them).

External Figure Sculpture

We have already noted the Normans' fondness for the corbel-table, with its elaborately carved corbels in the form of figures and monsters, and exterior string courses of figures and foliage continued to be used from time to time. Without doubt one of the finest examples is that at Adderbury, Oxfordshire, in which over one hundred carvings of rural scenes and weird animals and birds display a considerable sculptural imagination. Dragons, gryphons, mermaids are among the more identifiable fantasies, while reality is represented by minstrels with pipes, trumpets, cymbals, fiddles, harp and bagpipes, as well as other figures. Chedworth, Gloucestershire, (78) has several grotesques in the string course of the south parapet including an anthropophagist; Coates, Gloucestershire, also has an anthropophus eating his victim down to the waist.

Saxon carvings are sometimes to be found reset in later walls. Langford in Oxfordshire (79) has three, the largest of which is a big headless rood which shows Christ in a long robe with drooping hands. There is another little Crucifixion with, for some reason, St John and the Virgin Mary facing outwards, and on the tower there is a smaller, less distinct carving of two men.

Towers and porches were a favourite place for figure sculpture, but, although there are numerous niches, few of the original figures they once contained survive for they were particularly detested by reformers. Somerset, perhaps has the most, and the tower at Isle Abbotts the finest. Elsewhere in the county the figure of Our Lord surrounded by angels can be seen at Chewton Mendip and Batcombe. The church at Hartland, Devon, has a large figure of its patron saint St Nectan, whilst at Clanfield, Oxfordshire, there is a statue of St Stephen of early fifteenth-century date. The tower at Fairford, Gloucestershire, has quaint men at each corner and, even more unusual, on the side of the tower above the roof of the nave it has a statue of the Risen Christ.

78   Grotesque at Chedworth, Gloucestershire

79   Rood at Langford, Oxfordshire

Spires

Spires have no practical use but they enhance many church towers
and emphasize the monumental character of the structure. There is
little doubt that they developed from the low pyramidal roofs of the
Norman period, which were soon elongated – as at West Peckham,
Kent (80) before finally becoming the octagonal spire that is such

an outstanding feature of many thirteenth- and early fourteenth-century churches. At first these would not have been of any great height. The simple pyramidal roof was heightened and all four corners chamfered to create an octagonal spire, the diagonal sides of which were cut away to the four corners of the tower, the whole overhanging the walls of the tower. Soon they developed into spires of considerable size. In Surrey and Sussex these are very common, and in Kent, too, they are by no means rare. They may be squat (as at Old Romney in Kent), slender (Playden in East Sussex, Horsted Keynes and West Hoathly in West Sussex and Hever in Kent) or massive (Compton in Surrey, Bury in West Sussex (81) and Patrixbourne in Kent). Occasionally, instead of overhanging the tower, they would rise within a parapet on its top, as at West Tarring, West Sussex.

80　West Peckham, Kent

81 Bury, West Sussex

These spires were built of timber and generally covered with shingles or sometimes lead, that at Long Sutton, Lincolnshire, is the oldest. In Hertfordshire a needle spire, usually covered with lead, is a popular feature; often referred to as a 'Hertfordshire spire' it can be found on many churches in the county – for instance at Flamstead, Little Munden, Great Munden and Little Hadham – as well as in neighbouring parts of Essex and Cambridgeshire. At Baldock and Ashwell, Hertfordshire, there is a polygonal base to the spire.

These timber-framed spires were soon imitated in stone, becoming an integral part of the tower in all those areas where good-quality building stone was quarried, and particularly along the limestone belt. Almost without exception, these stone spires are octagonal in form, and the problem arose of fitting an octagonal

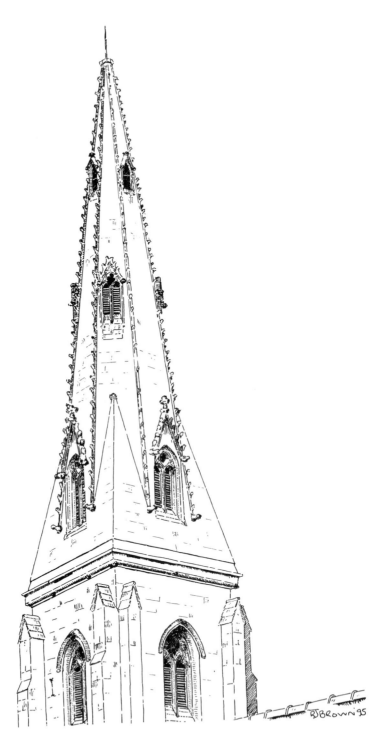

82   Broach spire at Walcot, Lincolnshire

spire onto a square tower. This was overcome by a number of methods. At first the spire overlapped the tower, with tall pinnacles placed at each corner. A characteristic of these early spires was the large dormer windows at the base of the spire on the four cardinal sides. This type of spire is to be found around Oxford, for instance at Bampton, Broadwell and Shipton-under-Wychwood, all of which are of early thirteenth-century date.

Later in the thirteenth century another type of spire evolved, the 'broach' spire – found only in England. The transition from the square tower to the octagonal spire was effected by 'broaches': half-pyramids of masonry leaning against one face of the spire at each corner of the tower. From a practical point of view the broach was most successful, throwing off the rain and snow which would otherwise fall on the tower's four angles, but aesthetically it can be less pleasing. A broach spire almost always overhangs the tower, and there are no pinnacles. In order to relieve the heavy appearance thus created, gabled lucarnes or spire-lights of two or more tiers replaced the dormer windows. The spire-lights may occur on the cardinal sides only, or on both the cardinal and diagonal sides, when they usually alternate in two rows. The object of these spire-lights, apart from being decorative, is to provide ventilation, rather than to light the interior of the spire; in later spires they were not always used and, if they were used, tended to be smaller and fewer in number. Another refinement is to be seen at Whatton, Nottinghamshire, where the lucarnes lean backwards against the face of the spire, so having little projection at their apex.

Broach spires nearly always date from the thirteenth century, and occasionally from the fourteenth century, when crocketing sometimes enriches the arrises and spire-lights; only rarely do they date from the Perpendicular period, as at Irchester in Northamptonshire. Broach spires can be stumpy like those at Holme in Nottinghamshire and Upper Hambleton in Rutland, or occasionally long and slender, as at Leckhampton and Shurdington in Gloucestershire. In most cases the tower and spire form an integral unit, and in Northamptonshire, south Lincolnshire, Rutland and the surrounding districts it is difficult to choose a few of special note from so many admirable examples. Certainly those at Walcot (82), Threekingham, North Rauceby and Frampton in Lincolnshire, at Polebrook and Warmington in

Northamptonshire or at Alconbury and Warboys in Cambridge-shire and Ketton (84) and Barrowden in Rutland are among the best.

83   Gaddesby, Leicestershire

84   Ketton, Rutland

From around the middle of the fourteenth century the broach spire was generally abandoned in favour of the more slender and graceful parapet spire – the grandest type of all. These spires, which do not overlap the tower but rise from within a parapet at the top of it, are more common than the broach type and once again, occur in areas with fine stone – particularly in south Lincolnshire, where many churches were enlarged or rebuilt, as at Heckington. A feature of these spires is the crocketed pinnacles at each corner of the tower with flying buttresses jumping across to the spire. Later spires had an abundance of crockets along their arrises as well, as at Whittlesey in Cambridgeshire. Once again many of the finest spires can be found in innumerable villages of the south midlands, south Lincolnshire and the surrounding areas. In Lincolnshire one can cite such villages as Claypole, Gosberton, Helpringham, Brant Broughton and Surfleet, with its leaning tower; in Northamptonshire, Bulwick, Easton Maudit, Wakerley and Weekley, with its diminutive spire; in Leicestershire, Waltham on the Wolds, in Rutland, South Luffenham and in Cambridgeshire, Great Gidding and Eltisley.

In the perfect combination the tower and the spire should be of equal height, but in those at Hemingbrough, North Yorkshire, and Glinton, Cambridgeshire, the height of the spire greatly exceeds that of the tower (that at Hemingbrough rises twice as high). The result is very striking.

The chamfered type of spire, so common in timber spires, was rarely used on stone spires but can be seen at Denford, Northamptonshire, at Etton and Bythorn, Cambridgeshire, and at Seaton, Rutland. Another small group of stone spires have rather a different arrangement in that they have double pinnacles, one above the other, at each corner. Examples can be found at King's Sutton in Northamptonshire, Laughton-en-le-Morthen in South Yorkshire and Ruardean in Gloucestershire. Yet another small but every attractive group, found in Northamptonshire and Rutland, has the combination of a square tower surmounted by an octagonal lantern and spire: Nassington and Wilby in Northamptonshire and Exton in Rutland, are all pleasing examples. At Quidenham, Norfolk, there is a round tower with an octagonal lantern and spire. The fourteenth-century tower at Patrington, East Riding of Yorkshire, has what at first glance appears to be an octagonal lantern but is in fact, an octagonal openwork screen surrounding the base of the spire, a unique and very pleasing arrangement. The spire was added during the Perpendicular period.

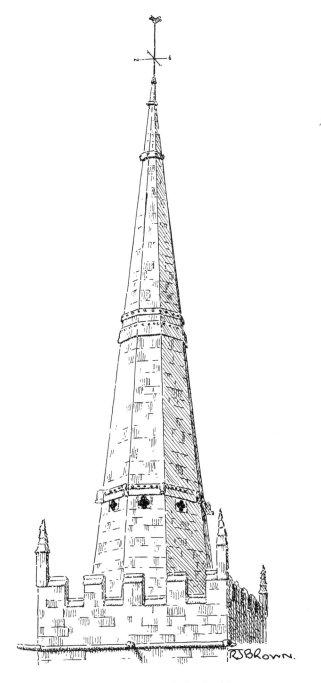

85   Spire at Bonsall, Derbyshire

Stone spires are more common in areas where good building stone was to be quarried, especially the Nene Valley, which yielded such a plentiful supply of oolitic limestone of excellent quality for the spires of south Lincolnshire, Leicestershire, Rutland and Northamptonshire. They occur also in Nottinghamshire, Derbyshire (85) and Warwickshire, and in the adjoining counties of Cambridgeshire, Bedfordshire, Buckinghamshire and Oxfordshire, as well as in parts of Yorkshire. They are also to be found, although less often, in Wiltshire, Gloucestershire and Worcestershire, and in

86   Bell-cote at Wormsley, Herefordshire

Dorset, Sussex and Cheshire they are far from common. Outside these areas – for instance in Kent, Hampshire, Hertfordshire and Surrey, or Cumbria and Northumberland – stone spires are rare or quite unknown. Other counties have only a few. The only medieval stone spire in Essex, for instance, is at Thaxted.

Bell-cotes, Bell-turrets and Belfries

In those parishes which enjoyed only limited resources churches were built with no towers, their one or two bells being hung either in an opening in the west wall of the nave, as at Sutton Bingham in Somerset, or more usually in an open bell-cote above the eastern or western gable of the nave. At the little Norman church at Stoke Orchard, Gloucestershire, one crowns the east gable of the nave, and those at Peakirk and Werrington, Cambridgeshire, are also of twelfth-century date. Bell-cotes are found in many parts of the stone-bearing counties; those at Wormsley in Herefordshire, (86) Kelmscot in Oxfordshire and Essendine and Little Casterton in Rutland are four typical thirteenth-century examples. More unusual is the wonderful thirteenth-century bell-cote at Boxwell, Gloucestershire (87): a very massive structure, with an octagonal stone spirelet on corbels. A similar example is to be found at Harescombe in the same county.

In some instances the bells were housed not in a bell-cote but in bell-cages in which the bells were partially enclosed; notable examples are on the little Norman building at Biddestone in Wiltshire (where it is perched on the east gable of the nave) and at Great Chalfield in Wiltshire and Brympton D'Evercy in Somerset, both of them small churches in the gardens of manor houses.

In areas where stone was scarce bell-turrets formed a cheap substitute for a tower. They are found in two main areas: the south-east, spreading northwards into Essex, and the west (Herefordshire and Worcestershire). Sometimes they are supported on the roof structures or more commonly, independently of the roof structures on cross-beams spanning from wall to wall, sometimes using a mixture of timber beams and uprights built into the walls. In other cases the turret is supported by the west wall of the nave and by oak posts framed into sill pieces on the floor of the nave (as at Copford, Essex, and Ford, West Sussex). In others timber belfries are not

87   Bell-cote at Boxwell, Gloucestershire

attached to the west wall and are supported on a structure of two, four or six (even, on occasions, eight) posts generally within the nave. Many of these belfries are to be found in Essex, fairly closely grouped together in the southern half of the county, like those at Mountnessing, Little Burstead and Doddinghurst (which dates from the first half of the thirteenth century), to name but a few. They can also be found in the south-east, particularly in Surrey – as at Dunsford, Alford, Thursley and Capel. In addition, there are a few belfries of similar construction in the west (for example at White Ladies Aston, Worcestershire), although here it is more common to use a timber cross wall to support the belfry and separate it from the nave, as at Bransford and Knighton on Teme. Most belfries stand at the west end of the nave, but at Thursley, Surrey, the bell-turret rises from the middle of the nave on four massive posts (placed close to the north and south walls, so as not to obscure the view of the altar), while at North Stoke, West Sussex, it is situated over the north transept. Some bell-turrets and belfries are little more than weatherboarded boxes with pyramidal caps, as at Ford

88   Heddon-on-the-Wall, Northumberland

and Coates, West Sussex, but others are a good deal more ambitious and are topped with good-sized spires, usually covered with wooden shingles. They may be of moderate height (as at Tangmere in West Sussex, Pyrford and Alford in Surrey, Brenzett in Kent or Aythorpe Roding and Birdbrook in Essex) or tall and slender (as at Crowhurst, Surrey, and Cowden, Kent).

Structures similar to these belfries were also built of wood outside the nave to form free-standing towers, with additional posts and braces forming aisles around the tower to ensure stability. Again these are to be found mainly in Essex, which has more examples than any other county and is justly famous for this form of construction. The earliest in Essex is the magnificent tower at Navestock, (89) which is dated to around 1190, while the finest – and perhaps the finest in England – is at Blackmore and was built, C.A. Hewett has suggested, in about 1480. Others of note in the county are at Margaretting, Stock and West Hanningfield (90); the last is unique in that the ground-floor plan is cruciform, and not square or octagonal, as is normal. Towers similar to those in Essex can be found in the south-east. Surrey has three notable examples at Newdigate, Great Bookham and (the finest) Burstow (91); others can be found at High Halden in Kent, Yateley in Hampshire and Itchingfield in West Sussex.

Some stone towers which might have been left unfinished – or have had their upper part demolished for some reason – are now often topped with a timber-framed belfry, usually with a pyramidal cap, as at Hampton Bishop and Winforton in Herefordshire, Defford in Worcestershire and Shipton and Bitterley in Shropshire. Also in Shropshire are a few stepped timber-framed belfries (for instance at Clun, Hopesay and More), all giving a degree of charm to the otherwise grim-looking squat towers.

Bells

The principal reason (and in the later Middle Ages the only reason) for building a church tower was to accommodate the bells. From the earliest times bells have been associated with religion, and by the seventh and eighth centuries they were in general use, the custom greatly increasing in England after the Norman conquest.

89   Tower at Navestock, Essex

90   Tower at West Hanningfield, Essex

91   Tower at Burstow, Surrey

In the later Middle Ages bells were rung far more frequently than today. They marked the divisions of the day, they summoned parishioners to worship, and they were rung at festivals, baptisms, marriages and funerals. Before funerals a 'passing' bell was always tolled to indicate the sex and age of the deceased. (These tellers, as they were known, were generally rung three times three for a man, three times two for a woman and for a child three times single, but there were many local variations. After this it would be rung once for every year of the deceased's age). This originated from the medieval belief that the sound of the bells drove away evil spirits, and in particular protected the passing soul from attack by demons. The bells were also rung during storms and tempests, in the belief that nature could be calmed, and they were rung in warning if fire, flood or other disasters threatened the parish. They were also rung when prominent visitors came to the district and on the occasions of national victories.

Most early bell-founders were, it seems, potters, and therefore it was the potter's tradition that determined the shape of early bells and that the sound bow, on which the clapper strikes, should be thickened on the outside like the rim of a pot.

Early bells were probably moulded on a horizontal 'lathe' – illustrated in the Richard Tunnoc bell-founder's window at York Minster – thus producing bells of small diameter (around 18 inches) and elongated form, with more or less straight sides and spreading sound bow, that gave rise to the term long-waisted bells. It was not easy to mould. As to date it is difficult to give an early limit to surviving bells; although a few may possibly date back to the twelfth century, it is safer to suppose that the majority belong to the thirteenth-century on the basis of the unique bell at Caversfield, Oxfordshire – England's earliest inscribed bell, dating from between 1207 and 1219. As a rule, however, these bells, like the pair at Little Braxted in Essex, ascribed to around 1230, are totally devoid of inscriptions or stamps. At first, different notes could only be achieved by altering the thickness of the metal, but during the thirteenth century bells began to be moulded in an upright position for it was not easy to mould a large, modern, shaped bell in clay horizontally. This new method enabled the founder to vary their height, diameter and weight to obtain the correct note. The shape of the bell therefore changed, so that the waist became concave, gradually thickening towards the convex-shaped sound bow.

Medieval bells did not always bear the maker's name but were frequently inscribed not only with beautiful lettering dedicating the bell to a saint – often St Agatha, patron saint of bell-founders – or engraved with a prayer or an inscription, but also with stops (ornamental patterns between each word), trade marks, shields, medallions and other decorations. After the Reformation the inscriptions, usually in English, consisted of rhymes of a somewhat secular nature, and it became normal for the bell to carry the founder's name and mark. The lettering employed on bells is of great interest; that on the early thirteenth-century Caversfield bell is Roman in form, but on later bells Gothic lettering appears. The earliest Gothic inscription is on bells at Chaldon in Surrey and Scawton in North Yorkshire, but even these are partly in Roman letters – a tendency that lingered on into the fourteenth century, especially where the letters M, W and T were concerned. During the fourteenth century Gothic capitals were used throughout, but subsequently Gothic initial capitals and black-letter lower-case letters, a combination known as mixed Gothic, was frequently used. In the sixteenth and seventeenth century Gothic was gradually replaced by Roman lettering.

It is estimated that over three thousand medieval bells still hang and ring in our churches, with the greatest number in Devon, Somerset, Norfolk and Suffolk. Although many churches have one or two pre-Reformation bells, only relatively few retain a complete set; one example is at Margaretting, Essex, where the early fifteenth-century timber-framed belfry contains a complete ring of four – still happily in frequent use. All four bells are by different London founders.

Until the fourteenth century bells were rung by a rope hung on a simple spindle but during the Reformation many bells were removed or silenced, and from Elizabeth's reign onwards the task of rehanging them provided the opportunity to experiment. Eventually a method was evolved in which the bell when mounted could rotate in a full circle, rather than just swinging back and forth, as before. To support the bell's weight, its main loop at the top (known as the argent) was reinforced by smaller loops (called canons) fixed to the massive timber headstock. The bells were rung by means of ropes turning large wooden wheels attached to the headstock and passing through the floor of the bell chamber to the ringer below. With the introduction of the slider and stay it was possible for the first time for the bell's movement to be stopped at will.

New methods of ringing developed during the seventeenth century. In 1668 Fabian Stedman, a Cambridge printer, introduced change-ringing, in which the bells could be rung with mathematical precision, one after the other, in constantly changing order. On eight bells 40,320 changes are possible. England is the home of change-ringing, and is almost unknown outside this country.

For many reasons bells were recast, and churchwardens' accounts abound with instances. Interestingly, the casting or recasting was sometimes carried out on site, and this is likely to have been done within the church or in the churchyard. Today there are restrictions on which bells can be recast; no bell cast before 1600 can be recast and those dating before 1750 cannot be recast either unless it is a poor example of its kind. If a pre-1750 bell (or indeed post-1750 bell) is recast, then its inscriptions must be reproduced in facsimile on the new bell.

Bells are rarely accessible to the casual church visitor, but in some instances an old bell which has become cracked has been preserved in the church where it can be examined in some detail. At Chaldon, Surrey, there is a bell dating from around 1250.

Although nearly all bells are housed in a belfry or bell-turret, there are a few which are not. At East Bergholt, Suffolk, (92) where the tower was never completed, a single-storey timber-framed bell-cage was built in the churchyard in about 1500 to house the five bells. It gives an ideal opportunity for the visitor to observe the bells. The bells at Wrabness, Essex, and Quarley, Hampshire, are also hung on frames in the churchyard.

In former days bell-ringers were paid for their services, and by the early eighteenth century change-ringing was performed mainly for money by local people. It was regarded as thirsty work, and ale and cider were often served, usually in a large earthenware jug kept handy in the ringing chamber or belfry for the benefit of the ringers. A few jugs or pitchers still survive. At Hinderclay, Suffolk, there is one dated 1724; another at Tawstock, Devon, is dated 1812 and inscribed 'Success to the hearty ringers of Tawstock' and 'The youngest ringers shall carry The Jug'. Hanging in some towers can be found painted boards recording the changes rung, or showing the rules of the ringers and the fines for faults or misdemeanours (there always seemed to be a fine for wearing a hat or spur).

92   Bell cage at East Bergholt, Suffolk

Doorways and Doors

Most churches had a north and south door to the nave and some a west door as well, usually into the tower. The north door was known as the Devil's door in medieval times (possibly because no sun ever fell on that side of the church) and was left open at baptismal services, so that when a child was christened the evil spirits thought to be in it could pass through the doorway to the outside. This door was also used on processional occasions, the procession passing through it into the churchyard, round the east end of the church, and in again by the south door – though after the Reformation many of these doors were blocked. Very occasionally the north door is used as the principal entrance if the village stands to that side of the church.

The earlier pre-Conquest doorways were openings with square jambs cut straight and without any recess for the door, which was hung on the inner face; later work generally had a small rebate for the door. Later still the door was hung somewhere around the centre of the wall. The typical Saxon doorway is tall and narrow with a semi-circular arch, large square impost stones and no recessed orders, all rudely constructed. In some instances the head is pointed or triangular, formed by two straight pieces of stone with their ends on the imposts and leaning inwards to form a triangle. Where large stones were available these run through the thickness of the wall. Sometimes the arches are made of brick taken from some Roman building, as at Brixworth, Northamptonshire (93). In the more elaborate doorways the opening is framed by flat pilaster-strips, in the fashion of a hood-mould, following the curve of the arch and continuing vertically to ground level, as at Earls Barton, Northamptonshire (94). Any attempt at moulding the arch is rare and gives no indication of date.

From the Norman period doorways, in particular south door-ways, became more ornate, and were often objects of some beauty – perhaps to reflect Christ's words 'I am the door; by me if any man enter he shall be saved'. The round arch continued to be used, and in the earliest examples the jambs and archivolt were without mouldings with a simple impost at the springing of the arch. Later, as the style developed, mouldings and other enrich-ments were introduced, usually with a number of recessed arches and corresponding shafts to the jambs. The arches are often highly ornamented, decorated with the typical Norman motifs, the zig-zag or chevron, pellet, diamond, star, beakhead (a type of decoration virtually unknown outside England), billet and cable. The lavish carving of some of these Norman doorways is truly remarkable – nowhere more so than in the group of Norman churches in Yorkshire – at Alne, Birkin, Brayton, Riccal, Stillingfleet and Wighill in North Yorkshire, Adel in West Yorkshire, Fishlake and Thorpe Salvin in South Yorkshire and Kirkburn in East Riding of Yorkshire. Elsewhere one can cite the west door at Iffley, Oxfordshire, where the bold beak-heads and zig-zag details contrast with the shallow medallions containing the symbols of the Evangelists and the signs of the Zodiac. St

Germans, Cornwall, and Tutbury, Staffordshire, both show seven orders of arches, and Kilpeck, Herefordshire, has elaborate carved shafts. The doorways at Dinton, Buckinghamshire and Barton Bendish, Norfolk (95), may also be mentioned.

93   Saxon doorway at Brixworth, Northamptonshire

94   Saxon doorway at Earls Barton, Northamptonshire

95   Norman doorway at Barton Bendish, Norfolk

A common feature in Norman times was the elaborate carved tympanum – the space between the door lintel and the containing arch. *Christ in Majesty* was a common subject for carved tympana, as at Water Stratford in Buckinghamshire, Eastleach Turville and Siddington in Gloucestershire, Rowlstone in Herefordshire, and Barfreston and Patrixbourne in Kent, to mention a few. The *Tree of Life* appears at Dinton in Buckinghamshire; *St George and the Dragon* at Fordington in Dorset, Ruardean in Gloucestershire and Brinsop in Herefordshire; and *Samson and the Lion* at Stretton Sugwas in Herefordshire (96). At Charney Bassett, Oxfordshire, two gryphons are held by a human figure and at Aston Eyre, Shropshire, there is a life-like depiction of the *Entry into Jerusalem*. The foregoing are all outstanding examples, but there are many others of note.

With the arrival of the Early English style the round arch of the Norman period was generally abandoned for the pointed arch. In large doorways the mouldings are numerous, and the jambs are generally cut into recesses to receive several small shafts with

96   Norman tympanum at Stretton Sugwas, Herefordshire

moulding between each. In most village churches of the period, however, the doorways are smaller, often with only one shaft in each jamb, or occasionally none cut at all. The capitals are frequently only moulded although many are enriched with stiff-leaf foliage, and the space between the archivolt of the arch and the shafts in the jamb is often enriched with dog-tooth ornamentation. There is almost always a hood-moulding over the arch, supported on a head at each end. In a few cases the head of the arch is formed into a trefoil or cinquefoil arch. Two typical Early English door-ways are at West Walton, Norfolk and Darrington, West Yorkshire.

The acute pointed arch of the Early English period was replaced in the Decorated period by a broader, though still pointed, arch with the doorway generally less deeply recessed. Most Decorated doorways are extremely plain. The shafts in the jambs are usually of slighter proportion than previously, and instead of being worked separately form part of the general mouldings. The dog-tooth orna-mentation was replaced with the ballflower and the four-leafed flower as the favourite motifs, and the capitals, instead of stiff-leaf foliage, might have the more natural-looking foliage of the period. Hood-moulds were almost universally used – often supported at each end with a boss of foliage or a corbel in the form of a head. Ogee arches are sometimes to be found on smaller doorways, the hood-mould crocketed and surmounted at the top with a finial, as at Crick, Northamptonshire, which dates from around 1300. The arches of a few doorways are beautifully cusped and foliated, as at Cley next the Sea, Norfolk.

In the Perpendicular period, although the pointed arch was often retained, the four-centred arch came into general use (often set under a square hood-mould), and the spandrel between the two was often filled with carvings of angels with censers, tracery or heraldry. Shafts are often, though by no means always, used in the jambs; they are generally small and worked in the jamb with other mouldings, and frequently are not clearly defined except for the capital and base. The capitals are usually octagonal – often plain but in some instances enriched with foliage or flowers. The jamb mouldings often have large hollows, the members lying on a cham-fer plane and divided into two groups by a deep and rather wide hollow, known as a casement. Generally the jambs continue up the same moulding as the arch. The chamfer plane is less rigidly adhered to in East Anglia where the shafts are often bolder. Niches for statues were often placed on either side of the door opening, and above the hood-mould a series of shields. The best examples are undoubtedly in the churches of the limestone belt and those of East Anglia.

Many of the finest Perpendicular doorways in our village churches are the west doorways. The one at Salle, Norfolk, is a notable example and has all the characteristics of the Perpendicular doorway: the shields above the hood-mould depicting the Royal Arms from 1400–1603, the coats of arms of local families, as well as emblems of the Passion and of the patron saints of the church. Similar doorways can be found at Great Cressingham, Hilborough and Cawston, all in Norfolk.

The seventeenth century saw the return of the rounded arch, though it was now handled in the Classical style, with projecting key-stones and large voussoirs. This style continued throughout the eighteenth century.

Medieval church doors were made of oak and were generally constructed in two ways. One involved two thicknesses of boarding – the inner one horizontal and the outer one vertical – fixed together with wrought iron nails driven from the outer face and cleated over on the inside. The alternative method used vertical boards nailed or pegged to a series of horizontal rails, known as ledges. This method of construction dates from the eleventh century, as shown by the remarkable survival at Hadstock in Essex (97), which is ascribed to around 1125. Constructed of four wide plain boards, it has three iron straps and an iron surround on the front, all riveted through to the D-shaped wooden ledges and surround at the back, the rivets being spread against lozenge-shaped iron washers which are wrapped around the ledges and surround. Another door of similar age is the north door at Buttsbury also in Essex. This was originally made of five boards and was fixed to circular ledges by the same riveting method. Later, probably during the Norman transitional period, the door was cross-planked – a process which has half submerged its circular Saxon ledges – and serpent-type ironwork was added. A similar construction can be found on the south door at Staplehurst, Kent, which has been authoritatively dated to 1050.

Generally, however, the ledges were of rectangular section, often seven or eight in number, relatively small in section and set into shallow housings cut across the width of the planks. An unusual

97 Doorway at Hadstock, Essex

arrangement can be found at Eastwood, Essex, where both north and south doors are ascribed to the late twelfth century. The south door is made of three planks, the middle one narrower with rebated edges while the ledges (originally four in number but now three, for the door has been reduced in height, apparently because the lower parts had rotted) are tapered and dovetailed in cross-section. These were driven into tapered dovetail trenches cut across the backs of the planks. Later, in addition to the ledges, a frame was introduced around the edge, consisting of stiles, a bottom rail and a shaped head piece.

A better method was to make the inner frame of a series of vertical and horizontal rails crossing each other, halved at their intersections and dovetailed to the outer frame (alternatively, the inner rails could be arranged diagonally). The boarding of the outer face was either square-butted, splay-butted, splay-rebated or V-edged, but rarely tongued and grooved. At Castle Hedingham, Essex, there is an unusual arrangement, in that the doors (no less than three, dating from its Norman origin probably around 1180) have the edges of the planks counter-rebated – a significant structural device which would have eliminated the need for ledges, although they are now fitted. Counter-rebated planks were again used on the west door at Kempley, Gloucestershire, which is made of three wide planks, but here there is further sophistication, with the introduction of free tenons between the planks.

Early medieval doors had no decorative timberwork either internally or externally. Indeed, up to the fourteenth century it was the smith who was entrusted to decorate the face of the door, and – from the many examples still remaining – his skill was remarkable. The most noteworthy and (if the date of 1050 is correct) some of the oldest ironwork still *in situ* in England is at Staplehurst, Kent. Although now much decayed, the ironwork tells the story of Ragnarok, the Norse Day of Judgement; it must be presumed that the ironwork was once distributed evenly over the face of the door, and not (as it now is) clustered at the top. The ironwork on the church door at Stillingfleet, North Yorkshire, continues the story, with figures of a man and woman – the only survivors of the end of the world – who hide in the cosmic ash tree Yggdrasil. Twelfth-century hammered ironwork can be seen in many old churches, some of the most remarkable being at Little Hormead in Hertfordshire, the two doors at Edstaston in Shropshire and the doors at Old Woking in Surrey and Hartley in Kent. The conspicuous C-shapes, split by big horizontal iron bands, which many of these early doors have, recall the symbolism of the crescent – rooted deep in the past and (like iron itself) said to have the power of averting evil.

Later in the thirteenth century iron scrollwork of straps and hinges was used, as at Eaton Bray, Bedfordshire, where the scrolled work completely covers the face of the door. This truly remarkable piece of craftsmanship was probably the work of the great medieval smith Thomas de Leighton, who made the grille of Queen Eleanor's tomb in Westminster Abbey and the ironwork to the doors of the churches at Leighton Buzzard and Turvey. Other notable early ironwork is to be found on doors at Skipwith, North Yorkshire, and Meare, Somerset, although more typical of our village churches is that at Little Leighs, Essex. Nonetheless, many church doors of this period were left plain, having only the heavy iron strap hinges to break up the surface of the door.

In the fourteenth century the importance of the smith declined, so far as church doors were concerned, and he was replaced by the wood-carver. At first the decoration was confined to an applied moulded frame and cover fillets masking the joints between the boards, with the heads of the nails that secured these to the surface of the door often providing additional decoration. In many cases the head of the door above the arch springing was decorated with tracery, usually following the window tracery of the period, applied in the narrow panels formed by the cover fillets. Sometimes the upper half of the door would have tracery while the panel below was left plain, but at Great Bardfield, Essex, the pair of doors is divided by a horizontal rail at the springing, the panels above left plain and the top part of the lower panels filled with tracery. At Addlethorpe, Lincolnshire (98), the applied frame and cover fillets were omitted, and the tracery to the head is the only ornamentation. In other cases the cover fillets stopped at the springing, and the entire head was filled with tracery, as at Wellow, Somerset. The panels could be filled in completely, either with tracery or some other pattern; on one of the most spectacular doors – the south door at Stoke-by-Nayland, Suffolk – the whole face is covered with carvings relieved by small figures of saints in niches. There is a similar door at Harpley, Norfolk.

Originally, it seems, these medieval doors were coloured, like so many other parts of the church. At Great Bromley, Essex, Kenneth

98   Door at Addlethorpe, Lincolnshire

Mabbitt has noted traces of ancient red colouring over the surface of the fifteenth-century south door, with green colouring on the framework and tracery. A kind of tempera was employed.

Doors were often hung in two leaves, suggesting the human and divine natures of Christ, but there was also a practical reason – such an arrangement lightened the weight on the hinges and eased opening of the doors. Most such doors date from the fourteenth century but there are some (as at Navestock, Essex) which date from the previous century. Unusually, the south door at Overton, Hampshire, is hung folding – its two leaves are hinged at the centre, so that one folds back upon the other. On occasions a wicket was provided, on the centre line in the case of simple doors. That at Thornham, Norfolk, is unusual in having an ogee head (there is another example at Humbleton, East Riding of Yorkshire). In many cases the main door was made first and the wicket cut out afterwards, so it is hardly noticeable. During the sixteenth century the old method of construction was abandoned, and framed and panelled doors began to make an appearance.

Several early closing-rings and knockers still survive, often decorated with beasts holding the ring: a monster swallowing a man at Adel (99), West Yorkshire; a demon at Dormington, Herefordshire;

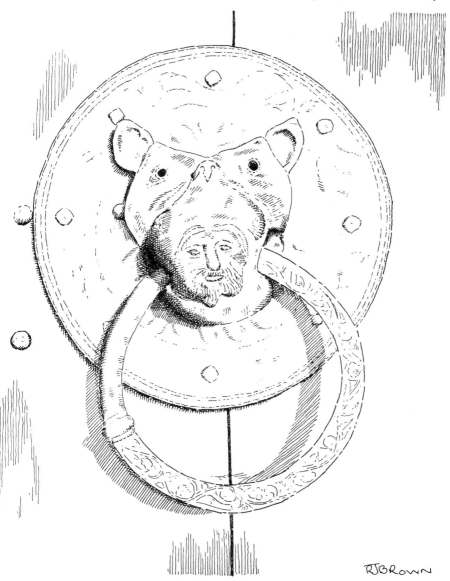

99   Closing ring at Adel, West Yorkshire

winged dragons at Iwade, Kent; and medieval salamanders at Withersfield, Suffolk. In many cases the back-plate of the closing ring is decorated with foliage or minute tracery, or pierced with holes to form various patterns as at Baltonsborough, Somerset. At Tunstead, Norfolk, the ironwork is in the form of a foliated cross.

Several kinds of lock were formerly used on church doors; the most common was the stock-lock, in which the mechanism was housed in a block of wood fixed to the inside of the door. Locks of this kind are still frequently seen on church doors.

100   Saxon window at Deerhurst, Gloucestershire

Windows

Until the early part of the thirteenth century most church windows were unglazed, for glass was expensive, and so only reserved for the larger churches. The windows of the average village church would have been unglazed or, at best, filled with oiled parchment, linen or even cow-horn (thin slices peeled or shaved from the horn) and supported on a wooden lattice-work. As a result, most windows of the time were sources of draught, and so were small, few in number and generally placed high up in the wall.

As with other developments in architecture, the change from one period to another was gradual, and one window can often combine both the earlier and the current styles. Saxon windows were, in the main, round-headed (often cut from a single stone), although some were triangular-headed, as at Barnack, Cambridgeshire, and the fine example at Deerhurst, Gloucestershire (100). When they were glazed the glass was set in the centre of the wall and a large splay was provided, both externally and internally (as at Tichborne, Hampshire), or else it was set flush with the external face of the wall, and the opening was splayed internally and had a chamfered edge to the external jamb. Windows that were originally unglazed, for instance in church towers, frequently took the form of one, two or more lights divided by a small baluster-shaped shaft without any internal or external splay to the jamb, as at Worth, West Sussex. (101)

In the early Norman period windows were still much like Saxon windows, of rather small proportions and with a semi-circular head. Later, though, they were often of some size and treated like doors, with two orders to the arch and perhaps to the shafts of the jambs as well. Most of the early Norman windows had very little ornamentation: only a small chamfer, or perhaps a plain, shallow external rebate round them – as at Adel, West Yorkshire (102) – and a very large splay internally. Externally, sometimes there is a small shaft to each jamb, which continues above the capital to form the arch, as at Kilpeck, Herefordshire. This form of decoration is typical of the Norman period, and, with the introduction of further orders, mouldings and ornamentation to the arch and shafts, sometimes produced a bold and rich effect.

In the main the windows are single small lights situated high in the wall with no attempt to space them out, although occasionally (as at Darenth, Kent) three might be grouped together. As in the Saxon period, unglazed windows were frequently divided by shafts into two or more lights – often placed in shallow recesses with arched heads, the whole placed under an all-embracing round-headed arch; this arrangement is usually found in belfry windows.

101   Saxon window at Worth, West Sussex

102   Norman window at Adel, West Yorkshire

RJBROWN.

103   Norman window at Cassington, Oxfordshire

A few circular windows from this period also remain; some have
no divisions (as at Lambourn, Berkshire), while others are articu-
lated by spokes radiating from the centre to make a wheel-window,
as at Barfreston, Kent, and Castle Hedingham, Essex. If they were
intended to be glazed, the inside of all these Norman windows was
usually splayed and often lacked any form of decoration, though
when decoration was used it was similar to that on the exterior,
both in character and mode.

Windows of the Early English period varied greatly in their proportions, but most were tall narrow lancet windows – windows without tracery (104). They were used singly, or combined in groups. These could be groups of two, as at Tangmere, West Sussex (although this is not common); of three, which was common in Sussex (for instance at Amberley, Barnham, Burwash, Climping and Udimore); of five, as at Bosham in West Sussex and Chetwode in Buckinghamshire; and even seven, as at Ockham in Surrey and Blakeney in Norfolk. For the first time the pointed (or two-centred) arch made its appearance, and when grouped together the lights were generally graduated, with the central one rising higher than those that flanked it. When so grouped they were sometimes

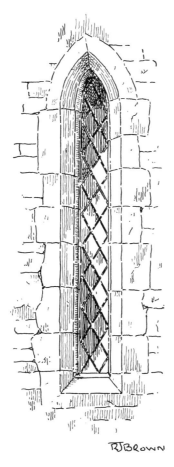

104   Lancet window at Burwash, East Sussex

placed so close to one another that the stonework between was reduced to little more than a mullion, with a single hood-mould embracing all the lights. The majority, however, were spaced further apart.

The decoration of Early English windows varied greatly. Many examples are completely plain internally and externally, and only have a chamfer and a small splay internally. Others, plain externally, have shafts and moulding internally; others are equally enriched both internally and externally; and yet others have the greatest amount of decoration externally. If anything, the majority has the greatest amount of decoration internally. Jambs are always splayed on the inside, and the inner arch does not conform to that of the actual window opening, usually springing from a lower level. Even when the jambs are plain, the arch always has either a chamfer or a moulding, generally projecting below the soffit and either dying into the jambs or supported on a corbel on each side, as at Luddenham, Kent.

The Decorated period saw the introduction of larger windows divided into separate lights by mullions, with the heads of each light filled with tracery. The heads of the windows vary in shape. Most common is the two-centred arch, although it generally is less pointed than that of the Early English style, but square heads were also common, and segmental arches (both plain and pointed) and ogee arches were also used. The arches are frequently of a different shape and proportion internally and externally, and even when the jambs in the inside are plain, they are often chamfered or moulded in much the same way as Early English arches. When the window is filled with elaborate tracery the jambs and mullions are often devoid of decoration, the mullion perhaps being only splayed, and the moulded jambs so popular at this time were commonly used. Transoms also began to appear, especially in unglazed windows like those of towers.

The main difference between windows of the Decorated period and those of the Perpendicular lies in the arrangement of the tracery and in the shape of the head which, although at first it was two-centred, grew more obtuse as the style became debased, until it developed into the four-centred arch. Unlike the windows of the Decorated period, in Perpendicular windows the mullions often continued upwards to the head of the opening, producing a stronger window than before. The result was to increase the overall size of the window – especially its height – enabling the small, humble church to be generously lit. So great was the height of many windows that the mullions themselves – so often over forty feet tall – required support, and this was provided by inserting a transom across the lower lights (as at Headcorn, Kent), and even on occasions across the tracery as well. The character of the mouldings also changed as the style developed.

Square-headed windows, too, were often used, especially in the north and in other less prosperous areas; these might have no tracery but for a few cusps at the top of each light. Circular windows also became a feature of some East Anglian clerestories, often alternating with ordinary windows, as in the remarkable clerestory at Cley next the Sea, Norfolk.

The Reformation generally saw the end of the Gothic style, with the introduction first of the Renaissance style and later of the Classical style, with its large, plain windows under semi-circular arches, generally with their keystones projecting.

As we have seen, in Gothic architecture tracery – intersecting rib-work in the upper parts of the window – played an important part in the overall appearance of the window in both the Decorated and Perpendicular periods. Evolving gradually, it first appeared with the introduction of plate tracery in the late Norman period, continuing into the early part of the Early English period. When lancets were grouped together and enclosed by a single hood-mould, the small piece of wall between the window and the hood-mould might be pierced with plate tracery (105).

Plate tracery developed into the bar tracery, and the window was for the first time considered as one entity. In bar tracery, introduced to England from France in around 1250, the intersecting rib-work, made up of slender shafts, continued the lines of the mullions up to the decorative head of the window. Characteristic of the period between 1250 and 1310 – although it continued to be used into the 1330s, as at Binsted, Hampshire – is geometrical tracery, which is similar to the bar tracery with the motifs chiefly consisting of circles and quatrefoils (106). The earliest form was the circle – at first plain, but later cusps were added. Y-tracery was used in two-light windows, with the mullion branching into two, forming a Y-shape. When the window was of three lights or more, each mullion branched out into two curved bars in such a way that each curve had the same radius as the containing arch, and all the curving bars intersected one another.

105   Plate tracery at Charlton-on-Otmoor, Oxfordshire

106 Geometrical bar tracery at Long Wittenham, Oxfordshire

This type of tracery is known as intersecting and, like Y-tracery, dates from around 1300. In both types the curves may be cusped or uncusped.

Typical of the early fourteenth century is reticulated tracery. This consists entirely of circles, drawn out at top and bottom into ogee lozenges and with internal cusps dividing the lozenges into elongated quatrefoils. The tiers of lozenges diminish in number as they rise towards the head of the window arch, and a net-like appearance results. Later still, flowing tracery became fashionable – in which, instead of tracery based on the circle, it is the curve of the bars that catches the eye. Flowing tracery developed in France into an even more elaborate style, known as Flamboyant, but in England it was abandoned for the style in which upright, straight-sided panels above the lights of the window played a prominent part. Rectilinear tracery, as this is known, is typical of the Perpendicular period and can be seen to perfection in the great churches of East Anglia (where, in some instances, small amounts of flowing tracery are to be found in the side lights).

Low-side Windows and Sanctus Bells

Peculiar to many village churches is what is termed the low-side window. There has been a great deal of controversy over the use of these windows. Sometimes they are erroneously called a 'leper window', and it has been suggested that they enabled lepers to witness the celebration of Mass at the High Altar from the churchyard; this is unlikely, however, as lepers were excluded from public society in the Middle Ages, and in any case their own hospitals had chapels. Also, many of these windows were so placed that they did not provide a direct view of the altar from the outside. Today most authorities agree that this window was used by an acolyte to ring the sanctus bell at the Elevation of the Host and the Elevation of the Chalice, so that those in the vicinity who were unable to attend the service might pause and pray, thus sharing in the celebration.

These windows are usually found on the south side at the west end of the chancel, or occasionally on the north side (particularly if the village was to that side) – even, on rare occasions, on both sides, as at Adstock, Buckinghamshire, Raydon, Suffolk and Tilshead,

Wiltshire. The lower part of the window was often separated from the upper part by a wooden shutter which could be opened, but these have generally now been filled in. Externally there was often a metal grille. A low-side window in the south wall of the chancel at Rampton, Cambridgeshire, still retains its wooden shutter and its iron grille, and there is another complete example at Saxthorpe, Norfolk. Melton Constable, Norfolk has a most interesting low-side window, which still has not only its shutter but also a hollowed-out stone seat and a stone desk for a book, from which the acolyte could follow the service and ring the bell at the appropriate time. Similar low-side windows can be found at Elsfield and Alvescot, both in Oxfordshire (the latter is of particular interest because it has desks at two levels, one for standing and the other for kneeling). In many cases, instead of a separate small window, a large window was extended and the additional portion at the bottom divided off by a transom, as at Garsington, Oxfordshire.

Not all the churches had low-side windows. Some had a special sanctus bell hung externally in their own turret – generally at the apex of the gable at the east end of the nave, above the chancel arch – and rung by a bell-rope within. Many fine examples survive, amongst which one can cite Fressingfield in Suffolk, Idbury in Oxfordshire, Preston Bissett in Buckinghamshire, Long Compton in Warwickshire and Rothwell and Isham in Northamptonshire. Those at Idbury and Long Compton still retain their original bell. Perhaps the finest of all is the turret at Castle Eaton, Wiltshire, where the original bell is housed in a massive structure complete with a spirelet. On occasions the turret is placed over the south-east corner of the nave; those at Adstock, Buckinghamshire, and Methwold, Norfolk, are both of this type.

At churches that could not afford a special bell, it is known that one of the ordinary bells in the tower was employed. In order that the acolyte could see the High Altar from the ringing chamber an opening was needed: a sanctus bell window. They vary greatly in shape and size, occasionally complementing the opening on the other faces of the tower. Generally, however, they were small – mere slits, small quatrefoils or small circular windows (at Swanton Morley, Norfolk, the opening is only four inches wide). They would not have been glazed and, because they were a source of draughts, many have been blocked up or obscured by hatchments, coats of arms, etc.

Priest's Doors

The chancel and sanctuary were the special responsibility of the parish priest and were only occasionally entered by the laity, so a small door into the chancel from the outside, usually on the south side, was provided for the priest's own use. The majority are relatively small and built in the style of the period, but a few are a little different. The one at Blythburgh, Suffolk, has a flying buttress over it, while at Trunch and Warham St Mary, Norfolk (107), the doors have a small porch built with a buttress centred above.

Holy Water Stoups

From earliest times it was customary to make an act of purification with water before entering the church. In medieval times a stoup – a receptacle for holy water placed at the entrance of the church – was provided for this purpose. The water was blessed every Sunday, and worshippers entering the church dipped a finger of the right hand in the holy water and made the sign of the Cross on their forehead and chest to remind them of their baptismal vows and the need of cleansing from sin. Nearly all stoups are therefore adjacent to the main door: generally within the porch, although sometimes just inside the church itself. In nearly all cases the stoup is on the right-hand side, and it is very rare to find one on the left, as in the porch at Crowle, Worcestershire. It is not uncommon for there to be two stoups, one inside the church and one in the porch; in such cases it may be taken for granted that the one inside is of earlier date. At Blythburgh, Suffolk, the stoup is on the outside of the porch, on the right-hand side.

Stoups were generally set in a niche formed in the wall and are often so plain that their date cannot be detected. However, there are many more elaborate examples, some dating from the Norman period. One such – at Broughton Astley, Leicestershire – consists of a slender shaft covered with the typical Norman chevron moulding supporting a cushion capital hollowed out to form a basin. At the north entrance to Wembury church, Devon, another uncommon Norman example has a partly engaged shaft built into the wall; its width at the top is some eighteen inches, while the basin itself has a diameter of twelve inches. Other Norman examples of note have

107   Priest's door at Warham St Mary, Norfolk

been identified at Lastingham in North Yorkshire, Stanton Harcourt in Oxfordshire, Castle Hedingham in Essex, Barton-on-the-Heath in Warwickshire, Great Gidding in Cambridgeshire and elsewhere. A fine example from the thirteenth century can be seen in the porch at Harlton in Cambridgeshire.

Fourteenth-century stoups with trefoil- and cinquefoil-headed

108   Stoup at St Endellion, Cornwall

niches, the cusp often tipped with a ballflower ornament, are to be found at East Dean, East Sussex, and Edgcote, Northamptonshire. Perhaps the largest is on the south porch of the redundant church at Caldecote, Hertfordshire, which is about six feet high, including its ornate canopy. The fifteenth century also produced some fine examples, including those at Northborough in Cambridgeshire, Albury in Hertfordshire and Beckley and Minster Lovell in Oxfordshire. Probably one of the most interesting stoups is to be found at St Endellion, Cornwall (108). Dating from around 1500, it is a projecting stoup beautifully carved with three coats of arms – those of the Roscarrock, Chenduit and Pentire families.

Not all stoups were formed in niches within the wall. Occasionally the angle between the porch and church was occupied by a substantial block of moulded stone with the top hollowed out, as at Wootton Courtenay, Somerset. Although stoups must have existed in every church, few survive intact today, for during the Reformation many were destroyed – or at least so mutilated that they could no longer hold the holy water.

Consecration Crosses

At the consecration of a church twelve crosses were carved, painted or depicted on the external walls – three on each wall – at a height of about seven to eight feet, so that they could not be brushed by passers-by. Each cross was anointed with holy oil by the bishop (who used a small ladder, which was moved round during the service of consecration, to reach them), and they were lit with candles on the anniversary of the consecration. These crosses have almost invariably disappeared, but examples of carved crosses survive at Uffington in Oxfordshire, Moorlinch in Somerset (109) and Bale in Norfolk; those at Great Sampford, Essex, are formed of flushwork.

Mass or Scratch Dials

Marks frequently found on the outside of many of our old churches, either on the south wall, a buttress or a south porch, are medieval mass or scratch dials – a form of sundial used to mark the

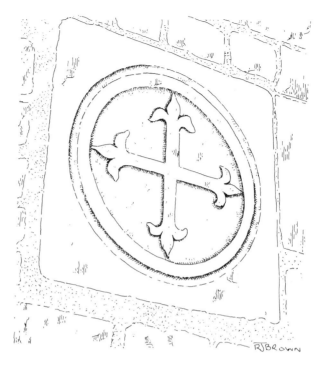

109   Consecration cross at Moorlinch, Somerset

time of church services. They vary widely in form, size and position, but are usually about six to ten inches in diameter with lines,
cut or scratched in the stone, radiating from a central hole to the
circumference of the lower part of the dial. A metal pointer, known
as a gnomon (from the Greek meaning 'indicator') was placed in
the hole and cast its shadow as the sun moved round. Each time the
shadow touched one of the radiating lines, it was time for Mass.

In their earliest form these dials often had only horizontal and
vertical scratches, with two intermediate scratches to divide the day
into three hour periods. In others the scratches were omitted, and
the circumference of the lower part of the dial was simply drilled
with holes at the appropriate intervals. On many dials a thicker line
can be seen, indicating the parochial mass hour of 9 a.m. The dials
were, of course, inaccurate. It was later discovered that, if the dial
was placed vertically and facing due south, and the gnomon was at
an angle of approximately 39°, a fairly accurate time indicator was
achieved. New dials were cut with the scratches corresponding to

each hour of the day and even (as at Barnardiston, Suffolk) had the appropriate numerals added.

Although many churches have only one Mass dial, many others have two or more. Barfreston, Kent, has several on one wall, and at Hales, Norfolk, there are six – three on the south-east corner, one on each side of the door and one at the south-west corner. Mass dials are found in most counties in the country, though they seem to be most common in Somerset and Hampshire and around the Cotswolds. One of the finest – at Farmington in Gloucestershire – has figures for the hours.

Sundials

Although mechanical clocks were common by the end of the seventeenth or the beginning of the eighteenth century, their cost was prohibitive. Many of our smaller village churches had to rely on scientific sundials, which were developed at about this time. Many of them are still to be found, usually above the entrance to the porch. A very fine painted example, dated 1720, is to be found at Ellingham in Hampshire (according to the Royal Observatory, its segments are 5 minutes and 35 seconds too small). Another, and highly complicated, one at Eyam, Derbyshire, shows the approximate times in various parts of the world, as well as giving astronomical information. The dial is said to have been made locally in 1755.

Most church sundials are from the seventeenth or eighteenth centuries, but, strangely, around twenty that date from the Saxon period still survive. The most famous is the one at Kirkdale, North Yorkshire (110), where the inscription proves the date of 1060. Others of note are to be found at Edstone, also in North Yorkshire, Daglingworth in Gloucestershire, Marsh Baldon in Oxfordshire (this one is surrounded by cable moulding), Warnford in Hampshire, and at Bishopstone, East Sussex (simply inscribed 'Eadric').

Clocks

An embellishment to many village towers is the clock, described as 'probably the most frequently used yet least considered pieces of

110   Saxon sundial at Kirkdale, North Yorkshire

church property'. Although mechanical clocks began to be used in churches as early as the twelfth century it was not until the fourteenth century that any of them had dials – and it would have been the late seventeenth century before many of the simple village church clocks had one. Early dials were simply painted onto the face of the stonework, or else a simple wooden dial was fitted. A number of clocks have only one hand, a sure sign that time was not so important as it is today. A notable example, dated 1796, is that at Garsington, Oxfordshire, whose swinging pendulum can be seen from within the church under the west tower. The adjacent village of Chislehampton also has a one-handed clock, and so (among others) do Groombridge in Kent, Long Stratton in Norfolk, Kedington in Suffolk, North Stoneham in Hampshire and Northill in Bedfordshire (the last made about 1663 and attributed to Thomas Tompion, the 'Father of English Clockmakers'). The largest clock of this type, some three hundred years old, is at Coningsby, Lincolnshire, where the huge dial is painted on the stonework. Instead of having figures at five-minute intervals, many churches have texts or other wording on the dial: Wootton Rivers, Wiltshire, has 'Glory be to God', and West Acre, Norfolk, has 'Watch and Pray'.

At the end of the fourteenth century a number of astronomical clocks made their appearance – the most famous is that at Wells Cathedral (its original workings are now in the Science Museum, South Kensington) – but their use was restricted to a few large churches. 'Jack' clocks – with their ingeniously devised automatic figures to strike the hours and its quarters – date from the fifteenth century; the most famous is the early sixteenth-century one at St Mary Steps, Exeter, which has three figures; the centre one is said to represent Henry VIII. A single 'Jack', witness to a clock long gone, can be examined in the church at Blythburgh, Suffolk.

Weather-vanes

One of the delights of the tower or spire is the weather-vane indicating the direction of the wind. Their use is ancient – one appears in the Bayeux Tapestry of the eleventh century – though generally surviving examples are from the seventeenth century onwards. A few are earlier, however: for instance the heraldic one at Etchingham, East Sussex, is fourteenth-century, and a sixteenth-century one, preserved on a beam in the nave at Alford, Surrey (a replica has been placed on the church tower).

Many weather-vanes are symbolic. The cock, signifying eternal vigilance, is the most common emblem. At Winchcombe, Gloucestershire, the richly gilded cock is made of wood and is nearly 6 feet long from beak to tail and 4 feet 6 inches high; it originally came from St Mary Redcliffe, Bristol, in 1872. Another splendid cock, also of wood, surmounts the central tower at Colyton, Devon. The cock at Priston, Somerset, is gold with a red comb, while the large one at Knapton, Norfolk, is combined with a pennon bearing the attributes of the church's patron saints: the crossed keys of St Peter and the sword of St Paul. The key is a symbol used on churches dedicated to St Peter, although it is sometimes used on churches not of this dedication, as at St Botolph's, Aspley Guise, Bedfordshire. The gridiron of St Lawrence surmounts the churches dedicated to him at Tidmarsh in Berkshire and Elmstead Market and Bradfield in Essex. A fish, an early Christian symbol, is also frequently used, as at Piddinghoe, East Sussex and Flamborough, East Riding of Yorkshire; the dragon is also a favourite, and an example with forked tongue and tail and bearing the date 1797 can be seen at Brookland, Kent. A ship is not an uncommon motif, and can be seen, for instance, at Tollesbury, Essex. There are weather-vanes of the pennon type, often pierced with the date (and perhaps with the churchwardens' initials), as at Wadhurst, East Sussex, or simply dated, as at Buxted, East Sussex; others may be heraldic, like that at Fotheringhay, Northamptonshire, which has the falcon and fetterlock, the badge of the House of York. Other motifs are more uncommon: for example the weather-vane at Great Ponton, Lincolnshire, represents a violin (a replica of the original). Perhaps the most unusual motif, however, is the bedbug at Kingsclere, Hampshire; the story goes that King John (some say Charles II) spent a night at the village inn and was so badly bitten that he decreed that the church should for ever advertise the fact on its tower.

6 Internal Architectural Features

The interiors of our village churches in medieval times would have presented a very different appearance to that of today. Unlike today, they were glorified by a blaze of colour lavished on stone, plaster and wood alike, but this, along with much of the church fittings and furniture, were in the most part stripped away during the Reformation, as we shall see. Even so, there is a great amount still to be seen – too much indeed for one chapter, so it has been necessary to split discussion of the internal features. In this chapter we shall examine the architectural features, such as roofs, arches, arcades and floors.

Vaulting

Stone vaulting in our village churches is very much the exception and is, for the most part, confined to cathedrals, abbeys and larger churches.

One of the simplest forms, used by the Normans, was the groin vault at the intersection of two plain barrel vaults. This can occasionally be found in small, square chancels, as at Darenth, Kent, and Coln St Dennis, Gloucestershire. Vaulting ribs were not used at this time. They were soon developed, however, to form the arches on which the roof was erected, its weight being carried down to the arch arcade by means of the vaulting shafts. The simplest type is quadripartite vaulting, in which the square or rectangular ceiling bay is divided into four cells by ribs that follow the diagonals of the rectangle, as at Elkstone in Gloucestershire, Kilpeck in Herefordshire and Steetley in Derbyshire. When there was an apse this was also generally vaulted, as at Kilpeck and at Compton, Surrey. The introduction of additional ribs increased the number of the cells and decreased their size. A very early example of sexpartite vaulting is at Tickencote, Rutland, which dates from around 1170.

In tierceron vaulting the ribs rise from springers on the side walls and meet not at a boss in the centre of the bay but at points on the ridge rib. This was used in high vaults of great churches and in the interior of towers and porches of our country churches, the arrangement of ribs often being contrived to form a star. There is a beautiful example at Sevenhampton, Gloucestershire, built around 1500, when a lantern tower was inserted over the crossing.

In the fourteenth century the lierne vault appeared, in which there are additional ribs that do not spring from the shaft or wall but cross the spandrels of the vault from rib to rib, producing elaborate star-like patterns. In a village church, this is best seen at Steeple Ashton in Wiltshire, where, at first glance, it seems to occupy the whole church. In fact the chancel and the nave aisles have lierne vaults in stone, but the nave vault is of wood. It seems that the whole interior was designed to be vaulted in stone, and it is not known why the nave was constructed in wood (it has been suggested that the nave roof was constructed in timber after the fall of the steeple). Usually these vaults in village churches were confined to limited, generally square, areas such as towers and porches. In the truly magnificent fifteenth-century south porch at Woolpit, Suffolk, there are 25 bosses; however, the majority of these vaults, some of which are uncommonly attractive, occur towards the south-west – in Wiltshire, Gloucestershire, Somerset and Devon. In the tower at Cricklade, Wiltshire, is a lierne vault of considerable complexity with 72 bosses. Most of these lierne vaults have bosses, usually with heraldic or floral decoration.

The fifteenth century saw the introduction of the fan vault, the most beautiful and purely English form of vaulting. This was built up of inverted trumpet-shaped conoids with all the ribs that rise from the same springer having equal curves and being spaced at equal angles to one another. Again, in village churches its use was generally restricted to towers, for example the central tower at Axbridge and the basement of the tower at Wrington (both in Somerset), at Castle Combe in Wiltshire and at Fotheringhay in Northamptonshire.

It is interesting to note that not all vaults are of stone, and there are a few made of timber. Of course, it is true that the vaulting was originally evolved to suit stone, but its form was easily translated into timber. The only ways in which wooden vaulting was inferior to that made of stone was that it was less durable and not fire-proof; its advantage was that its lighter weight exerted little extra thrust on the walls. Wooden vaults are to be found in some of our cathedrals and abbeys – the cloisters at Lincoln, the choirs at St Albans Abbey and Winchester and the central octagon at Ely – and sometimes in church towers (Ludlow, Shropshire, for example) but they are not often found in our country churches. The oldest is probably that over the nave at Warmington, Northamptonshire, thought to date from the thirteenth century; perhaps the most remarkable is the one already mentioned at Steeple Ashton, where the nave has a very good imitation of a stone lierne-vaulted roof in wood.

Timber Roofs

Whereas stone vaulting was very much the exception in village churches, timber roofs were almost universally used, for timber was plentiful and far less costly than stone. This was a form of construction in which the English excelled – and, considering the perishable nature of the material and the often ill-judged restorations of the nineteenth century, much still remains to be admired. One can only wonder at the medieval craftsman's skill, for there is not an iron bolt, strap or nail to be found; the elaborate structures rely solely on framing, and the various members are jointed together and secured with wooden pegs.

It is impossible to discuss timber roofs without some technicalities. They can be classified into two types. Single-framed roofs consist entirely of transverse members, such as rafters, which are not tied together longitudinally; in this type each pair of rafters forms a complete truss in itself. Double-framed roofs, on the other hand, consist of strongly framed principals at intervals, with longitudinal members (purlins and ridge-pieces) framed in between them, and these in turn bear the common rafters. The whole strength of the roof depends on these principals or trusses, and the common rafters merely rest on the purlins, either halved and pinned at the ridge or framed into the ridge-piece.

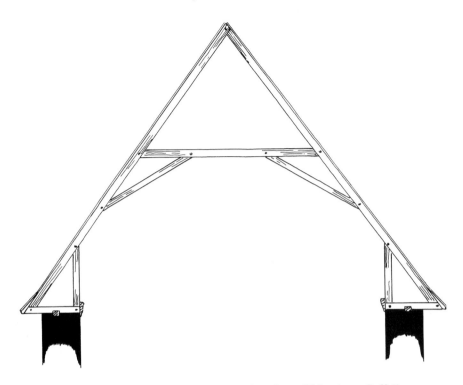

111   Single-framed braced roof based on Great Blakenham, Suffolk

Single-framed roofs are generally earlier in origin, and after the fourteenth century they were rarely used. The very early single-framed roofs consisting only of rafters (coupled rafter roofs) and relied on the roof-covering for longitudinal stability, and so were quite unsuitable for anything but a small span; they are therefore generally found only in porches, as at North Stoke, Oxfordshire (even here a collar has had to be introduced). The most common form of single-framed roof was the braced-collar rafter roof, in which each pair of rafters was strengthened by a collar beam, which in turn was braced (111). Although a large number of these roofs exist in the country, this was not a very satisfactory type of construction. The rigidity of the roof depends entirely on the joint between the collar and rafter to prevent the roof from spreading. When any one joint weakens, greater strain is put on the others, and a progressive weakness develops in the whole structure. In order to strengthen the foot of each rafter, a sole piece was introduced the full width of the wall, notched over the wall-plate, into which the foot of the rafter was

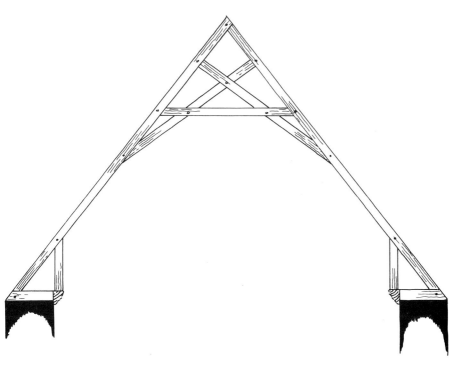

112   Single-framed braced roof with scissor bracing based on Belchamp St
Paul, Essex

framed, and an ashlar strut was introduced, framed to the rafter and
sole pieces, thus preventing any spread at the wall-plate. Even so,
nothing could prevent the collapse of this form of roof, once the
framing began to give.

A very early example of a surviving single-framed roof is at
Compton, Surrey, where an eleventh-century date is claimed for the
chancel roof. Others of note are at Chirton, Wiltshire (thought to
date from no later than 1200) and thirteenth-century roofs survive
at Chalvington in East Sussex, Forest Hill in Oxfordshire (reconstructed in the seventeenth century), Great Blakenham in Suffolk,
Chartham in Kent (dating from around 1300) and South
Burlingham in Norfolk; most of the fourteenth-century roofs in
Herefordshire and Worcestershire are single-framed.

In some instances tie-beams were introduced to prevent spreading, and these can be seen in the chancel roof at Inglesham in
Wiltshire and at Overton in Hampshire, both of thirteenth-century

date. Another variation was the introduction of scissor bracing – formed by continuing the collar brace through and beyond the collar framing into the opposite rafter – which was stronger than the general method (112). These roofs generally date from the thirteenth century, as do those at Shere in Surrey and Icklingham All Saints and Laxfield in Suffolk, or from the fourteenth century, like that at Burnham, Buckinghamshire. (The problem of these single-rafter roofs collapsing longitudinally can be seen at Burnham, where all the trusses lean towards the west; to alleviate the problem long timbers have been inserted that slope upwards towards the east.)

In the south-west and in parts of the midlands the straight braces of the braced-collar rafter roof was replaced by arch braces to form the arch-braced collar-rafter roof. This can be seen at Haccombe and Tawstock in Devon (113) and Halse in Somerset.

The earliest double-framed roof took the form of framed trusses

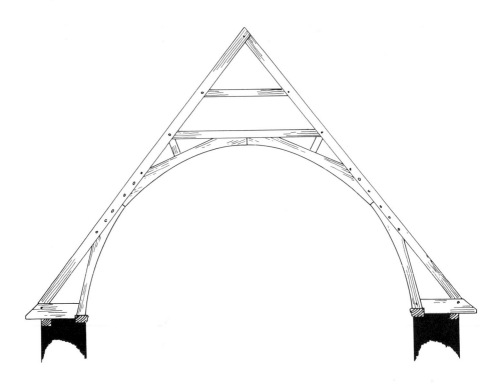

113   Single-framed arch-braced roof with arch-braced rafters based on
Tawstock, Devon (after F.E. Howard)

at intervals along the roof. The simplest version was the tie-beam roof, consisting of pairs of principal rafters tied together at their feet by a tie beam and with collar beams above, as in the thirteenth-century roof to the north transept at Harwell, Oxfordshire. One variation to this was to brace the collar beam, and another was to provide a king post rising from its centre to support a ridge piece at the apex of the roof. King-post roofs continued to be constructed until the end of the Middle Ages and even beyond, although they were generally more elaborate than early examples. Fine specimens are to be found in many parts of the country; those at Adderbury and Stanton Harcourt in Oxfordshire (114) – both dating from the fourteenth century – and Twyford, Buckinghamshire, from the fifteenth century, are exceptional. The tie beams at Twyford are supported on arch braces, and the principal rafters are supported on diagonal struts. All the main timbers are cusped.

In Somerset, especially in larger churches, by the end of the medieval period the roofs were basically of king-post construction, although of a flat pitch. Burton, Martock, Westonzoyland, High Ham and East Pennard all provide admirable examples, and

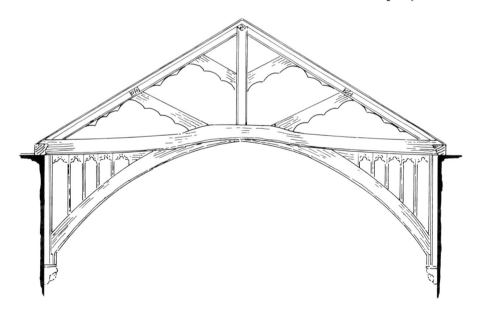

114 King-post roof based on Stanton Harcourt, Oxfordshire
(after F.E. Howard)

among those of a flatter pitch Somerton (built around 1520) is outstanding. They are all richly decorated; the tie beams, wall posts and cornices are finely moulded, and the space above the tie beams filled with tracery. At Martock the ceiling is divided into no less than 768 traceried panels; that at Somerton is divided into 640. The nave roofs at Evercreech, Wellow and Ditcheat are not panelled, and the rafters are left exposed; even so, the tie beams, braces and cornices are richly decorated. At Evercreech the angles with closed-up wings, the beams and bosses, all richly coloured and gilded, can be studied from the galleries.

Two other roof types popular in the thirteenth and fourteenth centuries were crown-post and queen-post roofs, both of which employed a tie beam. The crown-post roof was almost universally used for domestic building in the south-east and eastern England until around 1500 (and even beyond that date for the construction of barns), so it is not surprising that it also found favour in many of our village churches. In this form of construction the crown post rises from the centre of the tie beam, like a king post; however, it does not rise to the ridge-piece but supports a collar purlin that runs the whole length of the roof immediately below the collars. Framed into the tie beams at the bottom and the collar purlin at the top, crown posts thus support the collars along its entire length, and so support the rafters that bear the roof load. The crown post itself was braced to prevent lateral movement, while longitudinal braces were added to triangulate the roof (115). The bracings and the shape and height of the crown posts were the main variables in this roof type. The finest and earliest examples of crown-post roofs are to be found in the south-east, especially Kent and Sussex, and in eastern England: Essex, Suffolk and the surrounding counties.

There are various types of queen-post roof. The true queen-post roof has two vertical or curved timbers symmetrically positioned on the tie beam to support the purlins. A variation has vertical timbers placed towards the centre of the tie beam and supporting the collar rather than the purlins; this is known as a queen-strut roof. In some instances the queen posts support the principal rafters between the purlins – as at Sutton Courtenay, Oxfordshire, (116) – or between the purlins and ridge piece – as at Addlethorpe, Lincolnshire (which, in addition, is arch-braced). Both queen-post and queen-strut roofs and their variations are fairly common.

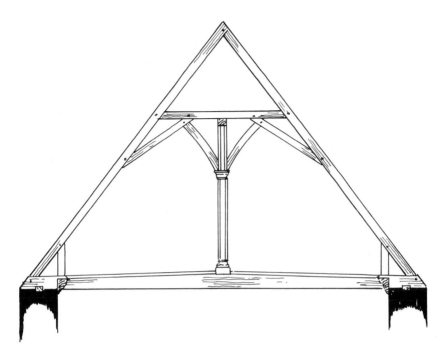

115   Crown-post roof based on Pattiswick, Essex

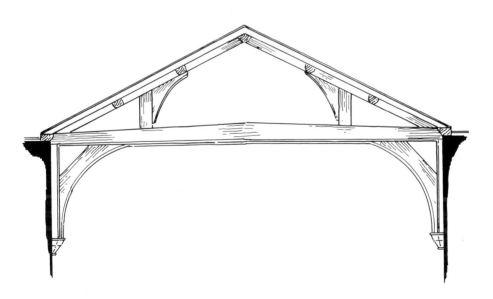

116   Queen-post roof based on Sutton Courtenay, Oxfordshire
(after F.E. Howard)

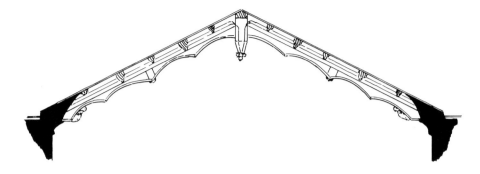

117   Couple-trussed roof based on Hinton St George, Somerset
(after F.E. Howard)

One of the disadvantages of many of these early roofs was that the tie beams, posts and struts were intrusive when an open roof was desirable. Roofs were therefore developed that had neither tie beams nor collars, thus increasing the effect of space. Couple-trussed roofs are not common – they exert great outward thrust, and tended to push the wall-plate off the wall – but they are to be found in the southern part of Somerset. The fifteenth-century one at Hinton St George (117) is a fine example, and there is another in Dorset, at Bradford Abbas. In East Anglia a wall-post and brace was introduced at the foot of each principal rafter, to overcome the outward thrust, transferring it to a lower level where the abutment was more stable, as at Middleton, Norfolk. Later the wall-post was elongated, and in the clerestory roof at Salle in Norfolk the wall-posts are actually tenoned into the ends of the aisle beams, which protrude through the wall and so ensure that the outward thrust is carried to buttresses on the outside of the aisle wall, thus acting rather like flying buttresses.

From these coupled roofs developed the arch-braced roof, widely used in East Anglia. A great many variations occur, the simplest consisting of only one pair of arch-braces to each truss, as in the nave roof at Rendlesham, Suffolk. In some instances the arch bracing is carried up in a true arch and tenoned into a pendant king post dropping down from the ridge, as at Great Glemham, Suffolk. The most common form of arch-braced roof incorporated a collar beam into which the arch braces were framed. Occasionally struts were introduced supported off the collar beam, either in the form of queen struts to support a second row of purlins (as in the chancel at Headington, Oxfordshire) or in the form of a king post (as at Chediston, Suffolk).

Wall-posts were again frequently introduced to give the roof greater stability, the arch braces being carried down and framed into them.

The arch-braced roof was common in the churches of the Welsh border counties and the adjoining areas of Worcestershire and Gloucestershire. Widely used in fourteenth-century domestic architecture, it was strengthened by wind-braces, often cusped, to form quatrefoil and similar shapes between the principal rafters and purlins. In Shropshire one can cite Alberbury, which has five tiers of windbracing, Wistanstow (four tiers, dated 1630) and Hopesay (three tiers).

In the West Country – Cornwall, Devon, Somerset and parts of Dorset – the arch-braced roof was developed into the elaborate wagon roof. This may be single-framed – with the braces supporting each pair of rafters and their collars forming a series of arches – or double-framed – with trusses placed at intervals along the roof supporting the purlins to form bays, with the arch-braced rafters between (118). These roofs generally date from the fifteenth century.

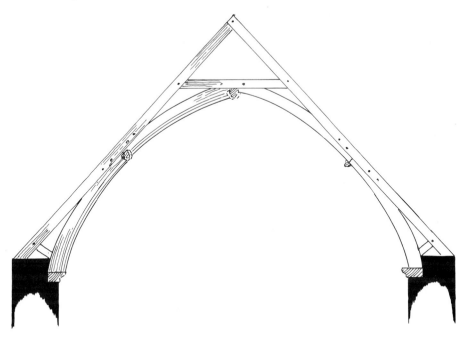

118   Double-framed arch-braced roof with arch-based rafters based on Ippleden, Devon (after F.E. Howard)

Sometimes the wagon roofs are left open, with the rafters exposed, but a good many roofs have (either originally or later) been ceiled, plastered and whitewashed, leaving only the principal rafters and longitudinal members exposed to divide the roof into panels. It is this resemblance to the canvas covering of a wagon that gives this roof type its name. It creates what Lawrence E. Jones has described as a 'homely effect' that adds largely to the attractiveness of many West Country churches. The wagon roof is almost universal in Devon; it can be seen at Alwington, Hennock, Hittisleigh and many other churches, mostly with decorative bosses at the main intersections. In Cornwall wagon roofs were also widespread, and, although many have gone, a good impression of their former beauty can be gained from visits to St Endellion, Blisland, Lanreath, Madron, Kilkhampton, Mullion and Linkinhorne. In Somerset, the three roofs at Selworthy, built around 1530, are notable; the one in the nave has remarkable decorative bosses at the intersections of the rafters and purlins. A feature of Selworthy and other west Somerset wagon roofs is the especially finely carved trellis which runs along the wall-plates, relieved by angels. Wootton Courtenay, Sampford Brett, Old Cleeve and Broomfield are all good examples.

The most remarkable are those wagon roofs in which the panels are themselves divided by cross-ribbing. The most outstanding example in a village church is probably at Chawleigh, Devon, where the whole roof is divided in this way; although this roof is largely late medieval, the chancel ceiling does date from around 1842. In the seventeenth century some wagon roofs received embellishments; three typical examples are in Somerset, at Axbridge and East Brent (both of which have patterns in plaster) and at Muchelney (which is painted). Wagon roofs are not exclusively the province of the south-west, however; they can be found in many parts of the country.

In East Anglia the arch-braced roof developed into the hammer-beam roof, the most ornamental of all roof types. Arch-braced roofs with wall-posts required large braces to keep the post and rafters at the same angle with one another. Since curved timbers of such length were not readily available, it was sometimes necessary to form the brace of two parts joined together, as at Edington, Wiltshire. However, in East Anglia the problem was overcome by introducing horizontal beams projecting from the wall into which the rafter, wall-posts and the two sections of the brace could be framed – thereby considerably reducing the width of the roof span, and hence the outward thrust. This beam is known as a hammer beam. At first the upper and lower sections of the brace had the same curve, but it was soon realized that this was no longer necessary, and braces of differing curves were introduced to form a trefoil outline – as at South Acre in Norfolk (119), and Palgrave in Suffolk (the latter still retains its original colour decorations).

Later, hammer beams projected more and more, and hammer posts were introduced, supported on the ends of the hammer beams into which the arch braces were framed. Single-hammer-post roofs, as this type is known, are a feature of Norfolk and Suffolk; among the most beautiful are those at Trunch, Banningham and Blakeney in Norfolk, and in Suffolk those at Badingham (where the spandrels are full of delicately carved wooden tracery) and Earl Stonham (probably the most ornate roof of this type in the country). Here true hammer beams, carved as prone figures, alternate with false hammer beams (that is hammer posts not resting on the hammer beams but pendant below it and relying for support on the joint between the two). The use of prone figures as hammer beams can also be seen at Hopton and Whelnetham Parva, Suffolk; however hammer beams terminating in winged angels are more common.

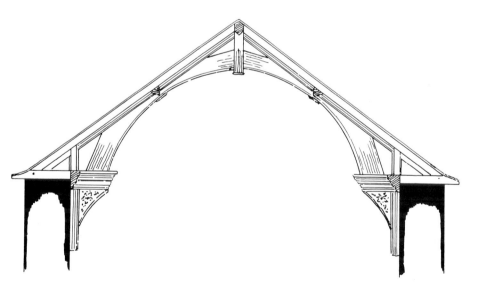

119 Single-hammer-beam roof based on South Acre, Norfolk

The double-hammer-beam roof, with its two tiers of hammer beams on each side, is perhaps the most beautiful conception of the medieval carpenter's work, yet it is doubtful whether it is structurally as sound as the single-hammer-beam roof – for in order to make room for the second tier of hammer beams and to maintain the graceful proportions, it was often necessary to raise the collar beam nearer to the ridge. Also there was often no hammer post to the upper hammer beam, and in some instances the upper hammer beam, the lower hammer beam and the purlin are all framed into the principal rafter at almost the same point. This can be seen at Bacton, Suffolk. Double-hammer-beam roofs are more usual in Suffolk than in Norfolk; notable examples are at Worlingworth, Gislingham and Grundisburgh (120) in Suffolk, and at Cawston and Knapton (where there are no less than 138 angels, some with colour) in Norfolk.

The roof at Woolpit, Suffolk is another fine example, with its niched wall-posts containing canopied figures, but the upper hammer beam is false: the arch brace to the collar springs from the back of it, and so makes no use of the projection. Wetherden, also in Suffolk, and Tilney All Saints in Norfolk (121) have roofs of another type. These are most ornate, with niched and canopied

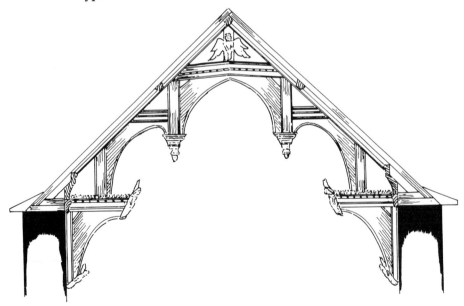

120   Double-hammer-beam roof based on Grundisburgh, Suffolk (after
F.E. Howard)

figures in the false-pendant hammer posts; in addition, the upper hammer beam is false, like that at Woolpit, with the arch braces to the collar making no use of the hammer beam's projection.

Hammer-beam roofs, both single and double, can be found in other parts of the country, notably Essex, where excellent examples equal to many in Suffolk and Norfolk can be found, as at Castle Hedingham, Gestingthorpe and Great Bromley. Although the type was not a native to the county, it was favoured in Shropshire in the seventeenth century, and many examples are to be found: Astley Abbots (1633), High Ercall (about 1660), Sheriffhales (1661), Benthall (1667), and Condover (around 1680).

With the introduction of large clerestory windows in the late Perpendicular period it became fashionable to construct almost flat roofs, with just enough fall to enable the rainwater to be shed to gutters behind the parapets. The only covering suitable for a low

121   False double-hammer-beam roof based on Tilney All Saints, Norfolk

pitch was cast lead, but lead is one of the most troublesome of our roofing materials, and the parapet gutters always proved vulnerable. Despite this, lead-covered roofs are to be found everywhere. Two types of construction were employed. In one, known as the cambered-beam roof, the camber of the tie beam gives sufficient slope for the roof to be drained. In the other, the firred tie-beam roof in which the slope is obtained by the use of firrings – tapered pieces of timber – laid on to give the necessary falls. In these low-pitched roofs the main decorative possibilities lie in the treatment of the underside of the roof slope.

Somerset and Wiltshire churches of the fifteenth century very often had cambered-beam roofs. Such roofs were naturally mostly employed on shorter spans, but this was not always the case – for instance, the nave roofs at Wrington and North Petherton. The best examples, though, are over aisles, porches or transepts. Somerset has three striking examples at Brent Knoll, at Mark in the Isle of Athelney and at Keynsham. At Mark the ridge piece is as massive as the tie beam, and the roof is divided into panels, each filled with decoration, which produces a most imposing effect. Wiltshire has a very fine example at Bromham.

Cheshire is noted for its fine wooden roofs, which are in the main of firred-beam construction, rather than the cambered-roof type. They have small braces, deep beams with traceried sides and richly panelled soffits. At the intersections of the timbers there are generally numerous elaborate and delicately carved bosses, usually composed of fretted leaves covered with a square boss of intricate tracery or strapwork in the form of a wreath enclosing a monogram. The roof at Astbury is uncommonly attractive, with openwork pendants to the main beams, as is the one at Barthomley. A rather uncommon local peculiarity, cambering of the common rafters between cornice and purlin and purlin and ridge piece, is to be found at Mobberley and Gawsworth.

In the north-eastern counties the firred beam is also preferred, but the decorative treatment is rarely as elaborate as in Cheshire. The wall-posts and braces are often omitted and, from an artistic as well as a structural point of view, this is disappointing.

Beam roofs occur occasionally in the eastern counties, and the results are most satisfactory. Cambered-beam roofs were generally preferred; the one at Burwell, Cambridgeshire (122), is a fine example, complete with wall-posts, arch bracing and gracefully traceried

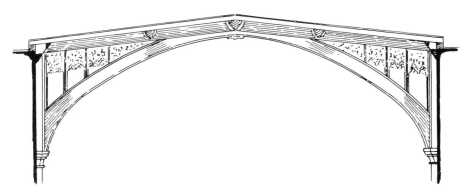

122   Cambered beam based on Burwell, Cambridgeshire

spandrels. In Suffolk excellent roofs of this type are to be found at Lavenham, Long Melford and Stoke-by-Nayland, and at Finchingfield in Essex, where the nave roof is inscribed '1561 W.B.S.L'. Perhaps the most outstanding of all is to be found on the south porch at Kersey – of its size there is probably nothing to equal it. It is divided into sixteen panels, with heavily moulded timbers with brattishing completely surrounding each panel, and the panels themselves are filled with diverse and elaborate tracery.

The firred-beam roof is rarer in the eastern counties, but Blythburgh, Suffolk, has a magnificent example, which still retains much of its original colour. Unlike elsewhere, the panelled treatment of the soffits is practically unknown, the rafters being left exposed.

A feature of some eastern churches is the lean-to roofs employed for aisles. They were generally provided with an inclined beam with wall-posts and deep arch braces, as at East Winch, South Acre and South Creake in Norfolk and Blythburgh in Suffolk. These roofs often acted as flying buttresses to carry the thrust of the nave roof out to the aisle buttresses. The spandrels are often large and filled with tracery, with the cornices and purlins moulded.

In the midlands flat beam roofs are more simplistic, with elementary mouldings as their chief form of decoration; carved bosses are rarely used, and other ornamentation seldom occurs. The firred-beam roof is generally used, and typical examples are to be found at Ewelme and Cogges, both in Oxfordshire, and in Bedfordshire at Dean (where there are a few carved bosses and angels) and Marston Moretaine. The inclined-beam type of lean-to roof is common over aisles, but rarely are the wall-posts and braces decorated.

In those medieval churches of cruciform type that dispensed with the chancel and transept arches, the ingenuity of the carpenter was tested to the full at the intersection of the four roofs. This can be seen in the wagon roofs at Luppit and Ilsington, Devon, where the crossing is emphasized in a most remarkable way by semicircular braces placed diagonally across the intersection. At Stody, Norfolk, the arch-braced roof proved a little simpler, coming together with a boss at the apex.

The majority of early medieval church roofs were purely utilitarian, with roughly hewn beams and posts, and the problem for the Gothic craftsman was to turn these into things of beauty. By the end of the fourteenth century most Gothic timber roofs in our village churches received some form of decoration, even if it was restricted to the moulding of the principal roof members. The spandrel above the arch braces or tie beams was by this time filled in by panels of fine pierced tracery. Later the wall-posts were elongated, finely carved and (as at Necton and Knapton, Norfolk, and Wetherden, Suffolk) had figures carved in niches beneath canopies. Necton has no less than sixteen such figures. Bosses were perhaps the most common form of decoration, and were often carved with a variety of subjects and figures. At Salle, Norfolk, the nine bosses in the chancel depict scenes from the life of Our Lord. Often the bosses depict saints (as at Selworthy, Somerset), and elsewhere they were carved with everyday subjects, as at Sampford Courtenay in Devon, where a sow and her litter and three rabbits are depicted.

Angels were another favourite subject particularly in East Anglia, where they are usually depicted with outspread wings, and in the south-west, where they have closed wings. In East Anglia the ends of hammer beams were often finished with angels, as were the ends of the wall-posts. Knapton, Norfolk, has no fewer than 138 angels with some coloured – a fascinating sight. At Blythburgh, Suffolk (123), many of the angels have lost some of their wings. Originally the loss was thought to have occurred in the seventeenth century at the hands of the Puritans, who are known to have tried to destroy some of the finest of our roofs by firing at them with shotguns. However, it has recently been established that at Blythburgh the buckshot was not the kind used in the seventeenth century, and it seems that the damage is attributable to a Georgian churchwarden's concern to rid the church of jackdaws which took shelter behind the angelic wings.

123   Angel at Blythburgh, Suffolk

Wall-posts nearly always rested on corbels, usually of stone and often decorated. These might represent human heads (as at Idmiston, Wiltshire), angels (Knapton, Norfolk) or grotesque monsters like those at Sharrington, Norfolk. These figures would have been originally coloured, like the four medieval musicians at Duston, Northampton.

Arches and Arcades

The arch has been used in this country since Roman times, and its introduction has had a great influence on church architecture. The principal arch in a medieval church was the chancel arch: the arched opening in the wall between the nave and the chancel. Only in Cornwall and parts of Devon – where the nave and chancel are usually in one unbroken line, originally divided by a screen – are they absent; elsewhere, with the exception of a few isolated examples, chancel arches are almost universal. Arched openings can, of course, be found elsewhere in the church and are frequently associated with the tower, particularly in those churches with a centrally placed tower. Arches in the form of arcades were used in all churches that have aisles.

An arched opening usually comprises responds (half-piers forming the jambs of the opening) divided into four parts; the base, the shaft, the capital and, above this, the abacus, from which the arch itself springs. In the case of an arcade the arch itself is supported on isolated piers, still divided into the same four parts, with responds at the terminations of the arcade. Each period had its own distinctive ornamentation, foliage and mouldings, all of which are important in dating.

The Saxon arch is usually semi-circular and generally springs not from a capital but from a massive impost, usually square in section but often roughly moulded with hollows and reeds – a very popular characteristic. Early arches are usually of only one order, the stones generally being the full thickness of the wall; only in a few cases, as at Escomb in Durham, is long and short work to be found. Some later and more ambitious Saxon arches show traces of the coming of the Norman style; the chancel arch at Selham (124) and the tower arch at Sompting, both in West Sussex, are two admirable examples. Saxon arcading is rare; the finest example is perhaps that at Great Paxton in Cambridgeshire (125), with its circular bulbous capitals carrying a square abacus, which is unrivalled anywhere.

Like the pre-Conquest builders, the Normans knew only one type of arch – the semi-circular – along with its variants, the segmental arch (used when height was limited) and the raised or stilted and the horseshoe arches (employed when a taller arch was required). Unlike those of pre-Conquest work, the stones of a Norman arch never ran right through the wall. Although plain arches were often used, this needed elaborate wooden centring when constructed and to avoid this the compound arch, made up of two or more superimposed concentric arches of increasing thickness and radius was usually employed. The first and narrowest arch, placed at about the centre of the wall's thickness, served as a centring for the second, which was thicker than the first and of greater radius. If the thickness of the wall required additional arcs, these could each be centred on the previous one. When each arc or order had been moulded or carved with the chevron or zig-zag – or, later in the period, with beakheads – the result was an arch of much splendour.

RJBrown96

124   Saxon chancel arch at Selham, West Sussex

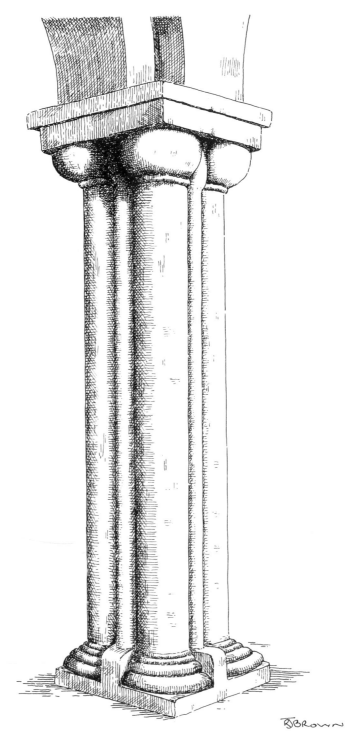

125   Saxon arcade pier at Great Paxton, Cambridgeshire

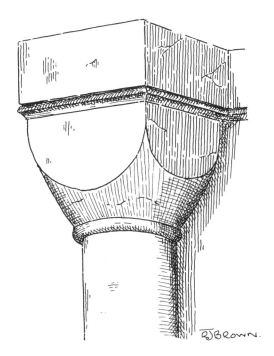

126   Cushion capital at Cassington, Oxfordshire

Whether plain or compound, an arch needs supports which corresponds with it. In the case of the responds of the chancel arch, or of an arcade, simple arches usually had simple square jambs. In the case of compound arches, though, the responds were worked into a series of recesses or orders, each of which was often worked into a shaft to carry each ring of the arch. The shafts of an arcade are rarely treated in this way and are usually circular in section, or on occasion octagonal; at Walsoken, Norfolk, and Castle Hedingham, Essex, the two forms are used alternately. At Compton Martin, Somerset, there is a rare example of a twisted column.

The base of the Norman respond or shaft was usually square and the projecting corners covered with leaf ornament. The capital was usually of the cushion-type (126), square above and circular below, to adapt the circular section of the shaft to the square arch it supported. Sometimes the capital could be cut with vertical flutes. Another type of capital from the late Norman period was the volute, which had four leaves springing from the neck of the

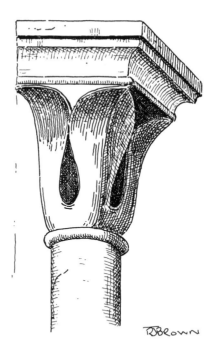

127   Capital at Easton, Hampshire

capital bending outwards – as at Easton, Hampshire (127), Harmston, Lincolnshire and Tilney All Saints, Norfolk. The abacus was rarely omitted, and the depth of its vertical face and the treatment of its lower edge is an excellent indication of dates: the narrower the vertical face, the later it is. Sometimes the capitals have elaborate sculpture, as at Wakerley in Northamptonshire, Adel in West Yorkshire and Liverton in North Yorkshire.

There are many fine examples of Norman chancel arches and arcades; the most magnificent chancel arch is at Tickencote, Rutland, but there are many others of note, including Adel in West Yorkshire, Kirkburn in East Riding of Yorkshire, North Grimston in North Yorkshire, Stoneleigh in Warwickshire, Elkstone in Gloucestershire, Stoke Dry in Rutland, Wakerley in Northamptonshire and Amberley in West Sussex. Norman arcades are less common, the finest being at Walsoken in Norfolk, Castle Hedingham in Essex, St Margaret's at Cliffe in Kent and Compton Martin in Somerset.

At the end of the Norman period the rounded arch began to be abandoned, and in Transitional churches the gradual change from one style to another can often be seen, massive Norman work with round arches being replaced by lighter Gothic work with pointed arches. A good example is the chancel arch at Walsoken: the arch is pointed, but the ornamentation is the zig-zag.

128   Early English capital at Holme Hale, Norfolk

Early English arches were usually constructed like the Norman ones in successive rings, but, owing to the deeply undercut rounds and hollows of the mouldings, the divisions are far less marked. The arch generally in use was the pointed arch often with a fairly acute point. In early work the jambs followed the Norman formula with recesses; often each shaft is detached and the recesses hollowed, which gives the effect of a shafted splay, rather than a series of recesses. In country churches the shafts were still generally round, although from around 1200 octagonal ones were gaining popularity, as at North Crawley in Buckinghamshire, Castle Bytham in Lincolnshire and Great Bookham in Surrey. Sometimes small shafts – often detached, as at Weston, Lincolnshire, and West Walton, Norfolk – were placed around the circular pier. The bases for the piers were deeply moulded with what is known as the waterhold moulding, while the capitals were either moulded (128) or had stiff-leaf foliage, usually with long stalks (as at Eaton Bray and Studham in Bedfordshire). Above the capital, the abacus was almost always rounded, with a rounded upper edge and deeply undercut. In addition to those already mentioned, some of the finest arcades are to be found at Ivinghoe in Buckinghamshire, Slimbridge in Gloucestershire and Sedgefield in Durham.

The pointed arch continued throughout the Decorated period but with less acute points than previously and rarely moulded with any elaboration – although the mouldings were more numerous, they were not so deeply cut. Characteristic of Decorated work is the roll or scroll moulding, in which the upper portion is rounded and overlaps the lower portion, which has an ogee curve. In many smaller churches splays were often used either by themselves or with other mouldings. In smaller churches the circular pier was gradually replaced by plain octagonal piers. In more ambitious churches the shafts comprised four semicircular half-shafts attached to a central square pier, as at Great Missenden, Buckinghamshire. In some instances the four half-shafts may be separated by a deep hollow or by a small shaft. The capital was sometimes omitted, and the moulding of the arch rose from the floor without a break. When a capital was provided it sometimes almost absorbed the abacus, by the abolition of the undercut hollow, and was practically always circular and moulded; from the second quarter of the fourteenth century, however, octagonal capitals, like those at Westhall in Suffolk, became increasingly popular.

Foliaged capitals are rare, but when they do occur they are extremely beautiful – for example, those at Patrington in East Riding of Yorkshire and Stoke Golding in Leicestershire. The foliage is life-like (very different from the stiff-leaf variety found in Early English work) and of a much broader character. It depicts the

129   Crossing at Blewbury, Oxfordshire

foliage of particular plants and trees – oak, ivy, maple, whitethorn, vine, etc. – and is generally well arranged and very compact, giving a bulbous outline to the capital. On the Oxfordshire –Buckinghamshire border several churches have capitals in the form of human busts with interlinked arms; those at Bloxham and Hanwell in Oxfordshire and Ludgershall in Buckinghamshire are of exceptional quality.

The pointed arch of the Decorated period continued in use throughout the Perpendicular period. However, its point became even more obtuse, and finally the four-centred arch (an arch which springs from four points) became fashionable. The mouldings became wider and less deep and, as the arches became more depressed, the piers occupied a greater proportion of the whole arcade. The octagonal pier was now usual, but two distinctive local styles emerged. In East Anglia semicircular half-shafts alternated with casement mouldings (wide, shallow hollows), and the shafts had small capitals with the hollows extending upwards to correspond with those of the arch. Good examples of this can be seen at Denston and Stoke-by-Nayland in Suffolk and at Salle, Shelton and Wighton in Norfolk. In the West Country four semicircular half-shafts were used, connected by wave mouldings (as at Broomfield, Somerset, and Altarnun and St Teath, Cornwall) or by deep hollows which extended between the capitals on the half-shafts to meet the similar hollow of the arch. This type of pier became almost universal in Somerset in the Perpendicular period; those at Martock, Long Sutton, Westonzoyland and Muchelney are a few of the many possible examples. The capitals were usually plain and octagonal, even if the pier itself was circular.

Foliage was less common in the Perpendicular period, and most confined to the West Country. In Devon undulating foliage surrounding the capital was popular, as at Swimbridge, Wolborough and Broadclyst. Similar capitals can be found in Somerset (for instance at Broomfield), while in Cornwall small leaves often occurred on each face of the capital, as at St Veep.

The vast majority of medieval arcades are of stone, though there are a few that are built of brick (St Osyth, Essex, for example). More surprisingly there are a number of timber arcades in churches that are largely built of stone. The earliest is probably to the south arcade at Navestock, Essex – now cleverly and very effectively disguised with plaster to imitate stone. Another of early (fourteenth-century) date is at Selmeston in East Sussex, and at Ribbesford in Worcestershire there is a very impressive arcade of five bays. Other timber arcades exist at Wingham in Kent, Crawley in Hampshire, Castle Eaton in Wiltshire, Langley Marish in Slough, in Berkshire and Nymet Rowland in Devon. The last has a three-bay arcade moulded as if it were stone; the reason why it was constructed of oak in an area where stone was plentiful and timber was not can only be one of economy.

After the Reformation, the Gothic style was gradually replaced by the Renaissance style, which was based upon Classical traditions. The round arch was again preferred, and the piers – consisting of base, shaft and capital supporting an entablature – followed the Classical orders. The capitals are the best indication of which of the five orders – Tuscan, Doric, Ionic, Corinthian and Composite – the piers belong to.

The Tuscan order is the simplest of the five. The height of its column, which is never fluted, is six times the diameter of the lower part of the shaft. The capital has a square abacus with a small projecting fillet on the upper edge; under the abacus is an ovolo and a fillet, and below this a neck. The base consists of a square plinth and a large torus.

The oldest and the simplest of the three orders used by the Greeks is the Doric order. The shaft has twenty flutings, which are separated by a sharp edge (not a fillet, as in other orders) and are less than a semi-circle in depth. The moulding below the abacus is an ovolo.

The distinguishing feature of the Ionic Order is the capital, which is ornamented with four spiral projections called volutes, generally arranged so as to exhibit a flat face on the two opposite sides of the capital. The shaft is sometimes plain but often has twenty-four flutes, separated from each other by small fillets.

With the Corinthian order the distinguishing feature is again the capital. This has two rows of acanthus leaves, eight in each row, plus a third row supporting eight small open volutes, four of which are under the four horns of the abacus. The Composite Order has the features of both Ionic and Corinthian capitals.

Squints

Many churches have openings cut obliquely through the wall or pillar at the side of the chancel arch, affording the priest at the side altar a view of the High Altar. This opening is known as a squint, or sometimes a hagioscope (a term introduced by the Camden Ecclesiological Society in the nineteenth century). Mass was often said at several altars at the same time, and these openings enabled the priests officiating at the side altars to synchronize their actions with those of the celebrant at the High Altar, and during the Mass to elevate the Host at the same moment that it was elevated at the High Altar. By standing at the High Altar and looking through the squints it is possible to locate the positions of the former side altars that they served (usually either at the east ends of the aisles or on either side of the chancel arch).

Squints are common and are to be found from all periods from the Normans (as at North Hinksey, Oxfordshire) right up to the Reformation. In size they vary greatly; at Newnham Murren, Oxfordshire (130), the squint is little more than a small round

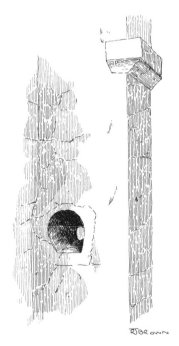

130   Squint at Newnham Murren, Oxfordshire

opening, while those at Scawton in North Yorkshire, and Tarrant Rushton in Dorset are particularly large. As a rule squints are quite plain, but there are many exceptions, and these often assimilate the design of windows, as at Irthlingborough, Northamptonshire, and Tarrant Rushton. Some squints are remarkably crude: simply a hole cut out diagonally through the wall and left rough, as at Wyre Piddle, Worcestershire. Others are particularly long; the one at West Chiltington, West Sussex, which is cut through the east respond of the aisle and the chancel wall, is some five feet long. At Quethiock and Landrake, Cornwall, the squints are combined with the stairway to the rood-loft, and at Woodchurch, Kent, there is a rare example of a double squint.

Encaustic Tiles

Most medieval village churches would have had no flooring other than beaten earth, perhaps mixed with ox-blood, strewn with rushes or straw for the sake of cleanliness. Stone slabs, clay pammets, bricks and tiles are generally of a much later date. The use of decorative encaustic tiles – clay tiles with a design burnt into them – was generally restricted to the great monastic and cathedral churches and, when used in smaller churches, would have been used only for the High Altar steps or the sanctuary. In those village churches that have a more or less complete tiled floor, this is often the result of the spoils from the suppression of the monasteries. The churches of Winchcombe and Hailes, Gloucestershire, both have some tiles taken from these former abbeys.

At first these encaustic tiles were imported from Normandy, but soon they were made in England. Kilns were set up in several places, the most important being those at Droitwich and Great Malvern. Later, manufacture gradually became more localized, and several centres emerged, the most prolific of which was that at Tylers Green, Penn, Buckinghamshire. The art of encaustic tile-making died out with the Dissolution of the monasteries and did not reappear until Victorian times (the floor at Kingsland, Herefordshire, is an outstanding example of these Victorian tiles).

The tiles were made of clay, formed by impressing the surface of the unfired tile with a wooden block, the resulting depressions filled with white slip (liquid) clay. This produced a white design in the red body of the tile. The whole tile was then covered with a thin surface glaze that, being slightly yellow in colour, tinged the white clay and imparted to the red a fuller and richer tone when fired.

The earliest tiles were decorated with crudely executed sacred symbols, but later motifs took a variety of forms. Most encaustic tile floors consist mainly of architectural and geometrical figures, interspersed with human or grotesque heads, symbolic figures (the fish was particularly popular) and a great number of armorial bearings. The fleur-de-lys was also very popular. Some patterns were made up of a number of individual tiles – from four to sixteen depending on the design. Although these and other examples survive throughout the country, many tile floors were destroyed when the chancel floor was raised, and now only a few churches – such as West Hendred in Oxfordshire and Hailes in Gloucestershire – have a more or less complete floor. Some of the best of these medieval tiles are to be found in Worcestershire and Devon. At Bredon, the early fourteenth-century tiles face the chancel steps, and are therefore probably in their original position, while those in the north nave at Cadeleigh are of thirteenth-century date. Other notable examples can be studied in Old Cleeve in Somerset, Westleigh in Devon, Brook in Kent and Launcells in Cornwall.

7 Chancel Furniture

In the early Middle Ages the purpose of the church-builder was to construct a shelter and shrine for the altar on which the Church's central service, the Mass, was performed. Around the altar clustered a number of accessories, all closely linked with the altar, and it is these that are the subject of this chapter.

Altars

Until 1076 most altars would have been wooden, but in that year Archbishop Lanfranc issued an order stating that all altars should be made of stone. There are many records of the subsequent destruction of wooden altars and their replacement in stone. In the main, these stone altars were all constructed in a similar manner, that is with a stone slab, or *mensa* (the Latin for 'table'), carried on two stone supports. The slab projected over the base at the front and sides and its edges were square or chamfered and usually undercut beneath. Five crosses were incised on the top surface – one at each corner and one in the centre, representing the five wounds of Christ – and were annointed at the consecration of the altar.

Holy relics were sought after by the early church, and those that possessed them incorporated them in the altar at its consecration. Sometimes they were placed in a cavity in the *mensa* and sealed with a stone, but more commonly it was in the supporting stonework that the relics were kept – one of the stones being hollowed out before being built in.

Even in the earliest and humblest of village churches there

would, in addition to the High Altar, be one or two minor altars. Even in those churches with no aisles, comparatively small altars were provided at the east end of the nave at either side of the opening to the chancel. In some cases recesses for these altars survive, as at Melton Constable in Norfolk, Barfreston in Kent, Boarhunt in Hampshire and Iffley and Stanton Harcourt in Oxfordshire. Later, when screens were erected across the chancel opening, these lateral altars were placed against the screen, which itself served as a background and reredos, as at Ranworth in Norfolk. When aisles were added there was no need to squeeze these lateral altars into the corners of the nave, and instead they were transferred to the eastern end of the nave aisles. Only rarely do such altar bays, screened off by parclose screens, retain their altars, although very often their piscinas survive. Minor altars are to be found elsewhere in the church: in the vestries, as at Adderbury in Oxfordshire, Warmington and Shotteswell in Warwickshire and Claypole in Lincolnshire; in towers, as at Brook, Kent; in the chamber above the porch as at Salle, Norfolk.

At the Reformation stone altars were ordered to be destroyed, but it is doubtful whether the destruction was on a great scale until after 1550, when stern injunctions caused most to be removed. The old stone slabs were not always destroyed, for it is recorded that many were used as pavings and in other roles, including hearths, fire-backs, sinks, steps, bridges and gravestones. With the revival of ancient rites under Queen Mary, high altars of stone were restored and those not destroyed were reused. Certainly many still remained in 1559, for the Injunctions issued by Elizabeth stated that 'in some other places the Altars be not yet removed' and that 'no Altar be taken down but by oversight of the Curate of the church and the Churchwardens or one of them at least'.

Original stone altars that survive *in situ* are rare; one church, at Peterchurch in Herefordshire, retains three – the High Altar and the side altars on either side of the entrance to the apse. A Norman altar remains at Forthampton, Gloucestershire, but many more churches have old altar slabs which have been found and replaced in the church, although not often in their original position. A few, such as the one at Chickney in Essex, have been restored to their original use.

Sometimes portable altars were used, perhaps the most remarkable is the one to be found at Newport in Essex (131), which takes the form of a chest dating from the late thirteenth century. The inside of the lid – which forms the reredos – is divided into five panels, each one painted (chiefly in red and green) with depictions of the *Crucifixion, The Virgin Mary, St John, St Peter* and *St Paul*, all under trefoiled canopies. There is a false bottom with a secret sliding panel for the altar stone.

Altar Tables

It was in the reign of Edward VI that it was directed that altars be replaced by wooden tables. The order was not universally obeyed, however, for it was not until after an edict of Elizabeth I in 1559

131 Portable Altar at Newport, Essex

that most stone altars were replaced by altar tables of wood 'decently made, and set in the place where the altar stood' – although the edict also stated that those who had stone altars could retain them if they chose. Subsequently, in 1564, it was required 'that the Parish provide a decent table standing on a frame, for the Communion Table'. These were at first ordered 'to stand in their place' when not in use, but were to be moved during the communion service to a position that enabled the minister to be better heard. From the frequent references in old records to 'tressles', it is possible that in some cases the altar table comprised no more than a table-top of boards supported on a light frame or trestle that could be easily transported. The flimsy nature of many of early Elizabethan altar tables probably explains why the only ones to survive date from the latter years of Elizabeth's reign, when more substantial tables were being built.

A few of these beautifully wrought late Elizabethan tables still remain, and their characteristic feature is the richly carved bulbous or 'melon'-type legs and the ornamental carving of the rails below the actual table. Fine examples can be seen at Blyford in Suffolk (132), Carleton Forehoe (still in use as an altar) and Carleton Rode in Norfolk, Jacobstow in Cornwall, Westonzoyland in Somerset and Ombersley in Worcestershire. These communion tables are frequently ornamented or inscribed on all four sides, and therefore must have been intended to stand free, rather than being set against the east wall of the church. Running all round the table at Ombersley is the inscription 'whosoever eateth and drinketh unworthily is guilty of the body and blood of our Lord'. Although Queen Elizabeth's injunction of 1559 had directed 'that the Holy Table in every church be set in the place where the Altar stood', the position of the communion table varied. It seems that in many churches the table stood north–south against the east wall of the chancel when not in use, but was turned east–west and sometimes brought forward into the body of the church when in use. When Laud was made Archbishop he was determined to rout out the new fashion of communion, and in 1634 he directed that in all churches the holy table should occupy the same position as the ancient altar.

Early Jacobean tables took a rather simpler form, retaining most of the Elizabethan characteristics, and although the legs were slightly bulbous, the bosses remained plain. The rails of the table were usually well ornamented and occasionally inscribed with the

132   Elizabethan altar table at Blyford, Suffolk

donor's name or a suitable text – a feature that was common throughout the seventeenth century. A typical example is the altar table at Dinton, Buckinghamshire, dated 1606.

As time went on the melon leg degenerated into an elongated bulb encircled by a shallow groove with a straight member beneath it. Later tables of the Stuart period have turned legs, like the simple table at Chelvey, Somerset. Twisted legs generally date from after the Restoration. At this time the altar tables were placed in their proper position against the east wall of the chancel, and many new tables were provided – hence the many dated, and still more undated, examples to be found from the reign of Charles II.

Occasionally one finds an example of a 'telescopic' altar table. These are almost certainly from the Commonwealth period and came into being after the suppression of the Prayer Book and the issue of the Directory of Worship in 1644. They are of considerable size and would be stored outside and brought into the church for use; the communicants would sit around it. One is to be found at Powick, Worcestershire; when closed it is 9'3" long and 2'9" wide, drawing out to 16'. Others had folding leaves.

During the eighteenth and well into the nineteenth century, communion tables were sometimes made of softwood. Many were small, but there are others of a grander nature. Table-tops of marble, often supported on an iron stand, also became fashionable, and notable examples remain at such churches as Bulkington in Warwickshire, Chesterton in Cambridgeshire and Welham in Leicestershire. Theddlethorpe All Saints in Lincolnshire has the distinction of having an Elizabethan communion table and a marble altar slab.

Altar Rails

Before the Reformation the chancel was closed off from the laity by the rood-screen, but before and during Elizabeth's reign many of these screens were removed and the altar table moved either into the centre of the chancel or even, on occasions, into the nave. This irreverence was opposed by some – and in particular Archbishop Laud, who in 1634 ordered that the altar be railed in so that it could not be moved from its original north–south position against the east wall of the chancel.

To many people these rails are, therefore, known as Laudian, though there appear to be a few which date from before 1634. (It is claimed that a few date from the end of Elizabeth's reign, but this is doubtful.) Examples that clearly date from before Laud's injunction can be found at Elton in Nottinghamshire, Maids Moreton in Buckinghamshire (where the altar table is dated 1623 and the altar rails were undoubtedly erected at the same time) and Poynings in West Sussex. It was, however, not until the early part of the seventeenth century that altar rails appeared in any numbers; the majority, therefore, do date from after 1634, and so can fairly be termed Laudian. Among them are those at Winchfield in Hampshire, Studley in Warwickshire and Northiam in East Sussex – the last given by Thankful Frewen, the Lord of the Manor, in 1638.

Some parishes proved recalcitrant and ignored Archbishop Laud's orders; evidently the churchwardens at Great Bromley in Essex were among them, for on 4 October 1638 they were excommunicated and ordered to pay 9 shillings and 4 pence for their absolution (according to the church records an altar rail was made and erected soon afterwards). When Bishop Wren was sent to the Norwich diocese he made the well-known order that 'the Rayle be made before the Communion Table reaching Crosse from the North wall to the South wall, neere one yarde in height, so thick with pillars that doggs may not gett in'.

Some puritanical parishes complied with Laud's order by erecting what are termed 'three-sided rails' around the altar, thus preserving access for the laity up to the east wall of the chancel and enabling the priest's actions to be observed from three sides. In some instances an additional set of seats was placed on the east side of the table, and this resulted in rails that surrounded the altar on all four sides. A fine example, bearing the date 1635, survives at Lyddington in Rutland. Here the vicar is said to have disregarded Archbishop Laud's order to move the table back to the east wall and rail it in. Bishop William of Lincoln, a bitter opponent of Laud who had a palace at Lyddington, supported the vicar. However, finding that he was to be cited before the Star Chamber, he instructed the vicar to rail the altar in – not as Laud had intended but on all four sides, thus keeping the altar table permanently away from the east wall. Another example, of mid-seventeenth-century date, is at Branscombe in Devon. Other churches which have, or had, this arrangement are Beckington and Milverton in Somerset, Deerhurst, Toddington and Winchcombe in Gloucestershire and Ermington in Devon.

Many altar rails went the way of other 'monuments of superstition and idolatry' during the Commonwealth. However, at the Restoration, when episcopal rule was restored and the taking of communion at the altar rail became accepted, they came into such widespread use that towards the end of the seventeenth century few churches were without them. Unlike those of an early date which have heavy turned balusters, these rails are frequently supported by posts which finish above the rail with turned tops; those erected after the accession of Charles II generally have twisted balusters. Even in poorer parishes where turned or twisted balusters could not be afforded, a cheap imitation can be found – as at Icklingham All Saints in Suffolk, where the balusters are cut from flat boards, reminiscent of the splat balusters found on domestic staircases in the seventeenth century.

Reredoses and Altarpieces

The wall behind the altar was usually decorated with panelling or carving, often enriched with a profusion of niches, buttresses, pinnacles, images and other forms of decoration that were usually painted in brilliant colours. Such decoration could be made of stone or alabaster, painted on wooden panels or, in its simplest form, just painted on the wall. Like the altar in front of it, the reredos suffered greatly at the Reformation, and relatively few pre-Reformation examples remain intact.

In the great churches, the reredos was an ambitious affair of two or three tiers of figures, as at Winchester Cathedral, but in small village churches it generally took the form of long, low bands of carving, or a series of niches or panels beneath the sill of the east window. Two fine examples in stone survive in Oxfordshire: at Bampton there are dwarf-like figures of Christ and the twelve Apostles under crocketed canopies, and at Somerton there are ten seated figures in a representation of the *Last Supper*, also under canopies. The introduction of alabaster in the fourteenth and fifteenth centuries saw the sculptured reredos gain in popularity, and from the surviving fragments some indication of their workmanship can be appreciated. At Drayton in Oxfordshire there is a fine six-panel reredos of alabaster which was discarded during one of the reforming periods and later discovered buried in the churchyard. Others of note can be seen at Elham in Kent, Yarnton in Oxfordshire (133) and Youlgreave in Derbyshire. From the examples remaining these alabaster reredoses must have been remarkable works of art, especially when coloured and gilded.

Some churches had a retable, comprising either a framed painting or a triptych with lateral shutters that could be closed to provide protection when the triptych was not in use. At the little church of Thornham Parva, Suffolk, there is a remarkable wooden retable in the form of a triptych dating from around 1300. Not only is the painting remarkably well preserved, but the framing is contemporary. The central panel depicts the *Crucifixion* with the Virgin and St John, while St Dominic, St Catherine, St John, St Edmund, St Margaret of Antioch and St Peter Martyr (who was a Dominican friar) appear on the side panels. Current research suggests that the panels were painted for the Dominican monastery at Thetford and after the Dissolution of the Monasteries was kept in a private chapel of a Roman Catholic family in the area. It was discovered in 1927 in the attic of Rookery Farm, Stradbroke, when Lord Henniker bought the contents at an auction, and later presented to the church.

133   Panel showing Christ bearing the cross in Reredos at Yarnton, Oxfordshire

In the seventeenth and eighteenth centuries altarpieces became fashionable. These often consisted of wooden panelling, sometimes in the Classical style with pilasters supporting a pediment and sometimes inscribed with the Ten Commandments, the Lord's Prayer and the Creed. A fine example is to be found at Chislehampton, Oxfordshire, a church built around 1763 in which most of its eighteenth-century fittings are intact. Early in the eighteenth century the practice was introduced of supporting the Commandments with the figures of Moses and Aaron and surmounting them with a sacred monogram surrounded by a sunburst. A great number exist, one of the largest being that at Redgrave, Suffolk, although it is not in its original position behind the altar. Another good example is at Clipsham, Rutland. In the nineteenth century this type of altarpiece was regarded as unsuitable, and many were removed.

Easter Sepulchres

Every church seems to have had an Easter Sepulchre – a representation of the entombment of Christ – as the focal point for the elaborate Eastertide ceremony that was so much a feature of the medieval church. The Host and the altar crucifix were placed on it on Good Friday and watched continuously until the early hours of Easter Sunday, when they were returned to the High Altar. The sepulchre was generally a temporary tomb-like structure enriched with hangings and situated on the north side of the sanctuary or chancel. From the many records remaining of their destruction in the reign of Elizabeth and the subsequent reuse of the material from them – in cupboards, chests of drawers, hen-coops and as firewood – it is obvious that a good many were made of wood. None of these pre-Elizabethan structures now exists, with the possible exception of one at Cowthorpe, North Yorkshire. It takes the form of a wooden chest decorated with traceried panels; posts at the corners carry a gabled roof with a fine cresting running along the ridge and eaves, and the gables are crocketed.

When there was already a canopied altar tomb in the north wall of the sanctuary, this was used as a pedestal for the Easter Sepulchre, as at Bepton in West Sussex (134), East Harling in Norfolk and Long Melford in Suffolk. That at Long Melford is

134   Tomb used as Easter sepulchre at Bepton, West Sussex

described by Roger Martin (who died in 1580) as a frame of timber to hold a number of tapers, and 'the sepulchre was always placed . . . at the North end of the high altar between that and Mr Clopton's little chapel there, in a vacant place of the wall, I think upon a tomb of one of his ancestors. The said frame with tapers was set over the steps up to the said altar'. This position was so greatly prized that tombs were specifically built so that they could be used as Easter Sepulchres. Many examples exist but it must be remembered that, although these tombs are usually called Easter Sepulchres, they are only the pedestals on which the temporary wooden structure of an Easter Sepulchre was placed.

From around the beginning of the fourteenth century stone sepulchres began to be built for the sole purpose of enshrining the Blessed Sacrament. These are not too common, although not rare, and are similar in design to the wall tombs they replaced. They generally consist of three stages: a raised base, on the front of which were carved panels containing sleeping soldiers; an arched recess in which the Sacrament was placed; and an elaborately sculptured canopy representing the Risen Christ. The most elaborate examples are all from the Decorated period. The finest, at Hawton in Nottinghamshire, is twelve feet high and divided into three bays, with four sleeping soldiers in the lower panels, and in the centre the *Resurrection* with the three Marys. Above is the *Ascension*, represented by the two feet of Christ showing beneath a cloud and the Apostles gazing upwards. The three-bay sepulchre at Heckington in Lincolnshire, with the sleeping soldiers below and the Risen Christ with the three Marys above, is noted for the exquisite foliage carved in low relief. Not so elaborate but very well preserved is the single recessed Easter Sepulchre at Patrington in East Riding of Yorkshire, which has three soldiers asleep below, and in the centre Christ rising from the tomb between two angels. Another noteworthy example is at Sibthorpe, Nottinghamshire, where there are two crouching soldiers on each side of the niche for the Blessed Sacrament; above, in the crocketed canopy, is the Risen Lord with two angels. Many other sepulchres are on a smaller scale, often with cusped and crocketed pediments with side pinnacles. One example is Stanton St John in Oxfordshire, and others include Hawstead in Suffolk and Gussage All Saints, a rare survival in Dorset.

In Northwold Church, Norfolk, is a fine example from a century or so later; of towering height, its base panel has the usual sleeping soldiers, and the whole structure is surmounted by rectilinear tabernacling. Dating from the later Perpendicular period is the sepulchre at Selmeston in East Sussex, a recess with a depressed (almost straight) arch and a cresting.

Easter sepulchres continued to be provided up to the Reformation. One of the last is that at Tarrant Hinton in Dorset, erected by Rector Thomas Troteswell (alias Weaver), whose initials – TW on one side and TT on the other – indicate a date of around 1532. Its detailing is in the Renaissance style, and it is remarkable to find work of this delicacy and sophistication in a remote village church.

Another form of Easter Sepulchre is found in West Somerset. This takes the form of a chest tomb – often wrongly described as an altar – with panelled work (usually carvings of the symbols of the Passion) on the front and west ends. They were placed in the north-east corner of the chancel with their backs against the north wall and one end – the plain one – against the east wall. One fine example is at Porlock, still in its original position, as is another at Milverton. Others, for instance at Luccombe, have been moved.

Sedilia

From the twelfth century onwards the sedilia – from the Latin *sedile*, meaning a seat – became a permanent feature of our churches. These recessed seats are invariably found in the south wall of the chancel near the altar and were used by the priest and his servers while the Creed and Gloria were being sung during the long ceremony of the Mass. Generally there are three seats, decreasing in height from the east: the easternmost was used by the celebrant, the centre one by the deacon, who read the gospel, and the westernmost by the sub-deacon, who read the epistle. Later, when rich endowments provided many churches with several priests, the seats were not graded but set on the same level. When this is found it clearly indicates that priests acted as assistants to the celebrant.

There are notable early sedilia, from the twelfth century at Castle Hedingham in Essex, Earls Barton in Northamptonshire and Wellingore in Lincolnshire. Those from the next century are fairly common, and in areas where good stone abounded they were made into decorative and architectural features with much delicate treatment expended on the enrichment of the canopy-work. In the earlier examples the stalls are divided by detached shafts or pillars, and the later ones by walling (which is not infrequently pierced). At Laxton in Nottinghamshire there are stone arm rests between the stepped seats, an unusual feature.

In the best examples a piscina, placed to the east of the seats, formed part of the overall design and was united with them under ornamental arches. Examples of this occur from all periods. An early one at Monyash, Derbyshire, known from documentary evidence to date from around 1200, is a fine example of late Norman or Transitional workmanship. It is the only example in Derbyshire of a triple sedilia in which the seats are graded. The sedilia at Uffington, Oxfordshire, is a fine Early English example. The finest sedilia from the Decorative period have lofty canopies – often with cinquefoil feathering, open bracing and richly crocketed finials over both sedilia and piscina. Notable examples are to be found at Cliffe in Kent and Sandiacre in Derbyshire. The most unforgettable sedilia are the exceptionally ornate early fourteenth-century ones at Hawton, Nottinghamshire, and Heckington, Lincolnshire.

Although three seats is normal, there are many instances where there are one (a sedile) (135), two or even four (the fourth seat being reserved for the clerk). Those with four seats are generally to be found in cathedrals and great churches – Westminster, Durham, Gloucester – but are sometimes found elsewhere; there are examples at Turvey, Bedfordshire, and Rothwell, Northamptonshire.

In some areas, particularly in East Anglia and the adjoining counties, the sedilia was formed by creating a simple seat beneath the window on the south side of the chancel. This type is generally referred to as a dropped-sill sedilia.

In many village churches a wooden bench or three chairs would have been used instead of purpose-built stone sedilia, and there can be little doubt that in those areas which had no good building stone, they would have been made of timber. At Rodmersham, Kent, there survives a rare example of a wooden sedilia under a canopy that forms a structural part of the parclose screen between the chancel and side chapel (which is what probably saved it from destruction). The seats are separated by shaped elbows, and the panelled backs support a handsome

135   Sedile at Lenham, Kent

coving with a moulded cornice and deep-carved cresting. At Upchurch, Kent, the sedilia bench of stone has a panelled wooden back that may have originally had some form of canopy, for the top is mutilated.

Piscinas

Piscina is the name usually given to the water-drain in the south wall of the chancel near the High Altar. Generally, it is a shallow stone basin with a hole in the bottom to carry off the water to the ground outside (water that had been blessed, or had come into contact with anything consecrated, had to be returned to the earth).

As early as the tenth century Pope Leo VI decreed that a drain should be made near every altar for the disposal of the water in which the sacred vessels were washed. In its earliest form this was no more than a drainage hole in the floor, but in Norman times the pillar-piscina (a basin supported on a stone shaft that had a drain-hole running down through it) became fairly common, as at East Hoathly, East Sussex, and Yatton, Somerset. Some of these early piscinas were supported on a bracket – a type known as a corbel-piscina. From about the middle of the twelfth century the basin began to be placed in a niche. The niche was usually surmounted by an arch, which was at first rounded, although later trefoil or even cinquefoil arches appeared. The ogee arch was common in the fourteenth century, and an example of a fifteenth-century piscina with a four-centred arch can be seen at Bloxham, Oxfordshire.

Early in the thirteenth century it became fashionable in some parts of England to construct piscina niches on either side of the angle between the chancel wall and the south chancel window, nearest the altar. These angle-piscinas had two openings, usually trefoil-arched, with a slender column on the corner of the window embrasure supporting the arches on the jamb to the south and the chancel wall to the east. They were particularly popular in north-east Suffolk, and there are admirable examples at Brampton, Uggeshall, Blyford, South Cove, Frostenden and Chediston. They are also to be found elsewhere in the county; two notable examples are at Coney Weston (136), where the corner pillar supports cusped openings with pedimented and crocketed arches, and at nearby Ickworth (a rare example of a fourteenth-century double corner-piscina). Although most common in Suffolk, angle-piscinas are also to be found elsewhere – for example, in Norfolk at Great Snoring, in the midlands at Quainton and Granborough in Buckinghamshire and at North Moreton in Oxfordshire.

136   Piscina at Coney Weston, Suffolk

Towards the end of the thirteenth century it was decreed that hands should not be washed in the same piscina as vessels, and so double piscinas began to appear. The nearest one to the altar, often with the most decoration, was for washing the chalice; the other, the lavabo, for washing the priest's fingers before the Consecration. Although these double piscinas are by no means rare, their popularity varied considerably in different parts of the country. In Cambridgeshire, (137) for instance, there are thirty or so, in other counties they are extremely rare. Although there are a few that are earlier (as at Doveridge, Derbyshire) and a few that are later, as a rule these double piscinas may be assigned to the reign of Edward I. At the beginning of the fourteenth century it became the custom for the priest to swallow the rinsings from the chalice, so once again a single piscina sufficed.

In the thirteenth century a stone shelf – the credence shelf – was included in the niche, above the piscina drain, on which the cruets and perhaps the ciborium for use during the Mass were placed. Usually these shelves were of stone, but in some instances they were of wood, and the grooves into which they fitted may be noticed. Occasionally the wooden shelves themselves remain, as at Ufford, Cambridgeshire, and Shalbourne, Wiltshire. At Westhall, Suffolk, the piscina niche has two shelves: an unusual arrangement. Now and again one finds a small recess within the piscina niche, usually on the west side (as at Hempstead, Norfolk, and Hawton, Nottinghamshire). Such a recess was clearly intended for keeping the cruets when not in use. In later examples there may be two very small niches in the wall, one on each side of the main piscina niche (as at Kirk Hallam, Derbyshire), and these two must have been intended for the cruets.

Some of the finest piscinas are those that are united with the sedilia in one design, the whole enclosed within a sculptured frame as previously described. The most remarkable piscina of all, at Long Wittenham in Oxfordshire, includes the diminutive figure of a cross-legged knight in armour, with shield and sword, lying with his head on a pillow and his feet on an animal. The recumbent figure is on the front of the piscina, with the head towards the east. Above the effigy the head of the niche is trefoil with the figures of two angels with extended wings.

In contrast to these elaborate examples there are other piscinas that have little decorative treatment. This is certainly true in the

137   Piscina at Trumpington, Cambridgeshire

midlands, where the shallow basin and drain is sometimes found in the sill of the window on the south side of the altar, without any niche or canopy at all. Instances can be found at Crich and Sawley in Derbyshire, Knipton and Goaby in Leicestershire, Sibthorpe in Nottinghamshire and Saltfleetby in Lincolnshire. Similar ones can be seen elsewhere, for instance at Orcheston St George (138) and at Pitton in Wiltshire. At Crawley, Hampshire (139), the piscina basin is in an unusual position – in the squint between the north aisle and the chancel.

It is not uncommon to find more than one piscina in a church. Occasionally there may be two in the same wall; this indicates that the chancel has at some time been extended, and the western piscina is the earlier of the two. Sometimes piscinas are to be found in other parts of the church, for instance at the east end of the aisles, their presence indicating that originally there was an altar nearby. At North Marston in Buckinghamshire there is a canopied piscina on each side of the great east window.

Aumbries

An aumbry was an oblong recess, originally with doors, in which the sacred vessels, books, linen and the chrismatory and its holy

138 Piscina in window sill at Orcheston St George, Wiltshire

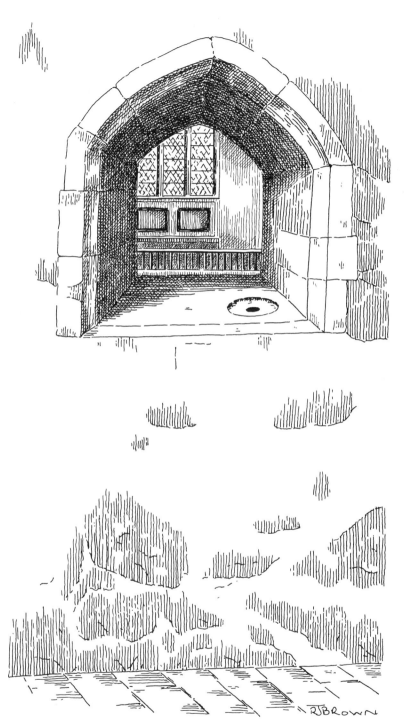

139 Piscina in squint at Crawley, Hampshire

oils were stored. It was frequently situated near the High Altar on the north wall of the chancel, but there seems no other reason for this than that the south wall was usually fully occupied by piscina and sedilia. Aumbries vary considerably in size, depending on what was being stored. All are rebated for a door, and some, like that at Lindfield in West Sussex, retain the iron pivots on which the hinges of the door once hung. A few retain their original wooden door, as do those at Rothersthorpe in Northamptonshire, Great Walsingham in Norfolk, and Higham in Kent (140). Inside, there was often a shelf, either of stone or wood; wooden shelves have generally disappeared but their former presence is indicated by grooves on either side and at the back of the recess, as at Rattlesden, Suffolk. Sometimes more than one aumbry was provided – two was most usual, but at Langford in Oxfordshire (141) there are six, in two rows of three, one above the other.

Stalls and Misericords

The chancels of most churches had wooden stalls placed against the north and south walls. Often they returned, being set against the back of the screen – three or four on each side of the entrance – facing eastwards towards the altar. In cathedrals and greater churches and chapels they were elaborately carved, often with marvellous tabernacled canopies. The number of stalls varied with the size of the foundation – Kings College Chapel, Cambridge, has for instance 118.

Stalls are also found in village churches, though here there was never more than one row of seats, which, at the most, would have had traceried backs (as at Tong, Shropshire) and a cornice. The elbow-rests might be adorned with angels and the fronts of the desks traceried (as at Salle, Norfolk), with poppyheads to the ends. These seats would have been occupied by the parish priest, the parish clerk and any chaplains or chantry priests, and by the patron, squire and leading members of the church. The choir was at first located on the rood-loft, then in the west gallery and finally, in the nineteenth century, in the chancel.

The finest sets of stalls are usually found in those village churches that were intimately connected to monastic or collegiate foundations. In the church at Minster-in-Thanet, Kent, there are eighteen beautifully carved stalls with particularly fine desk fronts, ends and arm-rests all dating to 1401–19. There is a fine group of stalls at Tong in Shropshire, where the chantry college was founded in 1410 by Sir Fulke de Pembruge; the church itself was rebuilt by Elizabeth, his widow.

140   Aumbry at Higham, Kent

141 Aumbry at Langford, Oxfordshire

Early stalls do occur, however, at purely parochial churches. In many cases these have been brought from monasteries which passed into secular hands at the Dissolution. The stalls from Fotheringhay Abbey, for instance, appear to have been distributed among various churches in Northamptonshire, including Benefield, Hemington and Tansor. In Suffolk none of the abbeys were retained for parochial use, but stallwork can be found (though some of it is fragmentary) not only in the larger town churches, like St Gregory in Sudbury and Southwold church, but in some twenty-four village churches. Some of the finest stallwork – not only in Suffolk but in the country – is to be found at Stowlangtoft, where there are six stalls backing onto the screen; all are magnificently carved, and the lateral stalls have traceried fronts with low benches for 'singing boys'.

Some stalls have tip-up seats with a smooth ledge projecting from the underside. When the seats were folded up, these ledges – known as 'misericords' or mercy seats (from the Latin *misericordia*, meaning pity, compassion) – provided support, especially for the aged and infirm, during long periods of standing during medieval services.

Misericords were often carved, and it is evident from the surviving examples that wood-carvers were free to give full rein to their imagination. Sacred subjects are comparatively rare, and the principal themes to be found are scenes from mythology, fables and medieval romances, scenes from everyday life (including scenes of domestic and working life and leisure pursuits), and depictions of creatures of fantasy, animals, birds and fishes, as well as humour and satire. Despite many differences in their style, English misericords nearly always have subsidiary carvings, known as supporters, one each side of the centre-piece. Only in a very few churches have the supporters been omitted, as at Wingham in Kent and Over in Cambridgeshire. These supporters generally differ in design and subject from the centrepiece and often depict human heads, animals, birds or foliage. These subsidiary carvings single out English misericords from those on the Continent, most of which do not possess supporters.

Over 3,300 still survive in England. Many are to be found in cathedrals, important churches, chapels and colleges, but many village churches have admirable examples, even though some contain only one or two. Misericords in cathedrals and greater churches date from the thirteenth, fourteenth and early fifteenth centuries, but those in our village churches are generally of fifteenth-century date. There are, of course, a few exceptions. The oldest is thought to be the one (the only survivor of four stalls) at

Hemingbrough, North Yorkshire; this is believed to date from the thirteenth century, although the church did not become collegiate until 1426. Another church containing thirteenth-century misericords is at Kidlington in Oxfordshire, where five stalls on the north side of the chancel have simple misericords with a plain vaulting of flowers. There are also a few from the fourteenth century. At Anstey in Hertfordshire there are seven which appear from the church records to be of early fourteenth-century date, and the headgear worn by the two men depicted on them was fashionable in the fourteenth century. At Fordham, Cambridgeshire, there are nineteen misericords thought to be from around 1350. There are others attributed to the fourteenth century, particularly in Suffolk (at Norton, Stoke-by-Nayland, Stowlangtoft, Occold and Wingfield) and in Kent (at Cliffe, Cobham, Westwell and Wingham).

Often a number of misericords in a church depict a common theme. Perhaps the finest example is to be found at Ripple in Worcestershire, where there are realistic representations of the occupation of the twelve months of the year. January is illustrated by two men gathering wood, February shows hedging and ditching, and for March and April there are scenes of sowing and bird-scaring. Rogationtide, in May, is indicated with flowers and a statue of the Virgin Mary, such as was often carried in a procession through the fields in this month. June was represented by a hunting or hawking scene, July by Lammas eve at the manorial bakery (142) (the only example of this subject on a misericord) and August by the cutting of corn. September shows two men carrying sacks (it is said, to the maltings); October is represented by the knocking down of acorns to feed the pigs; November has a pig-killing scene, and December a domestic fireside scene. In addition to these twelve carvings, four others represent blessings to help the crops; these were originally on the return stalls, two on each side, facing the altar.

Although most village churches that have medieval stalls have only a few misericords, some of them have notable sets. Twenty-six misericords survive at Salle in Norfolk. The majority are of flowers or fruit, and others show human heads, a leopard mask with human ears, a grinning lion mask with large ears, and a pair of dolphins facing each other. All date from the fifteenth century, for the whole church is of this period. The church at Greystoke in Cumbria has twenty misericords – ten on each side, of which three are returned. These are of different periods, six dating from the late fourteenth or early fifteenth century and the remainder, it appears, from the seventeenth century, possibly from the restoration of the chancel that took place in 1660. The fourteen misericords at Fairford in Gloucestershire, all of excellent quality, have been dated to around 1490. Various subjects are depicted. On the north side there is a fox running off with a duck, a demi-angel holding an uncharged shield, a hawk killing a duck, a man and woman sitting drinking from a barrel, a grotesque lion mask, a youth and girl teasing each other, and a domestic scene with a woman spinning. On the south side are two women plucking a fowl, two wyverns with tails interlaced, a man crouching with two dogs, two men sitting facing each other with an empty platter and flagon, reapers with short smocks, a man asleep beside a table with an empty platter, and a woman holding a man by the hair and beating him with a wooden scoop. Etchingham, East Sussex, has eighteen misericords, all dating from the fourteenth century, when the church was rebuilt. Each set of nine has the same carvings in the same order. Most are on columns with various types of floral ornamentation, but one scene of some interest depicts a fox in friar's cloak, holding a key and preaching to three geese on each supporter.

142 Misericord illustrating the Lammas Eve at the manorial bakery at Ripple, Worcestershire

8   Chancel Screens

We have seen that the medieval church was divided into two sections. The chancel and sanctuary at the east end were the preserve of the parish priest, while the nave, aisles and transept were the province of the parishioners. It was therefore usual to screen off the chancel from the nave by various means. In the simple Saxon church, such as at Escomb in County Durham, this division was achieved by forming a narrow chancel arch, which was doubtless closed by a curtain or veil. The use of veils, to add 'mystery' to the sacramental presence as perceived from the main body of the church, was customary in the medieval church. One well-known example is the Lenten veil: during the whole forty-day period of Lent the High Altar and its surroundings were completely shrouded by a great curtain or sheet of stained or painted linen or some other material. In a few churches the means of fixing the Lenten veil still survive; one example is at Shipmeadow in Suffolk, where in the walls above the altar rails, about six feet above the floor, there are two stone corbels pierced vertically and thought to have been connected with the fixing of the Lenten veil. In other churches hooks or rings are found in a similar position, as at Shillington, Bedfordshire, and Alfriston, East Sussex.

In the Western Church the idea of a more or less permanent screen or veil, secluding the sanctuary from the general worshippers, gradually gave way to that of a more open view that would give the congregation a better sight of the High Altar than a narrow single arch afforded. In some cases this was achieved by forming pierced openings on either side of the chancel arch; in other cases it took the form of a triple chancel arch. There are about a dozen churches that have pierced openings. One of the most interesting is the early Norman village church of Scawton in North Yorkshire, where on either side of the chancel arch, facing the nave, there are round-headed recesses pierced at the back by smaller square squints. There are openings of a similar nature on each side of the chancel arch in Hampshire churches of Otterbourne and Ashley. It is often difficult to know whether these openings are later than the chancel arch. Certainly at Inworth in Essex, where the arch and the general chancel construction is almost certainly pre-Norman, the openings on either side are clearly afterthoughts. At Pyecombe in West Sussex, however, the central archway and side archways into the chancel are all of the same date.

The remains of a triple chancel arch occur in a few of the earliest of our Saxon churches. At Bradwell-on-Sea in Essex, which was built soon after 563, the chancel has been demolished and only the nave remains, but there is evidence of the three arches that once opened up into the chancel. Triple arches are also to be found at Brixworth in Northamptonshire, built not later than 680. However, the idea of the triple chancel arches of coeval construction undoubtedly developed from walls with pierced openings. Initially these were often no more than three openings with arches above, piercing either the wall between chancel and nave or a wall that filled the chancel arch. A fine example, built in the thirteenth century, is at Westwell in Kent, where the three lofty trefoiled arches are carried on slender cylindrical columns. A very similar, but plainer, example is at Wool in Dorset. Other instances are to be seen at Sandridge, Hertfordshire, and Baulking, Oxfordshire. Another noteworthy example, dating from the fourteenth century, occurs at Capel le Ferne in Kent. Here the wall between the chancel and nave contains three small two-centred arches on octagonal shafts, but above the central arch is another opening, probably constructed to contain the Rood and its attendant figures.

There are other churches that have a screen wall in which only a central doorway was formed. This type may be noted at Eastwell, Leicestershire, where the screen of solid masonry is pierced by a central doorway with a traceried, unglazed window on either side. This dates from the fourteenth century. A similar arrangement can be found at Stockton, Wiltshire, where the chancel is divided from the nave by a solid wall pierced by a low doorway and two squints.

At Old Romney, Kent, there is a narrow chancel arch and beside it various squints – two to the left, one to the right – to enable the congregation in the outside pews to see the elevation of the Host during Mass. At Broughton, Oxfordshire, there is another fourteenth-century screen, a more elaborate example in which the solid base is surmounted by a range of traceried panels; each open panel has an ogee-arched head with decorated crockets and finials. In some instances low stone screens are to be found under the chancel arch. The one at Chelmorton, Derbyshire, which is of fourteenth-century date, probably carried an upper screen of wood.

Stone Screens

Most, if not all, of the aforementioned could not be classified as true screens, for they were merely openings formed in a solid wall. True screens of stone do exist from the fourteenth century, though, all of them consisting of three open arches supported on columns, the central opening forming the doorway to the chancel. One, of early fourteenth-century date, is to be seen at Bramford in Suffolk (143); the openings consist of two-centred arches, though their pierced quatrefoils and the battlemented coping are, it seems, later additions. There is another, built about 1330, at Welsh Newton in Herefordshire, where the arches spring from octagonal columns; here, however, the wall above (which is crowned by a cornice with ballflower ornament) is original. The lofty fifteenth-century chancel screen at Bottisham, Cambridgeshire, consists of three arches with pierced quatrefoils in the spandrels. There was usually a low wall in the side openings, but in some cases (as at Bottisham) this has been removed, thus defeating its original purpose.

Two of the most noteworthy examples of stone chancel screens are to be found in Essex, at Stebbing and Great Bardfield. In each instance the chancel arch has been filled in with stone tracery to resemble a large window of three lights, with clustered columns taken to the top of the arch. The screen at Stebbing dates from the early part of the fourteenth century, that at Great Bardfield from the following century. At Stebbing the screen was mutilated in the fifteenth century, when it was rudely cut away to make room for a wooden screen and rood-loft, but was restored to something like its original form in 1884. The one at Great Bardfield has also been restored.

143   Fourteenth-century stone screen at Bramford, Suffolk

Wiltshire has more stone screens than any other county. The finest, a late fifteenth-century specimen, is at Compton Bassett. The chancel arch is filled with an openwork screen; in front of this a lofty arcade of three four-centred arches rises to a height of 12 feet, and a panelled vault connects the two. The arches are delicately cusped, and the spandrels, cornice and supporting shaft richly carved. Other fine screens in the county are at Heytesbury and Yatton Keynell. In Dorset good stone screens can be found at Batcombe, Nether Compton and Thornford.

The number of stone chancel screens must at one time have been considerable. A large number disappeared in favour of timber ones during the fifteenth century, when it became fashionable to construct a rood-loft or gallery above the screen. It was more practicable to make these of timber, and so in most cases the old stone screens were removed and rebuilt in timber. At Stebbing, Essex, a timber screen with rood-loft was actually built alongside the stone chancel-screen as we have seen. Nonetheless, stone screens with rood-lofts were constructed – one at Harlton, Cambridgeshire, built in the fifteenth century, clearly had a rood-loft, for there is a newel staircase – however, it is not clear whether these stone screens had rood-lofts of stone or timber. Screens with rood-lofts came to be known as rood-screens. (It is interesting to note that the term 'screen' was hardly ever used until the seventeenth century; before that they were always referred to in official documents as partitions.)

Timber Screens

No other country can equal the superb wooden screens to be seen in this country, and they are perhaps the loveliest works left in many of our ancient village churches. By the late Middle Ages almost every village church was provided with a screen, complete with a secure door, to separate the chancel from the nave.

The finest rood-screens are of the late Perpendicular period (the second half of the fifteenth or the early part of the sixteenth century), but there are others dating from the fourteenth, and even a few of Early English style from the thirteenth century. The oldest in its original position is thought to be the one at Stanton Harcourt, Oxfordshire, which dates from around 1260; the old screen at Thurcaston, Leicestershire, is probably somewhat older but has been moved from the chancel to under the tower arch. Another is at Kirkstead, Lincolnshire. They are all of similar design – a rude solid base, and a row of light, open arches, supported by circular shafts with capitals and bases, carrying a plain beam. The screen at Stanton Harcourt (144) retains its double doors, complete with their original hinges, bolt and lock.

A good number of screens survive from the fourteenth century in our village churches. Essex has a fair amount of good screenwork from different periods of the century, for example at Little Canfield, Clavering, Castle Hedingham and Newport. Norfolk has three notable examples with fine tracery at Merton, Belton and Thompson (that at Belton still with full-height doors). Elsewhere good examples are to be found at Lavenham in Suffolk, which still retains its doors, Cropredy in Oxfordshire and Chippenham in Cambridgeshire.

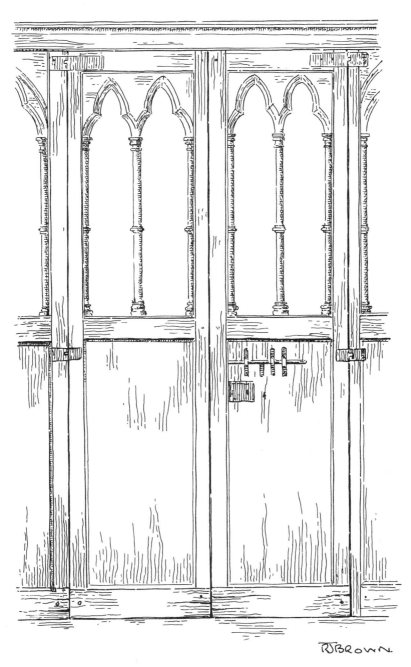

144   Screen doors at Stanton Harcourt, Oxfordshire

Although these early screens – and indeed many later ones – were placed exactly under the chancel arch, it must not be assumed that all those found in this position today, cut between the piers, are in their original position. Indeed it was more likely that most screens stood immediately in front of the chancel arch, so that, where possible, they could be extended the whole width of the nave. In some instances the screens extended across the entire church, incorporating both the nave and aisles. Visually, this is a most satisfying arrangement. It is most commonly found in Devon where many fifteenth-century churches were built with aisled chancels, allowing the screen to be carried right across the building without interruption. Even when an intervening column broke the uninterrupted line of the screen some provision was made. At Swimbridge, Devon, an opening was left for a small altar to be placed against the pier. In other churches the columns were sometimes cased with panelling and tabernacle work to match the screen – examples can be found at Bradninch, Broadhempston, Dunchideock and Harberton, all in Devon – and the result is most impressive.

The two principal areas for seeing rood-screens are East Anglia and the south-west. More survive in Devon than in any other county: some 150 or so, many of them of great beauty, but others only partly preserved. Their survival is due in no small part to the fact that when Devon churches were rebuilt in the Perpendicular period there was generally no chancel arch; consequently, the only division between the chancel and nave was the rood-screen, which remained as indispensable after the Reformation as it had been before it.

The screens in the south-west are generally of the vaulted type, consisting of a series of openings divided by stout muntins, the tracery to the head being bold and following the local Perpendicular window tracery. One of the delights of these screens is their ribbed vaulting (resembling fan vaulting), above the arches and, above this, the friezes of densely carved foliage (sometimes with figures of birds or men sitting or crawling in it) that cover the deep cornice, often in three or more bands. Most of the screens are coloured and gilded, many having been repainted and regilded within the present century. Few can rival those in Devon especially those at Burrington, Hartland, Plymtree (datable to about 1470), Swimbridge and Kentisbeare. Although most of the screens in the south-west are in Devon, there are some in Somerset – particularly in the west of the county – which are certainly of the highest quality. Those at Banwell, Bishops Lydeard, Halse and Timberscombe are certainly equal to the best in Devon. There are also a few screens of the Devon type to be found in Cornwall. The finest is perhaps the one at St Buryan, which was extensively but sensitively restored in the last century.

The screens of East Anglia differ radically from those of the south-west. In Norfolk and Suffolk they are much higher, with tall, narrow openings, slender posts between the bays and a general air of lightness and elegance. Most of the screens in East Anglia are of the square-headed type – that is without a vault (or, if there is one, it is not so pronounced as in the south-west) – often with charming pendant arches dividing the bays in place of the deep cornices. The tracery is also not so conspicuous and sometimes (particularly where there is a vault) there is no tracery at all, merely plain openings relieved only by a few cusps – as at Tunstead and Westwick in Norfolk, both of which have screens of great height.

Screens are more numerous in Norfolk than in Suffolk. In Norfolk the finest of the vaulted type to be found in village churches are at Cawston, Ranworth and Worstead, and of the square-headed type the best are at Broome, Happisburgh and Scarning. In Suffolk the finest screen is that at Bramfield, which still retains its original colour decoration unrestored. Although there has been much damage and restoration, the woodwork is of surprising quality; notable vaulting survives on both sides, but it is the decorator's art which is the chief glory of this screen.

Apart from the south-west and East Anglia most counties have something good to show, although screens are far less thick on the ground. Generally these screens are plainer and are not so distinctive. In the Welsh border counties both the vaulted and square-headed types can be found. The remote church of St Margarets, some four miles from Abbey Dore in Herefordshire, has a lovely example of the vaulted type, although it is supported not on a screen but a solid wall; in the north of the county at Aymestrey, by contrast, there is a screen in which the proportions are more reminiscent of those square-headed examples of East Anglia. Shropshire has a little gem of a screen at the tiny isolated church at Hughley, and there are others of note at North Lydbury and Bettws-y-Crwyn.

Fine screens can be found, too, in the counties adjacent to East Anglia. In Cambridgeshire the finest are at Balsham (built in 1401) and Tilbrook (restored in 1867), while in Hertfordshire there are good examples at King's Walden, Flamstead and Much Hadham. The screen at Baldock goes right across the width of the church. Lincolnshire, too, has many good examples, despite the widespread destruction of many in the second half of the nineteenth century under the guise of restoration. Those at Ewerby, Folkingham and Swineshead are all fine instances of fifteenth-century woodwork. The grand rood-screen of seven bays at Theddlethorpe All Saints is of early sixteenth-century date.

There are several of note in the Midlands, and in particular in Oxfordshire, where two of the finest are at Charlton-on-Otmoor and Church Hanborough. In Northamptonshire the screen at Bugbrooke has vaulted canopy, but by far the best instance in the county is at Ashby St Ledgers: a vaulted screen of delicate and admirable construction, beautifully carved and still with its original doors. In Derbyshire there is a beautiful screen at Fenny Bentley.

The northern counties of England have few rood-screens of note. There are a few in the north-west: for example those at Huyton (built about 1460) and at Sefton – where, in addition to the rood-screen, there is a side screen to the north chapel. Yorkshire was once very rich in rood-screens, but during the eighteenth century a great many were swept away on the orders of the archdeacons – without, it seems, any legality. The finest remaining are to be found in East Riding of Yorkshire. That at Flamborough is noteworthy, even in its mutilated condition, and at Watton (where there is no chancel arch) the late fifteenth-century screen is carried up in a curious fashion to the ceiling. One of the most interesting is the elaborate screen at the remote little church of Hubberholme, North Yorkshire, which was erected in 1558 at the end of Mary's reign.

On all these timber rood-screens the top part was open, and the lower part, except for the central doorway, was filled with panels. The panels, which corresponded with the openings above, usually had traceried heads, and within each panel was painted the figure of an apostle or another saint. Many of these paintings still survive, and in recent years there has been much careful restoration undertaken under expert supervision. They are in the main to be found on the screens of East Anglia and Devon. The figures in Devon are squatter than those in East Anglia and are considered to be of less artistic merit; nevertheless, they are of great interest because of the size of the panels and the number of figures in each screen. The finest of them is in the pretty village of Ashton, which contains over thirty figures including the *Four Latin Doctors* and the *Four Evangelists*. On the backs of the panels are a series of remarkable paintings of prophets with scrolls and the *Annunciation* and the *Visitation*. The screen at Holme has forty painted panels, as have the screens at Kenton and Torbryan, but at Wolborough there are no less than 66, including many unusual saints whose identification is a fascinating task.

In East Anglia the panels often incorporate a variety of designs in the spandrels, including beasts, grotesques, birds and flowers. The backgrounds are alternately green and red, with the costumes of the figures usually counter-changing. The figures depicted in the panels are numerous; the *Twelve Apostles* are the most favoured subject, but the *Four Latin Doctors* – at such churches as Cawston, East Ruston, Houghton St Giles and Tunstead, all in Norfolk – was also popular, as were angels, prophets, kings, martyrs and archbishops, many of them obscure. In Norfolk some of the finest are to be found in the area of the Broads. Barton Turf, Belaugh, Irstead, Filby, Ludham and Upton all have well-preserved examples, those at Ranworth being regarded as the finest because of the richness and delicacy of their detail, unsurpassed in the country. In addition to the rood-screen, Ranworth has two little side screens to separate the side altars, all adorned with figures. Outside the Broads there are screens that are equally fine; the *Twelve Apostles* at Beeston Regis is wonderfully preserved, the screen at Cawston has the *Four Latin Doctors* on the doors, and the screens at Carleton Rode, Morston, North Elmham and Thornham, to name but a few, are all truly magnificent.

A feature of many Suffolk screens is the rich gesso-work, which can be seen at its best in the village church of Bramfield, where the original colouring still remains, and the figure paintings of the *Four Evangelists* and *St Mary Magdalene* are superb. The most noteworthy of the many other fine examples are perhaps to be seen at Somerleyton, Westhall and Yaxley (the last is another church in which the gesso-work is of high quality).

Not all East Anglian panels depicted a single saint, angels or the like; in some churches there are complete scenes. At Loddon, Norfolk, the rood-screen has been cut down so only the bottom half remains, but it carries a most arresting series of paintings. Most of them are easily recognizable episodes in the life of Christ – the *Annunciation*, the *Nativity*, the *Circumcision*, the *Adoration of the Magi* and the *Ascension* – but on the left of the choir stalls there is one that is different. It depicts a small boy spread-eagled with one of his hands and one of his feet tied, and the others nailed, to a rough frame; an attendant figure holds a bowl to catch the blood from the pierced side. The lettering below, now faded, confirms that it depicts the story of St William of Norwich, a twelve-year-old murdered, it is claimed, by Jews in Holy Week, 1144. Another church where scenes are preserved is at Wellingham, also in Norfolk, where there are three panels, all wonderfully preserved. The first shows the King and Princess with others watching St George fighting the dragon, the second depicts St Michael weighing souls in a scale which devils are trying to pull down, and the third shows the Instruments of the Passion.

Outside East Anglia and the south-west painted figure panels are less common. Counties neighbouring East Anglia have many fine examples, including good panels at Guilden Morden and Cherry Hinton in Cambridgeshire. In the midlands they are rare. Perhaps the finest is at North Crawley, Buckinghamshire; in the same county nine of the twelve panels at Monks Risborough bear painted figures, and at Quainton the panels in the north aisle contain paintings of four prophets.

By the time of the Reformation it seems all our village churches would have had a screen of some sort dividing the chancel from the nave. During the early years of the Reformation many were destroyed, when the roods were almost universally torn down and their images destroyed as part of the violent reaction against Rome. When general participation in the services and the administration of the sacrament to the people became fashionable, many screens were removed, and the altar moved into the body of the church. Such was the destruction that in October 1561 Queen Elizabeth, in a Royal Order, directed that, while the great rood and its figures should be destroyed and the rood-loft taken down to the top of the vaulting, the screens themselves should remain, the Royal Arms or other suitable cresting replacing the rood. Where the screen, as well as the rood, had already been destroyed a new 'partition' was to be erected. It seems, therefore, that the Elizabethan view was clearly that the church should still be divided into two distinct sections.

Clearly, screens continued to be removed. In 1638 the Bishop of Norwich, Richard Montague, asked his priests, 'Is your chancel divided from the Nave or body of the church, with a partition of stone, boards, wainscot, grates or otherwise. Wherein is there a decent strong door to open or shut (as occasion serveth) with lock or key, to keep out boys, girls, or irreverent men and women, and are dogs kept from coming to besoil or profane the Lord's table?' Further destruction of screens took place when the Puritans gained the ascendancy during the Commonwealth, reflecting their desire to open up the church. We have already noted the destruction of screens in Yorkshire in the eighteenth century, when between 1720 and 1738 no less than 71 rood-screens were pulled down. It is probable that in the nineteenth century, during the restoration of so many of our village churches by the Victorians, many more were destroyed. F.B. Bond in the *Reports of the Devonshire Association* in 1902-3 compiled a list of 76 screens that had been removed, the great majority in the nineteenth century, with the last instance at Moretonhampstead occurring as late as 1897. In Kent it is a similar story; in 1907 Aymer Vallance in *Memorials of Old Kent* tells the sad tale of many rood-screens destroyed during the latter half of the last century, and of several other churches in which 'portions of the original screenwork have been egregiously worked up into seats, reredoses, pulpits or reading-desks'.

Before we leave the rood-screen, attention should be drawn to the instances, up and down the country, in which the lower panels of the screens are pierced with small openings. Many of these small openings are cut through with care (sometimes in the form of a small quatrefoil or of a Greek or Latin cross), while others are quite roughly cut. An opinion once widely expressed was that these holes were cut for the convenience of the penitent confessing to the priest seated within the chancel. This seems unlikely, for in several instances there are up to a dozen such holes in a single screen, and their proximity makes it impossible that they were used by several penitents at the same time. (If they were for confession one might naturally expect a single hole in a panel on each side.) It seems more likely that they were merely squints to enable kneeling worshippers to see the altar and more particularly the Elevation of the Host. Whatever their purpose, though, they could not have been in general use, for out of the several hundreds of screens still surviving only about forty or so have these openings.

Post-Reformation chancel screens are also to be found. They are not common, however, for (as we have seen) every village church had its medieval screen; these later screens were probably erected to replace those destroyed before Queen Elizabeth's directive of 1561. Good examples, some dated, are to be found at Countisbury and Washfield (1624) in Devon, at Croscombe, Elworthy (1632) North Newton (1637) and Rodney Stoke in Somerset, at Brancepeth and Sedgefield in Durham, at Empshott (1620) in Hampshire and at Stonegrave in North Yorkshire.

Roods and Rood-lofts

The rood (the old English word for cross) was the most prominent object in the nave for some three centuries, dominating the east side of the chancel arch. In its simplest form it was a great cross, but later a life-size (or even larger) figure of Christ was put on to what became the Crucifix, with Mary on the right and St John the Evangelist on the left. Behind this group of figures was usually the Doom, or *Last Judgement* painting. Surviving examples of these paintings (like that at Wenhaston, Suffolk), often have the unpainted spaces which were once covered by the Crucifix and figures. Such was the importance attached to the rood in the medieval Church, that walls were raised, clerestories built and windows inserted in order to give prominence to what was regarded as the greatest achievement in history.

No medieval roods survive, for nearly all were stripped away and their images destroyed during the Reformation. Their precise position and method of fixing is therefore uncertain and can only be deduced from surviving remains. From this evidence they appear to have been fixed either on the tympanum of the chancel arch (as at Ludham, Norfolk, and Wenhaston, Suffolk), on the wall above it (as at Cawston, Norfolk, and Kingston, Cambridgeshire), or, where the chancel arch was low, on a beam set against the east wall of the nave. This beam was usually supported on corbels either side of the chancel arch, around four feet above the springing – an arrangement that can be found at Raydon, Suffolk.

There are other churches in which the rood-beams look as if they were independent of the rood-loft. Some of these beams still survive. That at Denston, Suffolk, is so high that it was once thought that the rood was suspended from it; on inspection, however, mortices in the top were discovered, into which the rood group would have been fixed. Other examples in Suffolk can be found at Hacheston, Monk Soham and Ufford, all of them moulded and brattished. At Tunstead, Norfolk, a fine painted rood-beam is supported on carved spandrels considerably above the rood-screen. The beam at Potter Heigham in the same county is some six feet above the screen, but here the space between the screen and rood-beam seems to have been filled in. Other rood-beams in Norfolk can be found at Sutton, Blakeney and Bawburgh. In many churches there are fragments of substantial beam-ends (usually sawn off at the wall) which are set at such a level above the screen as to indicate that they were rood-beams, so this arrangement was by no means uncommon. This can be seen at Doddington and Ightham in Kent, Yaxley in Suffolk and Hawton in Nottinghamshire.

It was considered more desirable for the Rood group to be seen against a solid background, when viewed from the nave, rather than being silhouetted against the east window of the chancel. In Norman churches, with their low arches, this background was the chancel wall, but in the thirteenth and subsequent centuries, when the chancel arch was raised in the course of rebuilding or enlarging the chancel, it became necessary to fill the arch above the rood-screen with timber boarding or lath and plaster, generally referred to as the screen tympanum. This infilling generally carried the Doom or *Last Judgement* painting.

Many tympana were destroyed, particularly in the nineteenth century. Hayfield, Derbyshire, retained its screen tympanum, with the painting of the rood and its attendant figures, until 1818. There are many other examples: the churches at Bridestowe and Woodbury in Devon lost their tympana at the turn of the century; the one at Pytchley, Northamptonshire, was destroyed in 1843; and an old photograph of Yaxley in Suffolk, taken in 1867, shows a tympanic filling painted with the Commandments that has since disappeared.

Several screen tympana still survive. Over the fifteenth-century screen at Lockington, Leicestershire, is a fine tympanum with a large carved Royal Arms (dated 1704) and the Commandments, the Lord's Prayer and the Creed below. Another of great interest still survives in the village church of Ellingham, Hampshire. Here the space above the screen is filled up with lath and plaster and now bears the Commandments, Creed and the Lord's Prayer in black lettering within a Renaissance border; below are two texts from the Bishops' Bible of Elizabethan date together with the Royal Arms (inscribed C.R. 1671) and two further texts of the same date. Above the simple medieval screen in St Petrock's at Parracombe, Devon, is a solid timber tympanum entirely painted with the Royal Arms, the Creed, the Lord's Prayer, the Commandments and the names of the churchwardens. Baddiley in Cheshire, has another fine example, dated 1663, in which the Commandments, the Lord's Prayer, the Creed and other texts from the Scriptures are all contained within a framework of painted columns and arches, between which is the Royal Arms. Another most interesting example is at Ludham, Norfolk, where the chancel arch – some 15'6" wide – is entirely filled with boarding. The Royal Arms was painted on canvas and fixed to the front of the tympanum, but recently a painted rood group was discovered underneath, and the Arms were transferred to the east side. Above the pine screen at Warminghurst, West Sussex, a semicircular plastered tympanum bears the Royal Arms of Queen Anne painted on canvas and, on the east face, an early eighteenth-century painted text.

Many other tympana are plain. In the church of Bradwell-juxta-Coggeshall the tympanum still exists, and in this case – as with others in Essex – the plain side is to the nave, whilst old ornamental work remains on the side towards the altar.

Some churches show evidence of once having had tympana, for their chancel arches bear the scars of their removal. In other cases there is a rebate cut in the face of the arch, to give a flush, neat finish between the boards of the tympanum and the walls; sometimes the rebate is on the nave side of the arch, sometimes it is on the chancel side.

To give access to the rood, a narrow gallery, the rood-loft, was provided on the top of the rood-screen. There is no evidence of these lofts until the end of the thirteenth century. The loft stairs at Thurlby, Lincolnshire, belong to this time, as do the loft stairs at nearby Colsterworth; both of these appear to be built at the same time as the rood-loft, but it is probable that early lofts were reached by ladders. By the second half of the fifteenth century most screens in our village churches would have had a loft, but almost all were destroyed after the Reformation, and now less than a dozen remain in their complete state in England (although many are still to be found in Wales). Now the only evidence of the former existence of rood-lofts are the doorways or stairways which provided access to them, the ends of their supporting beams still embedded in the walls, or the corbels on the chancel walls which supported the beams.

The position of the rood-stairs varied greatly (145). The most common position was in the north wall of the nave, if there was no

145   Rood stairs at Garboldisham, Norfolk

aisle, or in the angle between the chancel arch and the arcade if there was. An alternative was to locate them in the wall flanking the chancel arch. In other cases rood-stairs were cut into a pier or a wall at one end of the screen. By far the most satisfactory arrangement was to construct an external stair-turret against the outer wall of an aisle, as at Long Melford, Suffolk. Here the entrance to the stairs was through a door at ground level, and at the top was a door which opened on to the loft. These projecting turrets on the north wall are a feature of many fifteenth-century Cornish churches.

An unusual feature to be found in Norfolk, at Cley next the Sea and in the neighbouring church at Wiveton, is that the stairs have two entrances; the reason for this is unknown. Lambley, Nottinghamshire, is unusual in having a set of stairs in the north wall and another in the south wall, both leading to the rood-loft. At Wrotham, Kent, a doorway in the pillar to the north of the Lady Altar gives access to a spiral stair which led to the former rood-loft, but it continues above the level of the rood to a passage running from the south to the north aisle with openings looking both east and west into the church; this is known as the Nuns' gallery, although how the name originated is unknown. The most unusual arrangement is to be found at Wouldam, Kent, where the rood-stairs, built into the outer wall of the north aisle, open on to a stone bridge with parapets on either side that crosses the aisle to the wall of the nave arcade, where a door gave access to the loft.

At the time of the Reformation, most rood-loft doorways were blocked up, and even many of the external stair turrets were taken down and the wall made good – as at Westerfield, Suffolk. (In recent years many of the doorways have been opened up and the hinges of the former doors discovered.) Consequently, not many original doors survive. A few churches still retain one door – perhaps the most remarkable being at South Cove, Suffolk, which bears a nearly life-size painting of *St Michael*; less commonly both upper and lower doors survive, as at Northleach, Gloucestershire.

The main purpose of the rood-loft was to give ready access for dressing and lighting the rood. In many cases the loft was so narrow that little else would have been possible, but wider ones were clearly used for other purposes. From documentary evidence it is abundantly clear that the rood-loft was used by musicians and singers, and there is frequently reference to the construction of a 'pair of organs'. The existence of rood-loft piscinas high up in the wall may be taken as evidence that altars were sometimes provided in the rood-lofts, and this is confirmed by documentary evidence. Such piscinas can still be seen at Burghill and Wigmore in Herefordshire, Maxey in Cambridgeshire, Bilton and Church Lawford in Warwickshire, Horningsea in Cambridgeshire, Great Hallingbury in Essex and Oddington in Oxfordshire.

That rood-lofts were well used is evident from a study of the steps of rood-stairs, which in many cases are remarkably worn – and in a few cases have been resurfaced, as at Horning, Norfolk. The narrowness of most surviving stairways and the often rough work of their walls would have made it almost impossible for anyone clad in church vestments to make a dignified ascent.

Generally rood-lofts were between three and six feet wide, with floors projecting beyond the screen to both front and back, and for safety had a four-foot-high panelled parapet on both sides. The beam crowning the parapet on the nave or west side was always referred to in old accounts as the candle-beam, indicating that it was used to illuminate the sacred scene. Because so few rood-lofts have survived in England it is difficult to say what the precise lighting arrangements were, but some information can be gleaned from the far more numerous examples to be found in Wales. Here the whole length of the candle-beam is generally drilled to receive the prickets (spikes on which candles were fixed). The beam on the chancel, or east, side was sometimes referred to as the rood-beam, indicating that at least in some instances the rood was fixed to it.

Only a dozen or so medieval rood-lofts survive in England. The finest are those at Flamborough in East Riding of Yorkshire and in the small market town Attleborough in Norfolk; there are other examples at Oakley in Bedfordshire, Warfield in Berkshire, Atherington in Devon, Coates by Stow in Lincolnshire, Avebury in Wiltshire, Besford in Worcestershire (a late example, dated 1538), Hubberholme in North Yorkshire (146) and St Margarets, Herefordshire.

Medieval rood figures have all disappeared apart from a few fragments, mostly in museums, but a number of roods have been erected in modern times. An especially beautiful reconstruction, with genuine fourteenth- to fifteenth-century figures, can be seen at North Cerney, Gloucestershire. Another can be seen above the admirable screen at Blisland, Cornwall, designed by F.C. Eden and built by local craftsmen in 1896.

146   Hubberholme, North Yorkshire, where the screen still retains its rood loft

Celures or Canopies of Honour

A feature frequently found in our village churches is the canopy of honour, usually associated with the rood, and so often referred to as the rood celure. Those related to the rood generally take the form of ornamentation applied to the eastern bay of the nave roof. In many cases this was achieved simply by colouring and gilding the structural timbers, in others boarding was secured below the rafters and ribs, with carved bosses introduced at the intersections, enriched by such motifs as suns and stars. There are examples at Braughing in Hertfordshire, West Camel in Somerset and in Devon at Hennock, Ideford, King's Nympton, Swimbridge and Lapford. At Dummer in Hampshire the roof is formed into a coved arch divided into eight panels with large square bosses, a most unusual feature but most effective. Other canopies of note are at Ditcheat in Somerset, Barton-le-Clay in Bedfordshire and Westwood in Wiltshire.

One of the finest examples is to be seen at Woolpit, Suffolk, where, high up on the east wall of the nave above the chancel arch, there is a most lovely canopy formed of five cusped panels divided by little shafts from which springs elaborate groined vaulting. The cresting, which has angels on it, is mitred to the hammer beams on either side and so forms an integral part of the roof.

Royal Arms

Royal Arms are a decorative and sometimes ancient feature in many of our village churches. Originally they were intended to replace the rood above the chancel screen (a position that makes it appropriate to mention them here). They are usually painted on boards or canvas or directly on the wall; very occasionally they are carved in wood or even stone (Beckington, Somerset) or moulded in plaster or made of cast iron. Sometimes they are set up and painted in a lozenge shape like a hatchment – as at Field Dalling, Norfolk – but this is unusual.

Royal Arms first appeared in the reign of Henry VIII, to mark the split with Rome and to confirm that the King was the head of the Church of England. It seems that early in the reign of Edward VI some order must have been made for the destruction of roods. Some writers state that in 1547 he directed that the rood be removed and replaced by the Royal Arms, and that stories and images of the Saints decorating church walls should be replaced by texts from the scriptures. Certainly there is documentary evidence that roods were being replaced with Royal Arms, the Ten Commandments, the Lords Prayer and other texts a few years later.

Like so many items within the church, the Arms suffered greatly through the various swings in religious orthodoxy. During the reign of Mary they were ordered to be removed from where they had been fixed over the rood-screen or altar and 'to be set in a place more convenient'. However, as so few survive, it seems most were destroyed. They reappeared under Elizabeth I, indeed Elizabeth directed their use and indicated that the tympanum to the chancel arch was the place to display them. Inevitably many were again destroyed during Cromwell's Commonwealth – in 1650 Parliament ordered 'the removal of the obnoxious Royal Arms from the churches'. It was not until 1660, at the restoration of Charles II, that an Act of Parliament made it compulsory to display the Royal Arms in every church, reminding clergy and congregations that the monarch was the head of the Church. Displaying the Royal Arms became popular again under the Hanoverian kings, but in the latter half of the nineteenth century it once again fell out of favour – when the restoration of our medieval churches was at its peak the Oxford Movement was anxious to emphasize the spiritual continuity of the Church, rather than any suggestion of secular control. Although not always destroyed, Arms were often relegated to less conspicuous positions.

Consequently, the Arms of Henry VIII are rare indeed. On the chancel arch at Rushbrooke in Suffolk there is a large one thought to be of this period (a truly magnificent example), but in 1976 Diarmaid MacCulloch, in *Proceedings of the Suffolk Institute of Archaeology*, queried its authenticity and suggested that it may be the work of Col. Rushbrooke, a Victorian amateur craftsman 'to whom the church owes its present appearance'. There is a Royal Arms from the reign of Edward VI at Westerham, Kent, but it is not until Elizabeth's reign that these Arms survive in any number. At Tivetshall St Margaret, Norfolk, there is a very fine example dating from 1587 in the tympanum of the chancel arch, painted on boards which previously would probably have had a Doom painting. This must have been one of the earliest examples, along with those at Lanteglos-by-Camelford in Cornwall, Badgeworth in Gloucestershire (dated 1591) and Ludham and Kenninghall (147), both in Norfolk. At Preston, Suffolk, the Royal Arms is painted on shaped board in the form of a tryptych of considerable size – the Arms on the inside of the two leaves and on the outside, visible when they were closed, various biblical sayings of a puritanical nature pertaining to images. The one at Elton, Herefordshire, is notable in that it is carved in oak in bold relief and shows no trace of colour. A most interesting example of the period is to be found at Lower Quinton, Warwickshire; this shows how the Royal Arms were employed to cover up the old wall-paintings, for it is positioned on the wall above the chancel arch, in the space formerly occupied by a painted Doom.

The Arms of James I are far from common, though good examples are to be found. The earliest dated example is probably the one at Blisland, Cornwall, which bears the date 1604, but by far the most magnificent painted panel, dated 1609, is at Winsford in

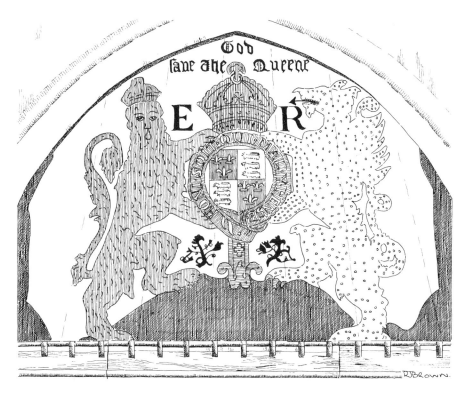

147 Royal Arms of Elizabeth I at Kenninghall, Norfolk

Somerset. Another magnificent example, dated 1616 carved in wood and incorporated in the chancel screen, is at Croscombe, Somerset. In some instances, earlier Royal Arms were brought up to date or altered for the new Sovereign, for instance at Troston, Suffolk. Above the tower arch at Tacolneston, Norfolk, is a silver and blue Royal Arms initialled for Charles I, but it is set in a wooden frame topped by a triangular gable which is dated 1620, for James I.

A few Arms survive from the reign of Charles I, the earliest (dated 1625) at Langley Marish, Berkshire. The finest example, however, is at Abbey Dore in Herefordshire, where it sits above the screen erected by Lord Scudamore in 1634. The majority from the seventeenth century come, of course, from the reign of Charles II, when Royal Arms became compulsory in churches. Some are painted on the plasterwork of the tympanic filling, as at Baddiley in Cheshire (1663) and Ellingham in Hampshire (1671). The one at

Wickhamford, Worcestershire, dated 1661, not only fills the entire east gable of the nave, the surrounding design is extended on to the horizontal roof panelling of the celure. Among the many other examples is a very grand one of Charles II, in nearly black oak, at Norham in Northumberland.

Perhaps the rarest of all post-Reformation Arms are those from James II's short reign (just three years, before he fled the country in 1688). In some instances, as at Great Snoring in Norfolk, an additional 'I' was simply added to the James I Arms. One of the treasures of one of Norfolk's loveliest churches, Shelton, is the Royal Arms of William III. Six feet by eight feet in size and made of carved, gilded and painted oak, it has luxuriant moulding at the top and a bottom panel beautifully carved with fruit and flowers. Other notable Arms are to be found at Wyverstone in Suffolk and Sible Hedingham in Essex, both carved in wood; the Arms at Vange in Essex are those of Charles II, although they are inscribed WR 1689.

Queen Anne was the last of the Stuarts, and a distinguishing feature of her Arms is the use of the motto *Semper Eadem* ('always the same'). There are many fine examples, since the Queen was held in high esteem by churchmen for restoring to the Church the tithes which had been appropriated by the Crown since 1534. Perhaps the most imposing example is at Lockington, Leicestershire, where the Royal Arms is made of moulded plaster and fills the upper part of the tympanum above the rood-screen. It has draped curtains on either side, and tables of the Commandments, Lord's Prayer and Creed below. Another of great charm, at Swilland in Suffolk, is finely carved in wood, while there is another fine carved set at Harberton, Devon.

The vast majority of Royal Arms in our country churches are Hanoverian, and they are to be found throughout the country. Like those from other periods many were adapted; there are several examples of Stuart Arms with the Arms of Hanover painted over the fourth quarter, and others from the reign of George I have had one or two numerals added to adapt them for subsequent Georges. A feature of many of these Arms is that it became customary to record on them the names of the churchwardens of the time, the donor and even the painter.

By the reign of William IV Royal Arms were thought to be somewhat perfunctory, and so the quality grew steadily worse, and by around the middle of the nineteenth century they virtually ceased to be erected. In Victoria's reign the Royal Arms were apparently mass-produced in standard sets cast in plaster (Washbrook, Suffolk) or fully moulded and cast in iron (Tonge, Kent).

9 Nave Furniture

Fonts

Fonts are often some of the oldest objects to be found in churches, and their variety is such that their study alone could occupy a lifetime. They change with the prevailing architectural styles and are of every possible type and variety. In the main, they are located in a prominent place inside the church, often immediately to the west of the south doorway or the principal entrance, or at the west end of the nave. In the Middle Ages the baptismal service began outside the church – in the porch, if there was one – and finished at the font.

In Saxon and Norman times fonts were quite large, deep and set low in the ground, so that adults could stand in them while the baptismal water was poured over their heads. A great number of fonts from these periods still survive. Those at Dolton in Devon, Melbury Bubb in Dorset (148), Deerhurst in Gloucestershire, Little Billing in Northamptonshire and Curdworth in Warwickshire are some of the finest of Saxon date. The one at Dolton is formed of three parts; the pedestal, which is modern, supports two blocks from a rectangular Saxon pillar cross, cemented together (the upper block is in fact upside down). At Melbury Bubb the font is simply hollowed out of a single block from the circular stem of a Saxon sculptured cross, again upside down.

More than a thousand fonts from the Norman period still survive. All are large, usually square or circular in shape, and the circular ones are often decorated only by an encircling roll moulding

148   Saxon font at Melbury Bubb, Dorset

halfway up (as at Poltimore, Devon) or by a cable band (as at Congresbury, Somerset). Many have their sides elaborately carved with figures, monsters or patterns. Some of the finest are to be found in the west, and three of them are truly magnificent objects. The one at Castle Frome in Herefordshire, is perhaps the most remarkable: a large bowl on a lavishly adorned but short stem squashing an evil monster. Almost as fine in their bold carvings are those at Eardisley in Herefordshire and Stottesdon in Shropshire. Perhaps better proportioned and with strong but more coarsely executed carving, is that at Chaddesley Corbett, Worcestershire.

Memorable fonts of the Norman period survive in isolation elsewhere. One at Bridekirk in Cumbria depicts the *Baptism of Christ*, with foliage, dragons and monsters from Norse mythology. It is of particular interest because one face is a representation of the sculptor himself, and it is unique for its date in having a runic inscription. At Southrop, Gloucestershire, there are sculptures of Moses, Synagogue and Ecclesia, with the Virtues trampling on the Vices. Some fonts, like the big, square ones at Lenton in Nottinghamshire, West Haddon in Northamptonshire and East Meon in Hampshire show biblical scenes and at Hook Norton in Oxfordshire Adam and Eve, Sagittarius and Aquarius are depicted. The square font at Locking, Somerset, has a figure at each corner stretching out long arms to join hands with snakes which look like beaded plaits.

Although Norman fonts are found in most counties in the country, in a few areas there are groups of them in a similar style. One such area is Cornwall, where over eighty Norman fonts survive. Their design, decoration, date and material vary considerably, yet two distinct types can be found. One type is found in the north and east of the county – at Altarnun (149), Lawhitton and Laneast, for instance – and follows the form of a Norman capital, having roundels on the bowl and large heads at the corners. Similar fonts can also be found in Devon, at Bratton Clovelly and Lifton. In later, more elaborately carved fonts, the cup-shaped bowl is supported on a massive central stem, with slender single shafts at each corner supporting winged faces, presumably angels. The finest is at Bodmin, but others can be found at Pentewan, Crantock and Roche (150).

There are two other notable concentrations of these Norman fonts. In Buckinghamshire there are seven or eight of the so-called

149   Font at Altarnun, Cornwall

Aylesbury fonts (named after the one in Aylesbury Church) which must be the work of the same man. Less ornate than those in Cornwall, for they have no figures, they are better proportioned and are chalice-shaped, with a circular bowl on what can only be described as an inverted square capital. Those at Chenies, Bledlow and Great Kimble (151) are perhaps the best.

150   Font at Roche, Cornwall

Less uniform, but possibly more remarkable, are the fonts found
in north-west Norfolk. Two of the finest are at Shernborne and
Toftrees, both of them well proportioned and richly decorated with
grotesque heads and interlacing work supported on four columns.
Four columns also support the very fine bowl at Burnham
Deepdale, one of the most interesting fonts in England, and three
of its four faces depict Labours of the Months. At South Wootton
the bowl is supported on nine pillars. Other outstanding examples
are to be found at Sculthorpe and Fincham, where there are large
square fonts with carved figures under arcades.

Arcading was widely used in font decoration, for it provided a
series of niches in which carvings of the Apostles or other subjects
could be placed. There are examples at Kirkby on Merseyside,

151   Font at Great Kimble, Buckinghamshire

Stoneleigh in Warwickshire, Wansford in Cambridgeshire, Orleton in Herefordshire, Darenth in Kent and Cowlam in East Riding of Yorkshire. Rude as all these are, the character of the figure sculpture marks them all out as of late twelfth-century date. Arcading was also used purely as decoration, frequently intersecting (as at Alphington, Devon).

The font at Cowlam forms part of another remarkable series of elaborately carved Norman fonts found in villages on the Yorkshire Wolds, all depicting a marvellous gallery of rudely sculptured figures. Apart from the one at Cowlam, those at

Kirkburn (152) and Langtoft in East Riding of Yorkshire and North Grimston in North Yorkshire, are all exceptional, and to these may be added that from Hutton Cranswick – unfortunately now in York Museum. At Reighton, North Yorkshire, there is another font of great charm, though different from the others; instead of figures its sides are decorated with richly carved patterns.

152   Font at Kirkburn, East Riding of Yorkshire

The majority of Norman fonts were made of stone and lined with lead, but there are around forty dating from the end of this period that are made entirely of lead and mounted on a stone base. They are to be found in many counties but Gloucestershire has eight of them; those at Frampton on Severn, Sandhurst and Tidenham, all with scroll-work alternating with figures under arcades, are possibly the finest in the county. This theme of figures under arcades, which was fairly common, occurs at Ashover, Derbyshire, on a fine example that has twenty figures under arches, and again at Brookland, Kent, on a remarkable font only 16 inches high with scenes of the signs of the zodiac and the labours of the months in two rows under arcading.

By post-Norman times the baptized were in the main children, and, as they were completely immersed, fonts were raised on a plinth. Later still it became customary to pour water over the child, and so the bowls were made smaller and raised higher on a pedestal or pillars. It is not uncommon for Norman fonts to be raised – which explains why many bowls are of earlier date than the bases they stand on. At Shilton, Oxfordshire, for instance, a square Norman bowl has been covered with fourteenth-century carving and set on legs with fourteenth-century mouldings.

Early English fonts were generally much plainer than many Norman ones and were rarely decorated with figures – although some of early date did so, for instance the one at Anstey in Hertfordshire, which has four sculpted mermen grasping their tails. Later, the main decoration was continuous arcading (of which there are literally hundreds of examples) and floral patterns. Some of the most attractive are the beautiful cup fonts, of which that at Eaton Bray in Bedfordshire, with stiff-leaf capitals on its detached shafts, is the finest (others include the fonts at Shere in Surrey (153) and Michelmersh in Hampshire). The detached shafts of the Norman period and the early thirteenth century slowly gave way to engaged shafts, as at Bradley in Derbyshire and Etchingham in East Sussex. A few have pedestals; they may be massive, as at Tickencote in Rutland, or slender, as at Studham in Bedfordshire.

From the end of the thirteenth century onwards, font bowls were invariably octagonal, rather than square or round. It is not uncommon to find square Norman fonts with their corners removed to form the later fashionable octagonal shape – a blatant example is at Ingoldisthorpe, Norfolk, where the bowl of the Norman font,

153   Font at Shere, Surrey

originally square with its faces covered with interlacings, has had the corners ruthlessly removed and the four new faces left undecorated. The font at Naughton, Suffolk, has been similarly treated; originally its large square bowl was ornamented with rude intersecting arcading, but it was subsequently roughly cut to an octagonal shape without regard to the pattern of the original arcading. The font at Braybrooke in Northamptonshire, has been similarly treated, as have those at Chelvey in Somerset, Thornbury in Gloucestershire, and Warham All Saints in Norfolk.

Fourteenth-century fonts therefore had either a polygonal bowl raised on a polygonal pedestal or, less commonly, an unmounted polygonal bowl. They were usually octagonal, but occasionally – for instance at Brill in Buckinghamshire – they were heptagonal. The simplicity and restraint of the previous century had gone, and, where it could be afforded, richly carved detail was lavishly applied. In a poor village the face of the bowl might be left plain, as at Lapworth in Warwickshire; in others the faces would be filled with window tracery, as at Brailes in Warwickshire (154) and Offley in Hertfordshire. By far the most popular form of ornamentation was a canopy, which at first had a straight-sided pediment, richly crocketed and cusped and crowned with a foliated finial. Examples of this are the fonts at Lowdham, Nottinghamshire, and Wortham, Suffolk. Some forty years later the straight-sided pediment gave way to the ogee arch. At first this was of a simple, homely form, but later it came to be worked with increasing richness – as at Rattlesden, Suffolk – until the niches they formed contained carvings of saints or other scenes. This can best be seen at Fishlake, South Yorkshire, and Tysoe, Warwickshire.

There are a few medieval fonts with projections from the bowl that have given rise to a great variety of speculations about their origin and use. There are five of these fonts in England, and the same explanation cannot be applied to them all. The most interesting is the late Norman font at Youlgreave in Derbyshire, where the projection takes the form of a round basin, or stoup, slightly lower than the rim. There is little doubt that this was used in connection with baptism by affusion, in which the surplus water poured over the head of the recipient was not allowed to return into the font containing the consecrated water but collected in a separate vessel. As it has no drain hole, the font stoup at Youlgreave seems to have held a removable basin. At Odiham in Hampshire the upper part of the bowl of the font has a bracket-like projection with an oblong hollow in its top and a circular hole at each end. Despite much speculation, its true purpose is not known. The fourteenth-century font at Pitsford, Northamptonshire, also has a plain projection from the rim, pierced with several small circular holes, and here

154 Early fourteenth-century font at Brailes, Warwickshire

again its purpose is not clear. At Sutton Bonington in Nottinghamshire (155) the font has three projections: one on the priest's left, which has a flat surface, and two smaller ones on the east and south sides of the font. The larger bracket would have been for the affusion bowl and the other two might have been for the salt and candle accessories in the baptismal rite. The fifth example is to be found on the Norman font at Rainham, Essex. Several other old fonts also show traces of projections which have been broken off.

155   Font at Sutton Bonington, Nottinghamshire

In the fifteenth century, fonts reached the zenith of their development. They were practically all polygonal – usually octagonal – and their ornamentation became bewildering in its variety. Many of the finest are to be found in East Anglia. One type outnumbers any other; it consists of an octagonal stem surrounded by lions sejant with, between them, buttresses of hairy men with large clubs (as at Happisburgh, Norfolk, and Chediston, Suffolk). Above the stem the corbel course generally has angels with outspread wings. Each face of the bowl itself is decorated with a variety of designs, a common motif being the symbols of the Four Evangelists, alternating with angels holding shields or musical instruments. Sometimes lions replace the Evangelists. The fifteenth century also saw the introduction of heraldic badges and shields to the panels of the bowl, with angels holding the coats of arms of donors or benefactors. Again some of the best examples are to be found in East Anglia.

Perhaps the finest fonts of all are those from the latter half of the fifteenth century which show representations of the *Seven Sacraments* – Baptism, Confirmation, Penance, Mass, Marriage, Unction and Ordination. They are almost exclusively confined to Suffolk and Norfolk (13 in Suffolk and 24 in Norfolk), with only two examples outside these counties: at Farningham in Kent, and at Nettlecombe in Somerset. These fonts are octagonal and, with seven panels representing the Sacraments, a subject was needed for the eighth panel; Christ's Baptism or Crucifixion were two of the most popular subjects. The finest of these fonts in Suffolk is the one at Cratfield, but those at Laxfield (where the font stands on traceried steps, the upper step in the shape of a Maltese cross), Badingham (where the eight panels are particularly well preserved) and Weston are also fine examples. In Norfolk the fonts at Loddon and Little Walsingham, like the one at Laxfield, have magnificent traceried steps which are works of art on their own. Another fine example is at Walsoken, and the best of the panels are at Gresham and Sloley. These fonts were probably originally painted, and a few still retain some colour – those at Westhall in Suffolk and Great Winchingham in Norfolk, in particular. Unfortunately, all the surviving sacrament fonts are mutilated; the best preserved may have been plastered over in troublesome times, apparently a fairly common occurrence.

Not all of the finest fonts of the Perpendicular period are to be found in East Anglia, and there are many notable ones to be found elsewhere. Perhaps the finest, that at Huttoft in Lincolnshire, is a variation of the East Anglian style of font. At the foot are the symbols of the Evangelists, in the niches on the stem are saints, and angels support the octagonal bowl; on the bowl are carvings of the Trinity (in the form of the Father holding the crucified Son, with the dove of the Holy Spirit above), plus the Virgin Mary and the Twelve Apostles in pairs.

In post-Reformation days the growth of Protestantism, and the Protestants' dislike of the sacramental aspect of religion, led to many fonts being destroyed – so many, in fact, that in 1564 Elizabeth I had to order 'that the font be not removed'. There are a few dated examples from Elizabeth's reign and subsequent reigns, those at Edlington in Lincolnshire (1599), Whixall in Shropshire (1608), Byford in Herefordshire (1638) and Rackheath in Norfolk (1639) among them.

During Cromwell's time, when the Puritans became influential, the use of fonts was strictly forbidden, and many of them were destroyed and replaced by a mere basin. Others were mutilated, their decorative features hacked away. With the Restoration, the old order of things returned, and new fonts were required to replace those that had been destroyed. Many dated examples exist from 1660 onwards, with those of 1662 naturally predominating (for that was the year that an Act of Parliament was passed making loyalty to the Prayer Book obligatory). Many are undistinguished, but those in Nottinghamshire are of decided merit, and the font at Orston is perhaps the most striking Restoration font in England. In some cases the date (perhaps accompanied by the churchwardens' initials) is to be found on a font of an earlier period – in which case it records the date when the font was brought back into the church again. This is the case with the Norman font of Parwich in Derbyshire and the fifteenth-century example at Church Langton in Leicestershire. At Rothbury in Northumberland a post-Reformation bowl with the date 1664 is carved on part of a shaft of an Anglo-Saxon cross.

As we have seen, apart from those Norman examples made of lead, fonts were almost always of stone – usually local stone, although Purbeck stone was widely used, and Tournai marble was also used on occasion. There are fonts in other materials, but they are very rare. There are brick examples at Potter Heigham in

Norfolk and Chignall Smealy in Essex, and wooden fonts can be found at Marks Tey in Essex, and Ash in Surrey.

Font Covers

In 1236 Archbishop Rich decreed that locked covers should be fitted to fonts to prevent the hallowed water (blessed only at Easter and kept in the font for the whole year) being stolen and used for witchcraft or black magic. The earliest form was a flat wooden lid, fastened down by a bar and staples, which was lifted off during the baptism service. The marks of the fasteners or the locks which secured the covers can often still be seen on the rims (Witcham, Cambridgeshire) and in some instances the broken metal staples remain in the stone. At Wickenby in Lincolnshire the original fastenings remain. They consist of an iron bar, one end of which is thrust through a hole in the upright wooden handle in the centre of the cover and into the staple at one side of the font; the other end has an eyelet or loop which is padlocked to a similar staple on the opposite side. At Ford in West Sussex, too, the iron straps, lock and staple survive.

Later medieval covers were often eight-sided cones; the panels rising from a moulded base were either straight (as at Monksilver, Somerset) or of ogee shape (as at Colebrook, Devon) and the cover was often ornamented with crockets and an elaborate crocketed finial. Jacobean covers are also found, particularly in the West Country; Lanreath in Cornwall, Banwell, Congresbury (156) and Rodney Stoke in Somerset and Aldenham in Hertfordshire all have splendid examples.

By the fifteenth century the font cover had developed into a canopy, often of splendid and large proportions and occasionally enclosing the entire font. It was in East Anglia during the medieval period that these covers became works of art – what L.E. Jones describes as 'the most splendid soaring mass of wonderful tabernacle work' often reaching almost to the roof. The finest of these is to be found at Ufford in Suffolk, where an amazing spire-like cover rises some eighteen feet high with three tiers of tabernacle niches that once contained the figures of apostles and saints (all, alas, long ago destroyed). How magnificent it must have been with all the figures in place, coloured and gilded! Other examples of these lofty

156 Norman font with Jacobean cover at Congresbury, Somerset

medieval covers can be seen at Castle Acre, Merton, Worstead and Salle in Norfolk. In Suffolk the finest example after that at Ufford is the one at Worlingworth, which is said to have come from the Abbey of Bury St Edmunds. Lincolnshire, too, has two beautiful examples; one at Frieston towers nearly to the roof, crowned with the figure of the Virgin Mary, and another at Fosdyke, almost as good, has three stages of openwork. There are also some fine font covers in the villages of Yorkshire, most notably those at Almondbury and Well.

The tallest of these covers were raised by means of a counterpoise: an engineering contraption, housed within the upper section of the cover, which enabled the lower sections of the covers to be telescoped up level with the upper section. Another fine fifteenth-century cover at Ewelme in Oxfordshire has the counterpoise outside the cover, and the whole cover moves. In a third variant only very occasionally used, the counterpoise is hidden by canopied panelling; two of the finest examples are the sixteenth-century cover at Pilton, Devon, and the seventeenth-century one at Astbury, Cheshire.

Unique in a village church is the elaborate, crown-like structural canopy at Trunch in Norfolk, which is supported independently of the font on six profusely carved pillars. This is an amazing structure to find in such a relatively small church, and it dominates the interior. One can only wonder what it must have looked like when new – with figure paintings of New Testament subjects filling the niches, flying buttresses connecting the canopies to the pillars, and the colours and gilding all fresh.

Not all covers were movable. Some rested permanently on the font and completely enclosed it, their sides being hinged to open when the font was required for use. A splendid cover of this type at Ticehurst in East Sussex has eight elaborate panels of fifteenth-century Flamboyant tracery, four of them hinged for opening. There are other notable medieval examples at Newington, near Sittingbourne in Kent, and Hepworth and Bramford in Suffolk. The covers at Marden in Kent (which sits on a contemporary font dated 1662), Burgh Le Marsh in Lincolnshire (dated 1623) and Walpole St Peter in Norfolk are all good post-Reformation examples.

Fine permanent covers encasing the complete font are those at Littlebury in Essex, which is of pre-Reformation date, and at Terrington St Clement in Norfolk and Stanford in the Vale in

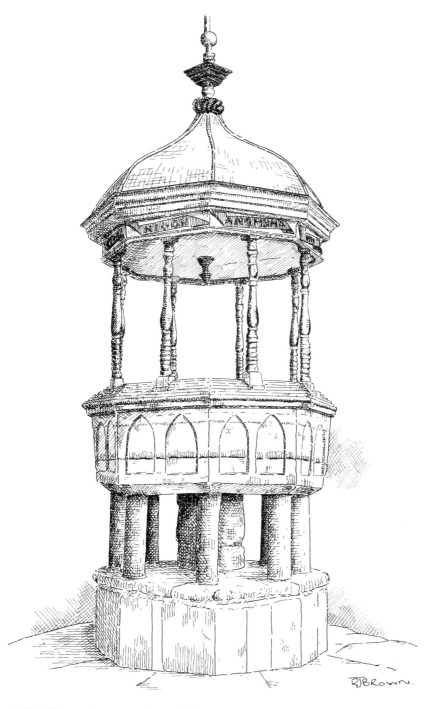

157   Thirteenth-century font with font cover dated 1704 at Knapton, Norfolk

Oxfordshire (both post-Reformation). Perhaps the finest of all is the early Jacobean cover at Swimbridge in Devon, which not only completely encases the font but also has a beautifully carved canopy above.

In the first half of the seventeenth century a simpler type appeared in which eight ribs rise from the flat octagonal font cover (one from each corner) to meet in the centre below a 'finial' of a shape that roughly suggests a crown. The ribs could be simply shaped in an ogee form (as at Poynings, West Sussex) or elaborately carved, as on the cover at Bolton Percy, North Yorkshire.

It seems that most of the more elaborate sixteenth- and seventeenth-century font covers were suspended from brackets, but nearly all have now disappeared. One example still remains in the village church of Warminghurst, West Sussex, where there is now no font cover but the iron bracket from which it was suspended is still visible; Salle in Norfolk also retains its original braced and traceried bracket. In the apex of the roof at Potter Heigham, Norfolk, there is an old wooden pulley that was once used to raise the font cover (which has long since disappeared).

Pulpits

Pulpits were introduced into churches in the fourteenth century and these were often hewn out of a solid block of oak. However, this ancient form of construction is by no means always a sign of early date; the pulpit at Chivelstone, Devon, although cut from a solid block, has linenfold patterns and shields that indicate a late fifteenth- or early sixteenth-century date. Another interesting early example is at Fulbourn, Cambridgeshire. By the fifteenth century preaching had become general, and many fine examples survive; those dating from before the Reformation are easily recognized by their perfect proportions – tall, narrow and usually polygonal – supported on slender conical stems and often having decorated panels.

There is evidence that on occasions the rood-loft was used for preaching, and now and again there seems to have been an adjunct to the rood-screen for this purpose, with access from the rood-stairs. One such example is at Walpole St Andrew, Norfolk (158), where there is a coved stone bracket immediately above the lower

158   Pulpit bracket at Walpole St Andrew, Norfolk

doorway to the rood-loft, with access from the rood-loft stairs. There seems little doubt that the bracket supported a small wooden pulpit of some sort.

Originally, it seems, the pulpit was usually fixed against the nave wall or the first pier west of the screen, but during the restorations of the nineteenth century many were moved further east and fixed to, or placed in front of, the screen. Today one rarely finds an ancient timber pulpit in its original position; stone pulpits (not so easily moved) are often found *in situ*, as at Combe, Oxfordshire.

Pre-Reformation pulpits, whether timber or stone, were generally either hexagonal or octagonal – although the one at Selworthy in Somerset is dodecagonal, which gives tall narrow panels, while that at Long Sutton, also in Somerset, has sixteen sides. The sides of the polygon were not always of the same width; on the nine-sided pulpit at Wendens Ambo, Essex, there are seven large and two small sides, while at East Hagbourne, Oxfordshire, narrow and wide sides alternate. Medieval pulpits, it seems, were generally provided with doors – on wooden pulpits these were formed by hinging one or two of the sides, as at Sandon, Essex – but these have now frequently been removed.

About sixty pre-Reformation stone pulpits are still in use today, the majority of them in the West Country – Devon, Somerset and Gloucestershire – with ten in Devon alone. Many are elaborately carved and incorporate figures, often depicting the four Evangelists or the Apostles, and most are richly coloured and gilded. One of the most beautiful anywhere, richly coloured with its original figures, is in the small country town of Bovey Tracey, Devon. Another with its original figures is at Dittisham in Devon; a very charming circular pulpit, full of grace, supported on a slender stem. At Harberton, also in Devon, is another richly carved and coloured pulpit, but here the figures are of seventeenth-century date.

Around Weston-super-Mare, there are some fifteen medieval stone pulpits, and most of them are of a similar design, with double-light fifteenth-century tracery and bands of foliage. The best examples are to be found at Banwell, Bleadon and Hutton, all in Somerset. Tracery was common on medieval stone pulpits and can be found elsewhere in the country. A simple but effective design is the stone pulpit attached to the north wall of the nave at Combe, Oxfordshire. Here each face has a double range of traceried panelling capped by an embattled cornice. Another of similar design at Berwick St James, Wiltshire, has simple traceried panels with shields within them.

More medieval timber pulpits survive – around a hundred – than stone ones. To judge from medieval illuminations they generally stood on legs formed by extending the angle posts, as at Wendens Ambo, Essex. Another early method, which continued throughout the period, was to support the pulpit on a stone base. The final and most beautiful form, however, was to support the pulpit on a slender stem, spreading out as a capital on a polygonal coving. The shaft might be of six- or eight-sided sections, according to the shape of the pulpit (or, in the eastern counties, occasionally circular) and usually had a moulded base worked out of the solid. In the West Country the stem was sometimes of stone, as at Long Sutton, Somerset. In some cases the sides were worked out of the solid, a method used in some of the Somerset pulpits, of which Queen Camel is typical. More often, however, the pulpit was built with a sill, top rail and angle-posts (the angles often ornamented with small buttresses) and filled in with panels – perhaps the most important part of the overall design – which were usually traceried. The tracery was usually to the head; in some cases, though, a band was introduced at the base of the panel, and in others the panels would be completely covered with tracery. Sometimes the panels were divided into two, with the tracery following the design of a two-light window. The most elaborate treatment of all, most common in the West Country, was to form a niche housing figures in each panel, though the figures have rarely survived.

Pre-Reformation wooden pulpits are most numerous in Devon and Norfolk, but they differ greatly in appearance. Those in Devon (and Somerset) are richly carved, whereas in Norfolk the sides are panelled and painted with figures. The pulpits of Devon are truly remarkable, and nearly all are to be found in the southern half of the county. So fine are the examples that it is difficult to select the best; Kenton (very richly carved but restored in 1882 and with modern paintings of West Country saints), Coldridge (with its most intricate canopy work), Ipplepen (canopied niches, foliage and colour) and Chivelstone (decorated with shields and retaining much of its original colour) are some of the finest.

Although there are fewer in Somerset, at least three bear comparison with the medieval pulpits of Devon. The most remarkable perhaps is at Long Sutton: a truly beautiful medieval wooden pulpit of sixteen sides. Its figures of the Twelve Apostles with their emblems are modern restorations, but the inscribed initials are supposed to be those of the rector and churchwardens of the time – around 1470. Equally fine is another fifteenth-century pulpit at Trull, which still has its original figures of the Four Latin Doctors, and St John the Evangelist. Angels in the upper part of each panel hold carved canopies above the figures, and the figures of two small saints appear on each of the dividers between the panels. The third remarkable pulpit in Somerset is the one at Monksilver, where the panels are filled with extremely fine tracery. Here, as in several other churches of the county, the pulpit was tight up to the front of the screen and approached through a doorway, which obviously at one time led up to the rood-loft.

As previously noted the medieval pulpits of East Anglia are not richly moulded, but their panels are painted with figures of Evangelists or the Four Latin Doctors. Perhaps the most remarkable is that at Burnham Norton, Norfolk, which dates from around 1475 and depicts the Four Latin Doctors. The base carries the name of the donor John Goldale, who appears with his wife as a kneeling figure in the other panels. The backgrounds are alternating dark green and red. The Latin Doctors appear again at Castle Acre, Norfolk, and at South Burlingham in the same county the green and red backgrounds have gold flowers and stars. At Horsham St Faith, Norfolk, the panels are painted with saints, including two abbots on the doors. It is curious that Suffolk, a county so rich in other medieval woodwork, has so few pre-Reformation pulpits. The best is perhaps the one at Stoke by Clare, only 21" in diameter but with good tracery. Others of note are at Creeting St Peter, Thwaite and Tuddenham St Martin.

Pre-Reformation wooden pulpits are also to be found in most parts of the country. Essex has seven that date from the fifteenth century, and those at Sandon and Leaden Roding are fine examples. Lincolnshire has one at Tattershall and there is another in Oxfordshire, at Handborough (159).

It seems that not all medieval churches had pulpits, for the severe restrictions imposed on preaching (not lifted until the reign of James I) meant that few churches felt the need for one. Until the Reformation most priests recited the service from the chancel, and reading desks were much more common than pulpits. Where both a reading desk and a pulpit survive, the reading desk is usually

159   Pulpit at Handborough, Oxfordshire

earlier; at Edingthorpe in Norfolk the reading desk is dated 1587, the pulpit 1632. With the sermon becoming of paramount importance, an edict of 1603 stated that in every church there should be a 'comely and decent pulpit to be seemly kept for the preaching of God's word', and this is probably why a number of wooden pulpits date from just after Elizabeth I's death in 1603 and the outbreak of the Civil War in 1642. They are usually termed Jacobean or Carolean, although their number is not large and most are undated. A feature of these pulpits is the tester or sounding board above, supported on a standard or back piece which was intended to magnify the speaker's voice.

Many fine examples from the period survive, including a splendid pulpit at Stoke D'Abernon in Surrey, given by Sir Francis Vincent in 1620. It is seven-sided and supported by a shaft with elaborately carved brackets and grotesques. On the standard is the shield with the Vincent arms, and the tester is upheld by elaborate ironwork. One of the panels bears the words *Fides ex Auditu* ('faith comes from hearing'). A slightly later or Carolean pulpit is at Stoke St Gregory, Somerset, where the panels are carved with the figures of Faith (with a sword), Hope (with an anchor), Charity (with a dove), Old Father Time (with scythe, skull and hour-glass) and the Virgin and Child, all beneath the rounded arches that are a very common feature of early seventeenth-century English woodwork.

After the Civil War, the normal Sunday morning service was conducted entirely from the reading desk, and only on the infrequent Sacrament Sundays would the service be conducted from the altar. As preaching became of increasing importance in the service, a focal point from which the sermon could be delivered, was required, and in the seventeenth and eighteenth centuries, at the same time as enclosed box pews with high backs came into fashion, two- and three-decker pulpits came into use. These are reading desk, lectern and pulpit combined, with seats at all levels. In three-decker pulpits the lowest tier was occupied by the clerk, who led the responses and conducted the singing, while the service was read from the second tier by the minister, who would climb to the third tier – the pulpit – to deliver his sermon. If a curate took the service then the rector would sit in the pulpit until it was time to deliver his sermon.

These multi-purpose pulpits became the centre of congregational worship, dominating the church, although the altar remained the focus. One of the earliest, the two-decker at Leweston in Dorset, is dated 1616, although others were adapted medieval pulpits (like that at Salle, Norfolk, which was made into a three-decker in 1611). As much importance was attached to seeing the preacher as to hearing him, and in churches that had galleries the pulpit was sometimes moved to a central position in front of the chancel screen, obscuring the sanctuary – as at King's Norton, Leicestershire, where the pulpit was built between 1757 and 1779. In some smaller churches without aisles the pulpit was moved down into the body of the nave, and the pews rearranged to face it. At Ravenstonedale in Cumbria, Gislingham in Suffolk (160) and Orton-on-the-Hill in Leicestershire the pulpits still stand part-way along the side of the nave.

Oak was used for most church furnishings, but in the eighteenth century mahogany, which had become popular for English furniture, began to appear. A few pulpits of this material are to be found – one at Kinoulton in Nottinghamshire, another at Hayfield in Derbyshire. Interestingly, many other pulpits were grained to imitate mahogany in the Georgian period, and a few still remain in this condition; Salle and Cawston, both in Norfolk, are typical.

Many three-decker pulpits were destroyed in the nineteenth century, when they were often felt not to harmonize with their surroundings, but many fine examples survive – the one at Bylaugh in Norfolk is typical. This has a tester and stairs that give access to the nave on one side and, on the other, descend into a mini-vestry shielded from the congregation by a curtain above the panelling. The pulpit has a semicircular seat for the preacher to use while the service is read; below, there is a spacious reading desk and an ingenious sliding block that enables its seat to be adjusted to two different levels. The clerk's pew is to the left and strategically placed to face down the nave.

Hour-glasses

These are generally thought to have been introduced into churches in the latter part of the sixteenth century, to control the length of sermons. However in Allen's *History of Lambeth* (1878) it is stated that an hour-glass was provided for a new pulpit placed in the parish church in 1522.

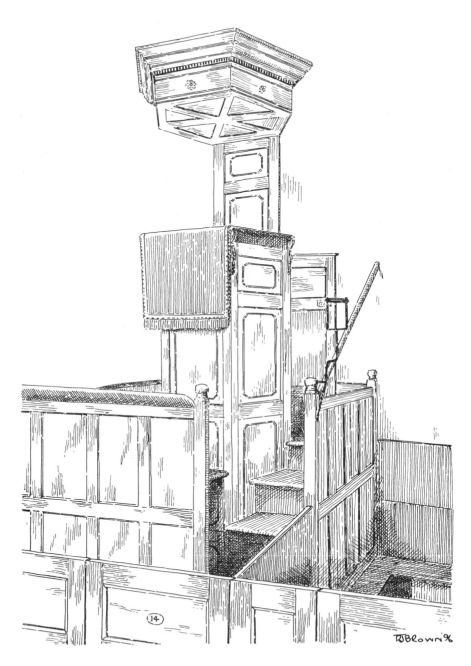

160   Eighteenth-century three-decker pulpit with eighteenth-century fittings
at Gislingham, Suffolk

Hour-glasses were either attached to the pulpit or fixed on an adjacent wall within the view of the preacher. Many of those that survive are simple, wrought-iron, utilitarian affairs, but a few show the blacksmith's art to the full. The two most elaborate are in Berkshire. The one at Binfield has a central stem supporting alternating branches, some bearing oak leaves and acorns, others shields and animals; the whole is painted and dated 1629. The hour-glass at Hurst, which is similar and has the date 1636, carries on the stem of the bracket the words 'As this glass runneth so man's life passeth'.

Dated examples are rare. The earliest is at Leigh in Kent (161) and its year is shown as 1597, although the 9 is a modern insertion. Another dated example – at Cliffe, also in Kent – is dated 1636. There are two unusual examples in Devon, at Pilton and nearby

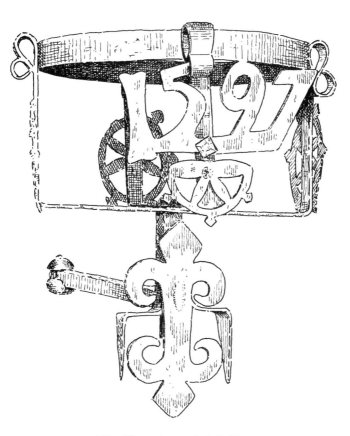

161   Hour-glass at Leigh, Kent

Tawstock, which are obviously the work of the same man; the brackets are of sheet-iron cut to the shape of a human arm with the glass in the hand. One of the largest examples is at Shipton Sollars, Gloucestershire, where the glass is 20" high and 6" across. At Earl Stonham in Suffolk no fewer than four glasses have survived, each of a different size. Of the some 120 hour-glass stands that survive, very few retain their original glass; Haversham, Buckinghamshire, has one which is from the eighteenth century. Others are to be found at Colby in Norfolk, Bloxworth in Dorset, Compton Bassett in Wiltshire and Stoke sub Hamdon in Somerset.

Lecterns

In the Middle Ages it was customary to have a desk or lectern in the chancel to hold the Bible. It stood in the middle of the chancel and moved to a position north of the High Altar for the reading of the Gospel during the Mass. After the Reformation it was normal for the lectern to be positioned in the body of the church in the place where it is found today, in the nave just west of the chancel arch.

The earliest form of lectern was a movable wooden reading desk about four feet high supported by a slender standard. A few still survive from the fourteenth century. Those at Lenham, Kent and Bury, Cambridgeshire, are single desks with one sloping side. Those at Hawstead and Blythburgh in Suffolk, which date from around 1450, and another fifteenth-century lectern at Shipdham in Norfolk, are double desks, having two sloping sides. The one at Detling in Kent (162), which dates from around 1320, is four-sided and has geometrical patterns.

The majority of medieval lecterns are, however, in the form of an eagle supported on a pillar, its spread wings supporting the open Bible. The eagle symbolized the carrying of the Gospel to the four corners of the earth, and the bird which soared highest and was therefore nearest to Heaven. Many of these lecterns have three animals at the base, symbolizing the evil powers conquered by the Word of God.

A variety of materials were used, brass and wood being the most common (although many brass lecterns were melted down to 'make pots and basins for new fonts'). Around forty brass and twenty wooden medieval lecterns are left in England. Brass examples are

162   Late fifteenth-century lectern at Detling, Kent

163 Fifteenth-century oak lectern at Leverington, Cambridgeshire

to be found at Cavendish in Suffolk and Long Sutton in Somerset, and wooden ones at Leverington in Cambridgeshire (163), Astbury in Cheshire and East Brent in Somerset; there is also a remarkably vigorous one at Bigbury in Devon.

Stone gospel lecterns are rare in our country churches; when they do occur they are simple in character and usually set in the north wall of the chancel. Most of them are in Derbyshire – for example at Chaddesden, Crich, Etwall, Mickleover, Taddington and Spondon. Elsewhere they occur at Chipping Warden in Northamptonshire, Roos in East Riding of Yorkshire and Walsoken in Norfolk. Stone desks are very rare; two survive in Worcestershire at Norton and Crowle, and there is another later and plainer one at Chesterblade, Somerset.

Benches and Pews

Until the fifteenth century churches provided virtually no seating for their congregations. The worshippers stood, when not actually kneeling.

Stone seats around the walls would have sufficed for the aged and infirm, (and were probably much more numerous in early churches than would appear from their surviving remains today – though, even so, such seats are more frequent than is usually supposed). The earliest churches in Cornwall seem always to have had stone benches around the walls, like those at the oratory of St Piran's and in the south transept of Tintagel. Elsewhere, too, stone seating was often provided against the side walls – at Rickinghall in Suffolk this runs the entire length of the north and south walls of the nave; Ufford in Cambridgeshire and Cotterstock in Northamptonshire have stone seats around the aisles; and at Chipstead in Surrey and Warmington in Northamptonshire there are seats in the chancel walls. Acton, Cheshire, is remarkable in that the stone seating runs all round both church and chancel. A few churches have stone seats encircling one or more piers (for example, Baumber, Moulton and Skirberk, all in Lincolnshire), and in a few instances they surround all the piers, as at Snettisham and South Creake in Norfolk and Sutton Bonington in Nottinghamshire (164). At Bratton, Wiltshire, there are seats around the piers of the central tower.

164   Stone seat at Sutton Bonington, Nottinghamshire

It was not until the middle of the thirteenth century, when sermons began to play a greater part in the service, that benches began to appear. The earliest that survive appear to be those at Dunsfold, Surrey (165), which are believed to date from 1270. Across the border in West Sussex, those at Didling and Loxwood are of a slightly later date (probably of the reign of Edward I), and the benches at Clapton-in-Gordano in Somerset are of similar date. These early benches are rude and low with carved ends.

Benches did not become general until the fifteenth or early sixteenth centuries, and even then they rarely filled the entire church. The blocks of seating were always arranged so as to leave ample passage-ways – particularly at the east end of the nave, where it was often necessary to leave a clear space of seven to ten feet to allow room for the side altars against the rood-screen. In a number of the larger churches of East Anglia, such as Blythburgh and Salle, there was never any seating at the west end of the nave, which was occupied only by the font. Many of these early benches were very uncomfortable, having no more than a plank for the seat and perhaps a single bar for a back support.

165   Late thirteenth-century benches at Dunsfold, Surrey

In East Anglia the older seats were often backless, though few have been allowed to remain in this condition. The most perfect remaining examples are at Icklingham All Saints in Suffolk and Cawston in Norfolk (166), both of which have happily remained in their original condition. At Blythburgh, Suffolk, and Ranworth, Norfolk, clumsy backs have been added to suit modern ideas of comfort. When backs were provided in East Anglia, they were generally low compared with those in other parts of the country. At East Winch, Norfolk, the benches have a stout moulded back rail with a thin panel housed into its undersurface and a plinth at the bottom; at South Creake, in the same county, muntins were provided to divide the panel. A favourite practice in Norfolk was to decorate the seat-back by piercing it with tracery; the examples in the churches at Harpley, Wiggenhall St Mary the Virgin and

166 Backless benches at Cawston, Norfolk

Wiggenhall St Germans are outstanding. In Suffolk the backs were often cut from a single-width board, beautifully moulded and carved with running patterns of tracery.

In the Midlands the backs were generally a little higher and framed with either a rail and a thin horizontal panel housed into or fixed to the back of the seat, or a rail with wide vertical boarding running down to the floor. The fronts and backs of each block were usually panelled with moulded muntins, and the head of each panel was often traceried – as at Ashby St Ledgers, Northamptonshire – or carved with linenfold patterns.

The backs of benches in the West Country resemble those of the Midlands in general construction. The boarding is almost always vertical, running down to the floor, but the fronts and backs are treated differently. In Somerset the front and backs are framed up, divided with very wide muntins (often with sunken tracery or foliage, as at Crowcombe and Broomfield) and the panels similarly carved. In Devon and Cornwall the backs are boarded and applied decoration added, consisting of a band of tracery at the top, a plinth and muntins between – as at Braunton and Frithelstock.

Book ledges were generally provided, some five or six inches wide and of the same thickness as the seat, but they never sloped, as in the post-Reformation pews. Sometimes seat and ledge were at the same level but generally the ledge was a little higher, about two feet from the floor.

Perhaps the most interesting feature of medieval benching is the design of the bench-ends, and it is these more than anything else that tend to affect the whole composition. There are two distinct types: those with square heads and those with shaped heads. They are of equal antiquity, the shaped ones being found mainly in East Anglia and generally square-headed ones in the south-west; in the central area both types are to be found.

Benches with square-headed ends can be divided into two sub-types: those in which the ends are framed-up with stiles, rails and panel, and those made out of the solid. The framed-up ends are generally to be found in the Midlands, and the benches at Cassington in Oxfordshire are probably the earliest example – they have been assigned to around 1300. At their simplest, the panels are left undecorated, with the stiles and rails moulded, as at Send in Surrey and Minster Lovell and Great Milton in Oxfordshire. Sometimes little buttresses were added to the stiles, a feature that can be seen at Byfield (167) and Ashby St Ledgers in Northamptonshire, Iron Acton in Gloucestershire and Hardmead in Buckinghamshire. This type was so popular that it can be found elsewhere: in Cambridgeshire (Horningsea), in Essex (Great Waltham) and in West Sussex (Climping). Generally, however, the panels were decorated with applied tracery, and sometimes the panel would be divided into two, with the tracery repeated on both halves – as at Eynsham, Oxfordshire. Linenfold panelling was sometimes used in the late fifteenth and early sixteenth centuries as at North Crawley, Great Hampden and Hillesden in Buckinghamshire and Iron Acton in Gloucestershire. At Tadmarton, Oxfordshire, the panel is framed on to a top rail and sill without stiles.

Solid bench ends with square heads are almost always carved. Sunken tracery is by far the most common form of decoration and can be found throughout the country. In the north there are good examples to be found at Hemingbrough in North Yorkshire and Stow in Lincolnshire. The carving in the midlands was rarely elaborate, and tracery was again the main form of decoration, but more elaborate examples are to be found, as at Kidlington, Oxfordshire. At Warkworth in Northamptonshire the bench ends have nicely carved figures representing the *Annunciation* and donors.

It is in the south-west, though, that most of these square-headed solid bench ends are to be found. Somerset and Devon have over a thousand each, while Cornwall has several hundred, and the considerable variety, artistry and liveliness of the carving still afford as much pleasure today as they must have done to past church-goers.

Tracery was a common form of decoration, particularly in south Devon, where it is generally in two tiers – as at Ashton, Plymtree, Kenn and Dunchideock. In Somerset, in the early fifteenth century, rectilinear tracery was used (as at Leigh upon Mendip and Cheddar), which changed somewhat later to a square-topped panel with tracery below. Tracery of a Flamboyant type, like that at Milverton in Somerset and Northlew in Devon is also fairly common. In north Devon, Cornwall and Somerset the panels were often carved with initials, shields, figures of saints and symbols of the Passion, as well as tracery and foliage. The Italian influence that brought early Renaissance forms arrived late in the south-west, and in many churches the old types continued unchanged; at Braunton, where the number of benches was increased six times between 1560 and 1593, the bench-ends include the usual instruments of the Passion, shields,

167   Bench-ends at Byfield, Northamptonshire

initials and some whole figures, but no Renaissance details.

There are, of course, local variations. In west Somerset, around the Quantock Hills, an uncommonly attractive type evolved in which the entire surface is covered with free-flowing foliage carvings; those at Broomfield and Crowcombe are truly remarkable. A feature peculiar to the extreme south-west is the trail of foliage around each bench end. Early benches – for instance, those at Kenn, Devon – lack this feature and have a simple moulding, but later, towards the middle of the fifteenth century, a huge twisted scroll of foliage was frequently employed.

A feature of many bench ends in the south-west is carving that depicts figures and objects of a secular rather than a religious nature. Altarnun in Cornwall has a large and interesting collection, including sheep grazing, a piper, a sword-dancer, a jester and a fiddler. Barwick in Somerset has a man holding up the date 1533, another man shooting a bird, a fox trotting off with a goose, and dogs hunting a rabbit. Mermaids were frequently carved (at Zennor in Cornwall and Down St Mary in Devon, for example) as were ships (St Winnow in Cornwall, East Budleigh in Devon and Bishops Lydeard in Somerset), obviously reflecting the importance of the sea to many in the south-west.

A remarkable series of bench-ends at Brent Knoll in Somerset shows the legend of Reynard the Fox. On one the fox is disguised as a mitred abbot, and looking up at him are three pigs in coats, geese and birds. Successive bench-ends show the fox stripped, put in the stocks and finally hanged by the triumphant geese all pulling on the rope. The carving is not of the highest quality, but it is full of vitality.

The earliest attempts to shape the top of bench-ends occurred in the thirteenth century. There is a good example at Dunsfold in Surrey, where the tops are in the shape of hollow curves between two scrolls, although the general rectangular shape is retained. At Kilmersdon in Somerset there are benches of another early type, in which almost the entire bench-end above the seat is cut away exposing the end of the seat-back but leaving a shaped elbow of sorts; a similar arrangement can be found at Clapton-in-Gordano, also in Somerset. Mark in the same county has a few benches, also of late thirteenth-century date, in which the elbows sweep up to a circular knob showing for the first time the vestige of a poppyhead. The poppyhead, which became the almost universal method of terminating these shaped bench-ends, resembles a kind of three-dimensional *fleur-de-lis* and derives its name, via the French, from the Latin *puppes*, meaning a curved poop or sometimes figure-head of a ship.

The problem with those bench-ends that have a shaped top is that the back is not in the centre of the bench end, and the end is rarely symmetrical, which is visually unpleasing. Several methods were used to overcome this difficulty. Sometimes it was avoided by not starting the shaping until the top of the back was passed, as at Westhall in Suffolk and Lowick in Northamptonshire. This, however, produced an unduly tall bench end, and in Lincolnshire the method was sometimes adapted by cutting away part of the end to form a sweeping elbow, though still covering the seat end. Sometimes the elbows were finished with a curly knob as at Coates by Stow (168).

168   Bench-ends at Coates by Stow, Lincolnshire

In Norfolk delightful carvings of beasts and animals sliding down the elbow are a common and effective ornament (170). Another device which produced excellent results, was to form a small buttress attached to the bench-end to take the end of the seat.

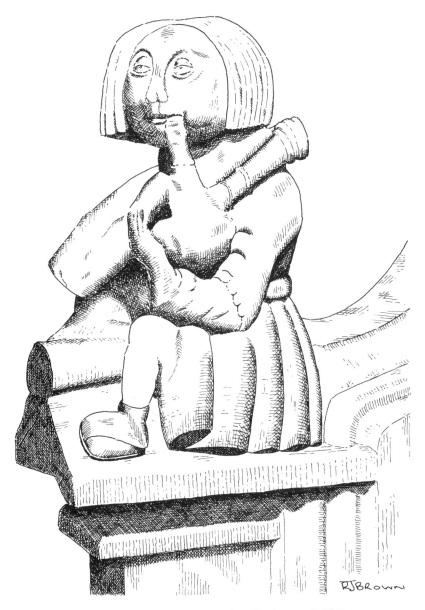

169   Figure on bench-end at Honington, Suffolk

The buttress is frequently finished with delightful carvings of human figures (169), animals, monsters and birds. This type is very common in East Anglia; Fressingfield, Woolpit, Mendlesham and Dennington, all in Suffolk, have admirable examples. Sometimes the buttress is applied to both sides of the bench-ends to produce a symmetrical end. This can be seen at Wilby, Athelington and Ufford in Suffolk and on the magnificent bench ends of the Wiggenhalls in Norfolk. The poppyhead was, in some instances, replaced by a grotesque head, as at Ranworth and Cley next the Sea in Norfolk, while at Earl Stonham in Suffolk there is a strange poppyhead with three grotesque heads. In others poppyheads were replaced by figures or animals; at Withersfield, Suffolk, there are two remarkable examples, one is St Michael weighing souls, the other St George slaying the dragon. In the same county, at Blythburgh (171), some of the poppyheads represent the vices, while others depict the seasons.

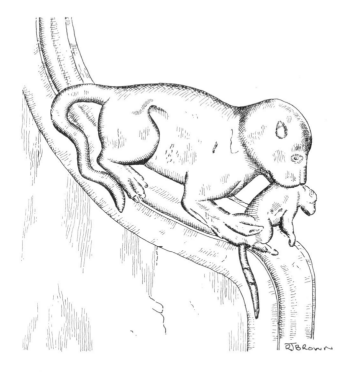

170   Cat with kitten carved on bench-end at Upper Sheringham, Norfolk

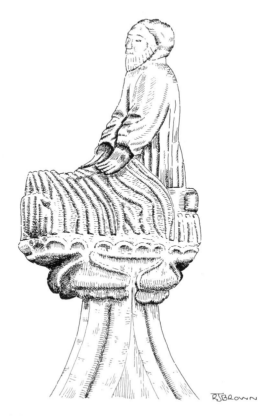

171   Poppyhead depicting sloth. One of the carvings of the Seven Deadly Sins
at Blythburgh, Suffolk

In East Anglia the faces of the bench-ends were often plain, but in
many instances they are richly carved with tracery and figures like
those in the south-west. Those at Athelington, Fressingfield, Woolpit
and Dennington are amongst the best in Suffolk – and the benches of
Wiggenhall St Mary the Virgin in Norfolk are regarded as some of the
finest and most complete sets in England. Beneath the poppyhead, on
the buttresses, are two seated figures with a large figure on a pedestal
under a canopy in the end itself. A mile or so away across the Ouse at
Wiggenhall St Germans there is a very similar collection of twenty-
five benches depicting the Seven Deadly Sins.

It was usual for bench ends to be framed into a continuous kerb
that surrounded the entire block. The purpose of this high and
sometimes richly moulded upstand was not only to add rigidity to
the benches but probably also to contain the straw and rushes that

used to be strewn on the floor beneath the seats, just as they used to be strewn on the floors of domestic buildings. In some cases wooden floors have been constructed level with the tops of these kerbs, making it warmer underfoot, but these are later additions.

The destruction of benches over the centuries has been widespread, but they did not fall victim only to the Puritans but rather more to the dictation of fashion. Towards the end of the seventeenth century enclosed box pews with high backs gradually replaced the low-backed medieval benches. Much was lost, too, during the restorations of the nineteenth century, when the Georgian box pews were themselves replaced by seating in the Gothic tradition. Although some of the replacements were good, many were commonplace and carried out not in the traditional material of oak but in pitchpine. Lastly, in recent years, churches all over the country have removed some, if not all, of their fixed seating and substituted chairs, which gives a temporary look.

Box Pews

The term 'pew' or 'peu' originally meant an elevated place or seat (from the French *puie*, or balcony), and so came to be applied to seats or enclosures in churches for persons of dignity or officials. Later, the word pew was assigned exclusively to an enclosed seat, and references in documents make it quite clear that pews were not general seating or benches. As early as the first quarter of the fifteenth century there are references to pews allocated to particular people, and by the second half of the century they appear to have had a door fitted.

It was not, however, until the late seventeenth and early eighteenth centuries that box pews came into favour in our country churches, replacing the medieval benches. Some, like those at Old Dilton in Wiltshire, are built on the original medieval benches. At first these pews were large and tall and, because of their appearance, were familiarly known as 'horse-boxes'. These high box pews were made for the gentry and often had seats on two or three sides, plus a door from the aisle, which helped to keep out draughts and ensure privacy for the occupants. So popular were these pews that by the eighteenth century smaller, lower box pews were built for the rest of the congregation, and the medieval benches were relegated to the back of the nave and aisles.

Early box pews are generally oak panelled, sometimes with strapwork or other decoration typical of the period. Those at Croscombe in Somerset, the ends and doors panelled and filled with tracery, are particularly fine and probably date from the beginning of the seventeenth century. Later box pews were often of pine, simply framed with the panels perhaps raised.

Pew rents were considered a legitimate source of church income. The pews were allocated by the churchwardens to various members of the parish, and in some churches (for instance West Chiltington in West Sussex) the names of the families were painted on the pews. At Clodock, Herefordshire, the pews bear the initials of their early occupants, while those at Shermanbury, West Sussex, have farm names on them. Often the pews were arranged to focus on the pulpit, which was sometimes sited part-way down the nave on one side; the seats east of it then faced west and away from the altar, which had become less significant as the Communion service was held less often.

In many medieval churches the box pews were destroyed in the 1830s when a new movement inspired by Augustus Welby Pugin, followed by John Newman's Oxford Movement, swept much of the eighteenth-century church furniture away. The reformers' vision was to revert to the truly Gothic church, and, since eighteenth-century church interiors were regarded as anathema, the box pews were removed and replaced by benches inspired by those of the Middle Ages. At the same time the system of pew rents was abolished. In spite of this, many medieval churches did retain their eighteenth-century fittings, and as many relatively unspoilt Georgian church interiors survived, so box pews are still fairly common.

Family Pews

The sixteenth century saw the introduction of the private pew. After the Reformation, when chantries were abolished, the Lord of the Manor retained the chantry space. In some instances the parclose screen was retained or adapted and the former chantry chapel converted into a family pew, as at Lavenham and Kedington in Suffolk. At Wensley, North Yorkshire, a ceiling with pendants was added and a Renaissance screen was placed within the older one, the whole painted white and partly gilded and the shields blazoned.

Early examples, like the splendid Elizabethan example at Holcombe Rogus in Devon, were open to the roof. Generally, though, family pews had a canopy, rather like a four-poster bed;

that at Tawstock in Devon is a very remarkable object – small, with two solid back panels and a miniature roof with rosettes – and probably dates from before 1550. Others of note, are Rycote in Oxfordshire and Stokesay in Shropshire; the latter is Jacobean in character, though no doubt dating from around 1660, after the rebuilding of the church in 1654.

Later such pews were often elevated – as at Tibenham in Norfolk, where the Buxton family pew, seating some 20 people, was erected in 1635 after permission had been granted by Archbishop Laud. This massive structure is housed in the end of the south aisle, right under the roof, and has its own staircase. There are similar elevated pews at Warbleton in East Sussex (set in the middle of the north aisle and accessed by a staircase in the aisle) and Croft in North Yorkshire (172) – a remarkable eighteenth-century family pew reached by a balustraded staircase.

172   Family pew at Croft, North Yorkshire

Later still the private pew developed into a cosy room, with comfortable upholstered chairs, padded benches, table, carpet, fireplace and a separate entrance from the big house. One of the most perfect surviving examples is at Gatton in Surrey. Fireplaces may also be seen at Heveningham in Suffolk, Colebrooke in Devon and Cottesbrooke in Northamptonshire. At Northorpe, Lincolnshire, the pew belonging to the Hall even had its own dog kennel – known as the Hall Dog Pew. At Easton in Suffolk canopied and screened pews, comfortably furnished, were built within the sanctuary on either side of the altar. At the same time the park wall was extended up to the west tower and enclosed the north porch, so as to give private access to the church from the big house.

Galleries

Church galleries (other than those on rood-screens or elsewhere in our larger churches and used for minstrelsy) existed in a few village churches before the Reformation. Three interesting examples from the early sixteenth century can be found in the Norfolk churches of Worstead, Cawston and Salle; all are situated within the tower. Several other towers in East Anglia no longer have their galleries, but their construction shows that they once had them; there are newel staircases with doorways to give access to such galleries on a level with the base of their west windows. One such church is Repps, Norfolk. These galleries are generally referred to as bell-ringers' galleries.

However, most west galleries date from after the Reformation, when the rood-loft was destroyed, and the choir, the village orchestra and the organ (if any) were moved to a purpose-built gallery at the west end of the church (the congregation turning round to face them during the psalms). The village orchestra and choir were a feature of most village churches until the middle of the nineteenth century, when the choirs were moved to the chancel. Sadly, many west galleries were swept away during the restorations of the nineteenth century, but there are still good examples to be seen. One of the earliest dated west galleries, of 1601, is at Worth in West Sussex. There is another attractive example, a low three-sided affair with the typical turned balusters of the period, at Dorney in Buckinghamshire. One of the finest occurs at the Dorset church of

Puddletown, which is dated 1635. There is another of the same date at East Brent, Somerset, and the finest gallery left in Shropshire, at Moreton Say, is dated 1634. In Gloucestershire there is a gallery at Bishop's Cleeve, while at Newdigate in Surrey the gallery carries the date 1627, the front being set up under the tower.

There are also some notable examples from the eighteenth century. That at Selworthy in Somerset, dated 1750 and one of the most elaborate, is a large, heavy classical piece with Doric pilasters carrying a metope frieze. There are many others less elaborate and perhaps more fitted to a village church.

In the eighteenth century additional galleries began to be inserted over the aisles in many old churches, so as to increase their seating capacity. In many new churches of this period integral galleries were provided on the north, south and west walls. The number increased in the nineteenth century to accommodate the larger congregations of the period. These side galleries have generally been removed by the Victorian restorers, for they detracted from the architectural character and were against the spirit of the Gothic revival of the period. Few now remain, though there is one fine example at Cameley in Somerset, where the side galleries are above the nave seating. At Hardingham, Norfolk, there is a board commemorating the construction in 1843 of a gallery to provide 143 seats – all of which were to be free, compared with the previous arrangement of 200 seats of which only 31 were free. The gallery, like the whole system of pew rents, has now gone.

Although galleries are found mainly at the west end of the nave, at Weston-in-Gordano in Somerset there is a small gallery above the doorway to the south porch, with a staircase giving access to it; there are traces of the same arrangement at the neighbouring churches of Clapton-in-Gordano, Kingston Seymour and Wraxall and at Westbury-on-Trym, Bristol. In the case of Westbury-on-Trym, there is a chamber above the gallery; it is believed these porch galleries were to accommodate the choristers who sang the *Gloria, laus et honor* on Palm Sunday.

10 Sepulchral Monuments

Commemorating the dead has always been among our deepest desires, and there can be few churches in England that do not contain a tomb or monument of some kind. For over five centuries English craftsmen have devoted much of their finest efforts to these works, and nowhere outside the great houses can such work be seen in such quantity. So vast is the subject, and so various in every period, that it can only be treated very cursorily here. Needless to say, we owe a great deal of our knowledge of English medieval dress and armour, not to mention heraldry and genealogy, to surviving medieval tombs and effigies.

Tombs, Effigies and Monuments

In the twelfth and early thirteenth centuries burials inside the church were few in number, the privilege being reserved for the bodies of the founders or benefactors. Their tombs were generally recessed under low arches in the north wall of the chantry, or were built into the outside of the church wall, as at Great Brington in Northamptonshire and Great Casterton in Rutland. Such recessed tombs, normally with a semi-circular or pointed arch above, would at one time have included an effigy, though not all do so now.

In the Middle Ages only the wealthy were buried in solid stone coffins. These were made by carving a coffin shape out of a block of stone, cutting off the top to form a lid and hacking out the centre. At first these coffins were buried in the churchyard so the top was at ground level, and the stone coffin lid was placed over it; eventually some were buried within the church, their lids forming part of the church floor, which was otherwise made of beaten earth. These early slabs usually bore the form of a Latin cross incised in the face of the slab – often with an additional symbol, such as a crosier, chalice, sword or key, to identify the deceased's calling or profession. They usually lacked inscriptions, and so are difficult to date; the style of the ornament and the various treatments of the cross have to be relied on to provide some clue as to the age. Before about 1275 the slabs were usually coffin-shaped, wider at the head than the foot, and the majority were flat, (although a few in the twelfth century were given coped tops); after this date they were generally rectangular. It is difficult to tell whether these slabs were in fact coffin-lids or flat sepulchral slabs which might or might not have been placed over a coffin (the body may well have been buried in the churchyard).

Later, these slabs were incised with a figure representing the deceased. The earliest examples of this are the fragment of a naked figure at Shillingstone in Dorset (around 1200) and a knight of around 1225 at Sollers Hope in Herefordshire. These incised slabs were not widely employed until the fifteenth and sixteenth centuries, a period from which some hundreds survive, some of them intact but many only in fragmentary form. Next the complete effigy appeared, carved flat and in low relief, before finally effigies in full relief developed. Initially they were still placed in the church floor; this was soon found to be impractical, so the effigy and its slab were placed at or nearly at floor level but in a low recess cut in the church wall. Occasionally the recess was elaborately decorated with cusps, finials and heraldry.

In the second half of the thirteenth century the semi-effigial figure, which combined the functions of coffin-lid and effigy, made an appearance. At first the head and shoulders was carved in relief above a cross (as at Bitton, Gloucestershire), then it was carved as though lying in a recess in the tomb slab (as at Lyddington, Rutland), and later a similar recess was carved for the feet (as at Elford, Staffordshire) to complete the illusion of a coffin-lid parts of which had been cut away to reveal the effigy it contained. Sometimes the space between the bust and feet was filled in with a carved sword, shield and helm. Fine examples of this can be seen at East Gilling, North Yorkshire, and Staunton, Nottinghamshire.

At South Stoke in Lincolnshire (173), a married couple is depicted as though at prayer in bed, the centre of the effigies being covered by a 'blanket'. At Stoke Rochford the feet of the effigies are exposed, but at Careby, also in Lincolnshire, the feet are covered. These semi-effigial figures remained fashionable until around the middle of the fourteenth century.

In the thirteenth century the rectangular sepulchral slab developed into the tomb-chest. The sides were decorated either with traceried panels or a series of quatrefoils enclosing the armorial bearings of the deceased or given a series of canopied niches with delightful diminutive figures, known as weepers. These weepers may represent either members of the family or angels or saints – the angels are feathered or, more commonly, dressed in albs (white vestments reaching the feet) and often carry shields (174). Tomb-chests could be free-standing within the body of the church, in which case they might be given a full canopy rather like a four-poster bed. More often, however, they were placed against the wall and perhaps given a backplate or, more likely, set in a recess within the wall under an arched canopy.

These tombs were usually surmounted by an effigy, and before the Reformation its pose was generally pious and humble: lying

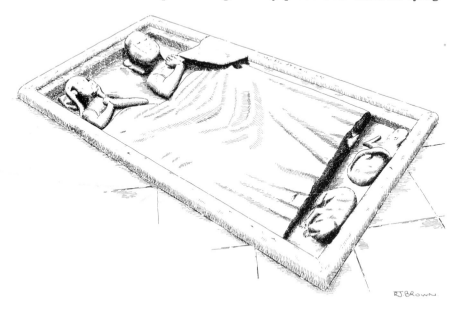

173   Tomb at Stoke Rochford, Lincolnshire

174   Weepers on de Roos tomb at Bottesford, Leicestershire

with the hands either folded on the breast or held together in prayer. Sometimes the effigies' hands, instead of being held up in prayer, would hold out the deceased's heart as an offering to God – as in the cases of the knight at Wickhampton in Norfolk and a lady at Denham in Suffolk, both of late thirteenth-century date. Another early feature is the use of a small canopy of tabernacle over the head of the recumbent figure.

Effigies were usually life-size, representing the deceased in the prime of life, and a great deal can be learned from them about the costumes of the medieval period – the armour of knights, the dress and hair-style of civilians or ladies' dresses and head-dresses. The earliest effigies are of ecclesiastics, but the majority of them represent knights, sometimes with their wives, which testifies to the growing power of the military. At one time the pose of the knight on the tomb was thought to have a meaning: if the legs were crossed, it denoted that he had been a Crusader; if he had a lion at his feet, he had died in battle, whereas a hound at his feet meant he had died in bed. All these oft-repeated legends have been disproved, and it appears that these differences of pose were simply due to changes in fashion. The straight-leg pose appeared around 1200, but around about the middle of the thirteenth century effigies with crossed legs appeared and lasted for roughly a hundred years before the straight-leg style reappeared.

Pre-Reformation tombs and effigies were mostly made of stone, wood or alabaster. During the thirteenth century and at the beginning of the fourteenth, tombs and effigies were carved from Purbeck marble: a dun-coloured, shelly, easily worked limestone that was capable of being highly polished. The desire for polychrome and to pick out details of the effigy in gesso, gilt and colour led to the abandonment of Purbeck marble for wood and freestone. Most wooden effigies date from between 1250 and 1350, although there was a brief revival in the fifteenth and sixteenth centuries after the best veins of alabaster had been worked out. There are good examples of wooden effigies from the fifteenth century at Wingfield in Suffolk, and from the sixteenth century at Slindon in West Sussex and Goudhurst in Kent (the last is remarkable for the colour and ornamentation on Sir Alexander Culpeper's armour). In all there are about eighty wooden effigies still in existence, of which ten are in Essex (175).

A number of freestones were used and can be divided into three main groups. Carvers in the south used various midland sandstones, Barnack oolite, Reigate sandstone and Petworth or Sussex marble; northern carvers used Tadcaster limestone from North

175　Oak effigy of knight at Little Horkesley, Essex

Yorkshire and Ancaster oolite from Lincolnshire; those in the south-west used oolite from Doulting (near Wells) and Dundry (near Bristol), Beer stone, clunch and Chilmark limestone. The design and quality of the work depended greatly on the nature of the stone. These materials continued in use until the close of the medieval period, although from 1350 alabaster largely displaced them.

Alabaster is a sulphate of lime (also called gypsum) found in abundance in the red marl of the upper Keuper beds in Staffordshire and Derbyshire and also at Buttercrambe in North Yorkshire. It was first used for effigies at the beginning of the fourteenth century (one at Hanbury, Staffordshire, dates from around 1300). It came into general use in the middle of the fourteenth century and continued in favour for some two hundred years; even then it remained in use, although to a lesser extent, until well into the seventeenth century. So expert did the craftsmen become that an extensive export market was established with France, Spain and Germany.

No matter what their material, effigies and tombs were at first richly decorated, but little evidence of this is now to be seen. They first suffered at the hands of the Puritans in the seventeenth century, when most were whitewashed, but even greater indignity was inflicted on them by nineteenth-century restorers, who, when not actually destroying the tombs, removed not only the whitewash but the coloured decoration beneath as well.

Gesso was used throughout the medieval period, and in the thirteenth and fourteenth centuries it was used on both wooden and freestone effigies to provide the smooth surface necessary to take painted decoration. It was also used on alabaster, although the fine quality of this material, which could be delicately worked, meant that it was only used for the very finest of details. Sadly very little gesso remains today.

In the sixteenth century a new material appeared: terracotta, an earthenware that was moulded or cast before firing and then left unglazed. Tombs of this material, which may have been introduced from Flanders, are to be found mainly in the eastern counties, and it is likely either that the material was moulded in Flanders or Flemish artists were brought to England. One of the finest terracotta tombs is the one at Layer Marney in Essex, dating from 1523. With the development of the iron-workings in the Weald, and later in Shropshire and Herefordshire, cast iron monuments also began to appear.

In medieval times, when the corpse or funeral effigy of an important individual was taken into the church, the coffin was often placed under a temporary gabled framework that supported the pall and also had sockets to hold the candles. This framework was known as a herse or hearse (it was not until about 1670 that the word took on its modern meaning of a carriage for conveying the corpse). Later, permanent herses, generally made of iron, were erected over the tombs of distinguished people, so that candles could be lit on the anniversary of their death. The finest is in a small church at West Tanfield, North Yorkshire, and surmounts the 1385 tomb of Sir John Marmion and his wife. The framework is of light construction, with standards at each corner surmounted by sconces; the side and top bars are battlemented, and the latter hold three more sconces.

Much more common was the provision of rails or grates around the tomb. These became popular in the latter half of the fourteenth century and consisted of top and bottom rails with connecting bars that were spaced closely enough to afford no foothold. The decoration was confined to the standards and perhaps an embattled top bar. Grates were produced in great numbers and varied from simple railings without any form of decoration to ones that were very richly ornamented. Grates continued to be produced until well into the sixteenth century. Sadly many have been destroyed during the last two hundred years or so, especially during the period of the Gothic revival; even at Westminster Abbey most were removed by the Dean and Chapter in 1822.

After the Reformation, the changing religious idiom and increasing Renaissance influence, brought changes in effigies. The recumbent attitude continued throughout the sixteenth and seventeenth centuries, but figures appeared in a variety of less devotional poses – in one of the most popular the effigy reclined on its side, resting on the elbows with the head supported on one hand. Other figures were shown seated, standing or kneeling, sometimes at a prayer desk; more usually, husband and wife knelt facing one another across a prayer desk, with their children kneeling behind them – usually the sons behind the husband, the daughters behind the wife. In some cases the sides of the tomb would be filled with numerous children (sometimes a child held a skull, to indicate that he or she had already died). There was also a deepening obsession with death, which was often expressed in the depiction of various symbolic reminders of death: skulls, skeletons and bones, scythes and coffins (obelisks signified eternity). Sometimes the monument had two effigies: one of the deceased in their prime, with another of a cadaver below it.

Although tomb-chests and effigies continued through the Stuart period and beyond, the wall-monument, either standing or hanging became increasingly popular. The standard type showed the husband and wife facing one another across a prayer desk with their children behind them. Later, standing wall-monuments began to appear without effigies, sometimes with Corinthian columns supporting a canopy. Another type of seventeenth-century hanging wall-monument was the frontal demi-figure (half-length figure of man or woman) often depicted in an oval niche or 'revealed' by cherubs holding back curtains. Later the demi-figure was replaced with a bust, again often in an oval niche or occasionally on a marble sarcophagus. The monuments of the period were often immense (particularly those of the first quarter of the seventeenth century), lavishly coloured and decorated with numerous coats-of-arms.

By the end of the century the highly coloured alabaster monuments were giving way to monuments made of imported black and white marble. Wall-monuments continued to increase in popularity, and their designs often showed Classical influences. Many of the monuments of this period are so large that they dominate the village churches that contain them. The sculpture, in most cases, is excellent, but there is a general lack of reverence; figures are now often depicted standing: a pose that does not convey much humility and typifies the self-satisfaction of the age. They were often attired in Classical costume with wigs, and their epitaphs habitually described the innumerable virtues of the deceased in the most pompous and verbose language.

Despite the undoubted importance of the grander eighteenth-century monuments they are by no means the most common, for hanging wall-monuments were far more numerous. Many of these showed busts or medallions of the deceased, and many others included allegorical figures, cherubs or urns. The majority, however, consisted merely of an inscription in an ornamental setting or frame; few village churches lack examples of this type.

Cartouche tablets also became popular in the eighteenth century and are to be found in many of our churches. These wall-monuments were usually of marble and designed to look like a scroll – a sheet of paper with the sides curled – containing an inscription in the centre, and perhaps a coat-of-arms and a crest above.

Heart-shrines

Heart-shrines are rarities that relate to the medieval custom of piecemeal interment – especially when death occurred abroad. For instance, when a knight died on campaign abroad it was impossible to convey the body home; in this case, although the body was laid to rest in a foreign land, the heart was returned to the knight's own village church for burial. Perhaps the finest of these rare heart-shrines is in the little church at Coberley, Gloucestershire, where an oval plaque in the sanctuary contains a bas-relief of a knight in chain armour with mailed hands holding an extra-large heart; it is believed to represent Sir Giles de Berkeley, who died in 1295. Another, at Leybourne church in Kent, contains the heart of Sir Roger de Leybourne who died in 1271 on the final Crusade. The shrine is a small traceried recess of two lights, in the base of which stand two caskets one containing Sir Roger's heart. A different type of heart-shrine, in which two hands hold a heart aloft, is to be found in Yaxley, Cambridgeshire (176); in this case a wooden box containing the remains of a heart, thought to be Abbot William Yaxley's, was found in 1842 in a cavity behind the monument and is now displayed in a nearby alcove. Similar heart-shrines exist at Careby, Lincolnshire, and Bredon, Worcestershire. Another type, usually from the early fourteenth century, consists of a miniature effigy, recumbent and holding a heart in his hand; there are examples at Adwell in Oxfordshire and Mappowder in Dorset.

Memorial Brasses

An alternative to an effigy carved in stone or wood as a memorial was an engraved plate of latten, today popularly known as a brass. It is estimated that around two thousand brasses still remain, (though most have suffered some damage), but these represent only

176   Heart shrine at Yaxley, Cambridgeshire

a fraction of the number that once existed. Brasses suffered whole-sale destruction during the Dissolution and Reformation and the upheavals that followed, because of the value of their metal. In many churches one can see the recess in the stone from which a former brass has been taken. Even so, there are many more in England than the rest of Europe put together.

Latten (an alloy of roughly two-thirds copper and one-third zinc with small amounts of lead and tin, although the exact proportions varied) was first imported into England, mainly from Cologne and the Low Countries, in the latter part of the thirteenth century. It was cast into slabs and subsequently beaten into plates of variable thickness. It seems that there must have been some limit on the size of plate, for most large brasses consist of several pieces carefully cut and fitted together. Once the plate or plates had been cut to the required outline and the surface engraved, the completed brass was set and bedded in pitch into a stone slab – often Purbeck marble – and held down with brass rivets. Sometimes areas of the surface of the latten were removed and inlays of lead or enamel inset to enhance the design (though little of this now remains). The stone slabs were then placed on a tomb-chest or, more commonly, set in the church floor (or, from the mid-fifteenth century, the walls).

Medieval brasses can be found in most counties, but the highest concentrations are in eastern England, the south-east and the Midlands – with Norfolk having more examples than any other county. At first their style was largely influenced by the work of the alabaster craftsmen, but by the middle of the fifteenth century both their size and quality began to decline. In the early part of the sixteenth century a large number were laid down, often small and rather crudely executed, and by the middle of the seventeenth century the use of figure brasses as memorials died out. Apart from figures shown under canopies, which were imitations of effigial carving, the brass engravers introduced more modest memorials depicting chalices with inscribed tablets, as at Colney and Burlingham St Edmund, Norfolk, hearts as at Trunch, Norfolk, and floriated crosses as at Cassington in Oxfordshire (sometimes with a small figure incorporated at the base or the centre of the cross) or with the deceased standing on a cusped bracket on a raised shaft, as at Bray, Berkshire and Cotterstock, Northamptonshire.

The chief centre for the manufacture of these brasses was London, but it appears that there were also workshops in several of the major medieval cities, such as Norwich, Bristol and York. It is evident that brasses were often commissioned during the lifetime of the person to be commemorated, because in some instances the date of death was left blank and never subsequently filled in.

Brasses were at first confined to the wealthier classes, and all the early ones are of knights; the earliest brass in England is the one commemorating Sir John Daubernoun (1277) at Stoke D'Abernon in Surrey. Brasses depicting knights in armour continued until the sixteenth century and so form a most complete history of armour. Notable examples are to be found at Trumpington, Cambridgeshire (1289), Acton, Suffolk (1302), Pebmarsh, Essex (1323), Cobham, Kent (1365), Drayton Beauchamp, Buckinghamshire (1368 and 1375), Spilsby, Lincolnshire (1410) and Middle Claydon, Buckinghamshire (1542). Priests, at first in Mass vestments, appeared during the fourteenth century (Horsmonden in Kent, Crondall in Hampshire, Edlesborough in Buckinghamshire and Shottesbroke in Berkshire); those in copes are generally from the late fourteenth or early fifteenth centuries (Balsham in Cambridgeshire and Watton-at-Stone in Hertfordshire). The rise of the merchant class by the fifteenth century is clearly indicated by the increasing proportion of brasses memorializing its members; these often carry some form of identification – vintners standing on wine casks, or wool merchants with woolsacks at their feet. In some instances merchants' marks were incorporated in the composition, often in the form of a small shield. The ladies of the wealthier classes are also well represented, those at Trotton in West Sussex, Digswell in Hertfordshire and Isleham in Cambridgeshire being outstanding, and such brasses provide an excellent record of women's fashions (ladies' clothing, and particularly head-dresses, can be an aid to dating brasses). Especially during the fifteenth and sixteenth centuries, many brass memorials show children, often as miniaturized adults, below or behind their parents.

The deep obsession with death that occurred between the mid-fifteenth century and the early sixteenth century, which we have seen reflected in stone monuments, is also reflected in some of the brasses laid down in this period. They show the dead person either in shrouds as at Loddon and Cley next the Sea, Norfolk, or as a skeleton or an emaciated body in a funeral shroud tied top and bottom – as, for example, in the memorials to John Hampton at Minchinhampton, Gloucestershire. Even more macabre, the body is sometimes shown being devoured by worms, as on the brass to Ralph Hamsterley at Oddington, Oxfordshire.

Because of the high cost of the raw material, brasses were quite often re-engraved on the reverse side. These are known as palimpsests (a term originally referring to reused parchment manuscripts). There are several possible reasons for reworking the material – an error might have been made in a first attempt, for instance – but it is more likely that an earlier brass, or part of a brass, was appropriated from another memorial and set in a new slab. This could happen centuries later.

Not all brasses were made in England, and Flemish brasses, famed outside their country of origin, found their way to England – especially to the eastern counties, which had sea links with the Low Countries. Unlike most English brasses, which depicted the outline of the deceased, suitably engraved, Flemish brasses consisted of a rectangular plate engraved all over, showing the deceased surrounded by attractive, decorative patterns.

A magnificent brass is a great treasure for any church, but there are a few churches which have wonderful collections; Cobham in Kent, has no less than nineteen, many with fine canopies, commemorating members of the Cobham family and the priests who staffed the collegiate church. The chancel floor, which is covered with brasses, is a most splendid sight, the finest display of such memorials not only in this country but in the world. Northleach in Gloucestershire, which was one of the major centres of the medieval woollen trade, also has a fine collection, mostly depicting wool-merchants. The sanctuary floor of the medieval church at Digswell, Hertfordshire, is also covered with many fine brasses, the most outstanding being the memorial of 1415 to John Peryent and his wife.

Ledger Stones

When the art and use of monumental brasses declined in the first half of the seventeenth century, massive floor slabs (known as ledger stones), carved by a newly appeared school of heraldic sculptors, replaced them. Many different materials were employed; carboniferous limestone, a bluish-grey stone from Belgium known as black 'marble', was a popular choice, but stones such as limestone, sandstone, slate and granite were all used where they were locally available. These stones – incised (some quite deeply) with a coat-of-arms and a crest at the head of the slab and bold epitaphs below – were let into the floor of the church so they would not impede those walking on them. They are a study in themselves (many carry marvellous inscriptions) and should not be overlooked. They are to be seen in many churches throughout the country especially in eastern England and the south-east.

In the south-east, close to the Wealden iron industry, iron slabs were used instead of ledger stones. Because of their weight it was not possible to transport them any great distance, and so their use remained confined to the areas of manufacture. In Kent they are usually found singly – a fine example is that to John Bottinge (1622) at Cowden – but across the border in East Sussex, the churches have many more. The largest number is at Wadhurst, which has no less than 31 ranging in date from 1625 to 1771.

A feature of many of these slabs is that the lettering of the text filled out each line completely, even if the line-ending fell in the middle of a name or word. Because they were cast in reverse the letters are sometimes to be found back to front. Not all these slabs carry inscriptions; some carry just the initials and date, while others (for instance one at Rotherfield) simply have a raised cross with no lettering. Most of these iron slabs date from seventeenth and eighteenth centuries, but at Burwash, East Sussex, there is one dating from the fourteenth century.

Achievements

Occasionally to be found in churches are 'achievements'. These are the shield, helm, gauntlets, crest, spurs, tabard and other accoutrements placed on the coffin at a knight's funeral, deposited in the church and suspended above his tomb as a symbol of respect. The helms, swords and gauntlets were often specially made, because genuine armour was too expensive to be used for this purpose.

In recent years many of these sets have been stolen, and others have been removed for safety. Some churches still display these examples of the armourer's art, although often no longer in their original positions. At Fletching in East Sussex there are two good sets comprising helms, sword, gloves and spurs of the Nevill family, which date from about 1720. There is also a good representative selection at Aylesford in Kent, with two helms in the chancel and two more, together with swords, in the north chapel. Perhaps the finest – with helm, tabard, gauntlets and badge – is at Compton Wynyates in Warwickshire.

Funeral Hatchments

A fairly common feature on many church walls are hatchments: lozenge-shaped frames filled in with wood or canvas on which are painted armorial bearings, crests and mottos. Sometimes they bear family mottoes, but usually they carry the word *Resurgam* ('I shall rise again') on a black or black and white background. Early hatchments were around two feet square but some later ones are as much as four feet square.

They originated in the Low Countries in the seventeenth century, evolving from the medieval achievements through the transitional stage of the armorial panel. The custom was for these painted boards to be carried in the funeral procession of the holder of the Arms, before being displayed at the family's house during the period of mourning and then transferred to the church. They were popular throughout the seventeenth and eighteenth centuries and continued into the first half of the nineteenth century. Very occasionally their use continued into this century – one of the most recent (at Orsett, Essex,) dates from 1927.

The heraldic description of the coat of arms on a hatchment are couched in terms of the viewpoint of someone *holding* a shield. The dexter side, which refers to the male member of a married couple, is the holder's right-hand side (or the viewer's left-hand side), the sinister side, which refers to the woman, is the holder's right (or the viewer's left). The background of a hatchment is significant in that it indicates the sex and marital status of the deceased. The rules are very simple (177). If the background is all black, then a widower, widow, bachelor or spinster is commemorated; in the cases of a widower or a widow, the shield carrying the arms is divided into two, with the dexter side showing the husband's and the sinister side the wife's arms (the arms of a bachelor or spinster are not divided). The shield bearing the arms of a spinster or widow is lozenge-shaped. When the background is half black and half white, then the deceased was married. If the husband died first, the dexter side is black and the sinister side white; if the wife dies first, then this is reversed. If the wife is an heiress, her paternal arms are shown in pretence (on a small shield in the centre of her husband's).

Hatchments are pleasing in that they evoke some of the human element associated with a church's history. In some cases they display excellent heraldic painting, but unfortunately many are hidden away and hard to see clearly. Although some are being cleaned and restored many hatchments of heraldic and genealogical importance are still neglected.

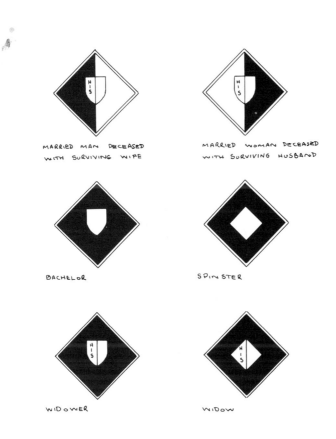

177 Hatchments

Maiden's Garlands

An old and rather quaint custom used to be observed at the funeral of an unmarried woman of unblemished character who was born, baptized and died within the parish. A garland of real or imitation flowers was placed upon the coffin, or carried by two young virgins, together with the gloves or a handkerchief of the deceased; afterwards they were hung above her empty seat in the church. The gloves or handkerchief represented a challenge to anyone who might wish to dispute the worthiness of the deceased. There are various theories about how this practice originated, and it is generally thought to have some connection with the legends of virgin saints, so prevalent in medieval times. The custom started before the Reformation and continued in a few churches until this century.

These garlands, made of a rush or wooden frame covered with ribbons and flowers, are rare today, though they are still found in a few churches. There are a number at Minsterley in Shropshire; dating from between 1726 and 1794 they hang from the west gallery, some still retaining their gloves. Also in Shropshire, at Astley Abbots, there is another garland (also with a pair of gloves) dated 1707. Ashford in the Water, Derbyshire, has four garlands (until 1936 there were five) hanging in the church, each one carefully preserved under a perspex dustcover; a recent copy is also displayed in the church for visitors to inspect. The church that contains the finest collection is Abbotts Ann, Hampshire, where some forty or so still hang – the earliest dated 1740 and the latest from the 1950s. Some still retain their gloves. The earliest surviving maiden's garland is probably the one at Walsham le Willows, Suffolk, which dates from 1685.

11 Miscellanea

In many of our village churches there are items which do not fit
into any of the foregoing chapters. Many are of a civil rather than
religious nature, for the medieval church was not only the spiritual
focus of the village but also the centre of village life and often the
only substantial building in the village. It was natural, therefore,
for these objects to be kept at the church. Unfortunately, many
objects have been discarded as they fell into disuse, and so have
been lost for ever.

Chests

During the Middle Ages the parish chest was an important item of
church furniture that housed the churchwardens' accounts and the
vestments used in the church services and processions. In addition,
it was where the tithe books and parishioners' wills were also kept.
These valuables must have been very safe, considering the number
of locks and bolts that were attached – usually three or more (that
at Stonham Aspal in Suffolk has fourteen hasps for its locks: seven
for each of its two lids). The keys were distributed among the priest
and his churchwardens, so all of them had to be present when the
chest was opened.

The earliest of these chests date from the twelfth century and are
of extraordinarily primitive construction. Known as 'dug-outs'
they are large logs, roughly squared, with the top sliced off to form
a lid and the remaining part hollowed out. They are usually bound
with iron and provided with three or more padlocks. Surprisingly,
there are a number still to be found. There are several in
Warwickshire – among them those at Curdworth (some ten feet

long) and Shustoke (nine feet long and said to weigh half a ton). Norfolk has a very ancient one at South Lopham (178) that some authorities believe could well date from the 1100s. Essex has four- teen examples, perhaps the most notable being at Messing: a partic- ularly long example with the lid in two sections. In contrast to this, the one at Langham – the oldest in the county and one of the oldest in the country – measures 4'7" x 1'6" x 1'3", but the cavity is only 13" x 7" x 6". It is thought that this chest was probably made in obedience to the decree of Innocent III of 1166, under which money raised was used for the projected conquest of Jerusalem.

178   Dug-out chest at South Lopham, Norfolk

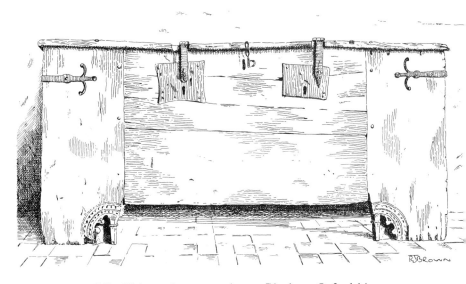

179   Thirteenth-century chest at Bloxham, Oxfordshire

Thirteenth-century chests have two features peculiar to the period. One is that they are built on very broad uprights, or stiles, at the front and back, which extend beyond the body of the chest to form legs and are sometimes shaped or even carved, as at Bloxham, Oxfordshire (179). The other is the working of the lid on a pin or pivot hinge. The stiles are unmistakable. They are formed of slabs of oak – usually cleft and not sawn – into which the front, back and ends of the chest are mortised; the front and back boards are often single pieces of timber. Roundels in the form of chip-carving adorn many chests of this period, like those at Earl Stonham in Suffolk and Felpham in West Sussex. Early English arcading, such as that on the chests at Climping in West Sussex and Hindringham in Norfolk, was another form of ornamentation.

In the fourteenth century the chests were made of thick oak planks clamped and bound together with ironwork. In many cases this was for strength, though in some (like the one from Icklingham All Saints in Suffolk – now in nearby St James – and that at Church Brampton in Northamptonshire) it was ornamental and took the form of elaborate scrollwork.

Some fourteenth-century chests have elaborately carved fronts. The stiles are divided horizontally into panels filled with carvings (dragons and grotesque figures were popular) and the central section filled with tracery. Most of the finest specimens appear to be Flemish work; the chests at Brancepeth in Durham, Chevington in Suffolk and Hacconby in Lincolnshire are all good examples of this. The fine fifteenth-century chest at Brailes, Warwickshire, has distinct traces about it of the Flemish chests of the previous century but the elaborate foliated tracery and the Tudor roses leave no doubt that it is Perpendicular.

Chests of sixteenth- and seventeenth-century date are also to be found. Unlike earlier examples, which rarely carried a date, initials or inscriptions, these later ones are often dated; they are fairly common, and those at Combs in Suffolk (1599), Chelmorton in Derbyshire (1630), Flintham in Nottinghamshire (1663) and Fillongley in Warwickshire (1729) are all typical. In most cases these chests are plainly panelled, but at Rushbrooke, Suffolk, there is a very ornate Stuart chest with the front, ends and the inside of the lid covered with drawings of figures of the period and with patterned borders containing hounds and the crests of the local Jermyn family.

The vast majority of chests were made from oak, but elm (Eckington and Cleeve Prior, Worcestershire), sycamore (Gestingthorpe, Essex) and cypress (Cheveley, Cambridgeshire) were all used. Not all chests were wooden, though; in the Weald of Kent and Sussex – famous for its iron-working in the fifteenth and sixteenth centuries – some were made of iron. An example, still banded with iron strips, can be found at Seal, Kent.

Small money slots are to be found in the lids of many chests. It is often asserted that these were for Peter's Pence, but this seems to be unlikely, for the collectors of this Roman due were specially appointed officials who gathered the money from the different deaneries on a regular basis and on a certain date. It seems more likely that these pre-Reformation money slots were either for contributions to some general parochial fund or, if the chests originally belonged to a guild, for the monthly, quarterly or other payments required from each of its members. It must also be remembered that many of the slots may have been made long after the chest was built; in these cases it may have been a cheap way of complying with the sixteenth-century orders to provide a 'Poor Man's Box'.

Alms Boxes

From earliest times alms-giving has always been considered a Christian virtue, and it has always been encouraged at churches. Before the Reformation, when there was no public responsibility for poverty, it was also considered an individual's Christian duty. Pre-Reformation alms boxes still survive and are generally made from roughly hollowed tree-trunks, with iron bands to strengthen them. The ingenuity in making the contents of these boxes safe can be observed at Loddon, Norfolk (180). At Bedale in North Yorkshire the box is secured by three padlocks, while the one at Blyth in Nottinghamshire, is bound with iron and secured to the wall by an iron band. In Suffolk, the box at Kedington is let into the floor of the nave aisle, and that at Parham, a round tub, is chained to the Stuart altar rails. The alms box at Steeple Bumpstead, Essex, dates from around 1500. The lower part is shaped into an octagonal shaft with roughly traceried sides, a chamfered base and a moulded and battlemented capital supporting a plain iron-bound box; the whole

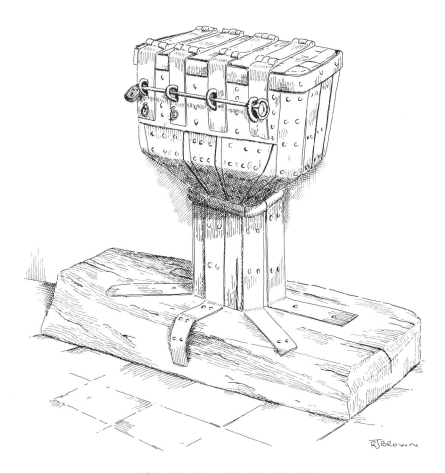

180   Alms box at Loddon, Norfolk

thing is apparently carved out of a solid log, and the lower end is embedded in the floor. Perhaps the best pre-Reformation alms box (dated 1473) is the one at Blythburgh in Suffolk (181), which is designed to stand against a wall; in plan it is a half-octagon, with the sides decorated with very simple but beautiful tracery.

After the Dissolution of the Monasteries caused an abrupt halt to the relief normally afforded to the poor, some other means of relief became a pressing necessity, and in the reigns of Edward VI, and Elizabeth I parishioners were enjoined to provide alms. Although old boxes continued to be used, solid, well-padlocked new boxes were generally provided. A dated Elizabethan alms box remains at Hargrave, Northamptonshire. Seventeenth-century boxes (182) are

181   Alms box at Blythburgh, Suffolk

182   Poor man's box at Watton, Norfolk

183   Alms box at Giggleswick, North Yorkshire

fairly common and many are dated: Stoke Hammond in Buckinghamshire (1618), Rewe in Devon (1631), Monksilver in Somerset (1634) and Watton in Norfolk (1639). Others, like the one at Giggleswick in North Yorkshire (183), dated 1684, bear the words 'Remember the Poor'. Sometimes they incorporate figures of beggars (Watton, Norfolk), while at Pinhoe in Devon there is a fine figure of a well-dressed man – presumably the parish beadle – carrying a book inscribed 'Ye poor man of Pinhoe, 1700'. Tunworth in Hampshire has a unique box on which two sides have carved human faces with open lips serving as money slots (one of them puts out its tongue when money is inserted). Two unusual ones are to be found at Witley in Surrey and St Teath in Cornwall; the one at Witley is made of iron with enamel decoration, the one at St Teath has painted figures.

Collecting Boxes

It is not known when collecting boxes or shoes, alms dishes or basins first came into use for collecting the alms of the faithful. In the Church of England's first Reformed Prayer Book of 1549 no collection of alms by wardens or clerks was contemplated, since the offerings for the poor were to be placed in the fixed poor box. In the second Reformed Prayer Book of 1552 this was repealed – probably because of the disturbances arising as the congregation clustered around the fixed poor box – and it was laid down that the church-wardens, or other persons appointed by them, should collect the offerings and place them in the 'poor mens boxe'. It was not until 1662 that the rubric ordered that the alms were to be collected 'in a decent basin to be provided by the parish for that purpose' by the churchwardens, who were then to bring it to the priest. Latten or pewter dishes or basins were usually provided for this purpose, but at Billingshurst, West Sussex, there is a wooden dish hand-painted on the inside in blue-green, black and gold.

Some churches still possess collecting shoes of wood, often dated. The pair at Blo Norton (184) in Norfolk lined with green velvet, are dated 1910, although the carver obviously made a mistake by carving the six upside-down. An example at Worlingworth, Suffolk, is inscribed 'W.G. Gave ME 1622'. The three shoes at Bressingham in Norfolk, are all dated 1631, and those at Troutbeck, Cumbria, carry the date 1692. Later, wooden collecting ladles were used, like the eighteenth-century one at Warnham, West Sussex (185).

Inscribed Boards and Wall Texts

During the Reformation it was the custom to clear the church of all decorations and adornments, which were thought of as 'Popish', and one can imagine from this the unsightly state of many of our

184 Collecting box at Blo Norton, Norfolk

185 Wooden collection ladle at Warnham, West Sussex

churches as a result. In 1560 Elizabeth I, through her ecclesiastical commissioners, wrote a letter complaining of those who spare no cost on their private houses but in God's house permit 'open decaies and ruins of coverings, walls and wyndowes and leave the place of prayers desolate'. The Queen ordered Archbishop Parker to see 'that tablets of the Commandments be comely set or hung in the east end of the chancel', not only for edification but also 'to give some comely ornament and demonstration that the same was a place of religion and prayer'. As we have seen, the tympanic filling to the chancel arch, which suffered much from the bareness the Queen complained of, was often used to comply with this order usually accompanied by the Royal Arms.

In many cases, however, the tables of Commandments were produced on boards, and in 1561 more explicit instructions were given that the boards were to be fixed on the east wall of the chancel above the communion table. A few of these decalogue boards still survive from the period; the most interesting is the one at Preston, Suffolk, which takes the form of a triptych and was obviously made at the same time as, and to match, the same church's triptych bearing Elizabeth I's Arms, already described. When it is closed various passages from the Scriptures are visible on the outside, and when it is open, the 'Tenne Commaundement' on the central panel are revealed on the inside, flanked on either side by further biblical texts. There are still a few other decalogue boards of Elizabethan date; one lovely example is at Lanteglos-by-Camelford in Cornwall, which has a typical West Country ornamental border, and another at Bengeworth in Gloucestershire, dated 1591.

In 1614 Archbishop Abbot more or less reaffirmed the order of 1560, enlarging it 'to wrighte in fayre text letters the tenn commandements, the beliefe and the Lord's Prayer with some other fruitful and profitable sentences of holye scrypture', and so the inscribing of both boards and walls continued unabated and unchecked through the next two centuries.

By far the most magnificent examples are those at Terrington St Clement, Norfolk, where one board exhibits the Lord's Prayer and the other the Creed. Both are beautifully painted with a typical border design; the one bearing the Lord's Prayer is dated 1635 and inscribed at the top: 'God is near to all that call on him by faithful prayer'. Of similar date are a set engraved on brass at Little

Gidding, Cambridgeshire, where they hang on the east wall of the chancel to form a reredos.

Many churches still contain these boards. Most, however, have been removed from their original position behind the altar (although Westfield, Norfolk, still retains two boards, one on either side of the altar) and hung on a convenient wall of the nave or aisles. Not all text boards were rectangular, for a feature of many of the churches on Romney Marsh is black ovals; Ivychurch has no less than nine, while Snargate (186) has seven.

During the eighteenth century the Commandments were often flanked with figures of Moses and Aaron, and a good number of these survive – many of them taking the form of altarpieces, while others are placed above the chancel arch. There are examples at Hillesden, Buckinghamshire, and Woodrising and Great Snoring, Norfolk. The painting is often rather crude, and was obviously undertaken by local artists.

Judging from the number still to be seen, many thousands of boards containing the Commandments, the Creed and the Lord's

186   Inscribed board at Snargate, Kent

Prayer must have been produced for our churches during the eighteenth century. However, like the paintings of the Royal Arms, their artistic quality steadily declined, until in the late eighteenth and early nineteenth centuries cheap printed sheets were produced showing the Commandments, Moses, Aaron and Joshua. At one time these could be found in many churches, but most have now disappeared; a few survive, for example at Bruisyard in Suffolk (dated 1794) and Rougham in Norfolk.

Testament boards with beautiful lettering were also popular and can be found in many village churches throughout the country. Some of the finest are at Bottisham in Cambridgeshire, dated 1639-1728 and 1762, the last high above the chancel arch. Another fine example is to be found at Little Waldingfield, Suffolk.

We have seen that not all Commandments, Creeds, Lord's Prayers and other texts were written on boards. Many were painted directly on to the surface of the walls – the tympanic filling to the chancel arch was the most popular place, but they are to be found in many other positions too. The walls at Stokesay in Shropshire carry the Commandments, Creed, Lord's Prayer and many texts, allegedly executed during the Commonwealth. The walls at Fincham, Norfolk, are also covered with texts, very well painted with red initial letters.

Instances of 'fruitful and profitable sentences of holye scrypture' – or improving texts, as they are often called – are common enough, especially in churches which are largely unrestored, and the practice of displaying them on church walls was obviously widespread from the time of Elizabeth to the end of the nineteenth century. In many instances appropriate texts are placed in certain parts of the church. Near the porches at Abbey Dore and St Margarets in Herefordshire and Ringsfield in Suffolk is found 'I had rather be a doorkeeper in the house of my God than to dwell in the tents of ungodliness', and again above the door at St Margarets is 'Go and sin no more'. 'Suffer the little children to come unto Me and forbid them not, for of such is the Kingdom of Heaven' is to be found beside the font at Tichborne in Hampshire, and near the altar at St Margarets are the words 'I will wash my hands in innocency O Lord and so will I go to thine altar'. Encouragement to give alms is very common; incised and coloured on the arcade pier above the alms box at Bramford, Suffolk, is 'Remember ye pore the scripture doth record what to them is geven is lent unto the Lord 1591'. At

Ringsfield in Suffolk there are two texts: 'In all thy gifts show a cheerful countenance and dedicate thy tithes with gladness' and 'Give unto the most high according as hee hath inriched thee, and as thou has gotten give with a cheerful eye'.

Not all texts were directed at the congregation. Some were exhortations to the clergy. At St Margarets one finds the words 'Cry aloud, spare not, lift up thy voice like a trumpet and show my people their transgressions and the house of Jacob their sins'. And carved in the back of the pulpit – dated 1635 – at Yaxley, Suffolk are the words 'Necessite is laid upon me yea woe is me if I preach not the Gospel'.

Before leaving the subject of inscribed boards and texts one must mention those boards unique to Cornwall of which Charles I wrote, in a special letter, dated 10 September 1643, 'To the inhabitants of the County of Cornwall' thanking them for their loyal and gallant conduct. They must at one time have been displayed in nearly every Cornish church, but now, sadly, few remain. One of the finest is at St Minver, beautifully written on a board measuring 7' x 4' 8". Another is to be found at Breage.

Another type of inscribed board to be found in our churches is the benefaction or charity board. These boards were commissioned to record and perpetuate the name of the donor, often referring to a bequest of an earlier date. They were common in the eighteenth and nineteenth centuries, and many date from after the Tithe Act of 1836, when odd unaccountable acres of land came to light. In some counties, such as Kent, most churches still display these boards, although they have sometimes been relegated to the base of the tower or to the vestry. They often provide a fascinating insight to local social history, showing how help was provided for the old and infirm, schooling and apprenticeships for poor children, and money for the poor to buy bread or other food.

Dole Cupboards

After the Dissolution, the monasteries were no longer available to feed the poor. Consequently benefactors left money to the church for a dole of bread to be distributed to the needy, on condition that they attended the church service, and dole cupboards were needed to store these loaves. They were shallow but varied considerably in size. Some were open-fronted, like the highly coloured one at Milton Ernest, Bedfordshire; others were open, with the fronts divided by turned balusters, like that of 1717 at Coughton in Warwickshire, which has above a tablet recording the generosity of the donor William Dewes. Yet others were cupboards with doors – either solid, like that dated 1639 at Wiggenhall St Mary the Virgin in Norfolk (187), or pierced for ventilation, as at West Chiltington in West Sussex. If a cupboard could not be afforded, shelves were provided, where the charity loaves were placed before distribution. At Maids Moreton, Buckinghamshire, a bread-basket was provided. A similar custom existed at Goudhurst, Kent, where John Bathurst left an endowment for the provision of loaves of bread; they were placed on his memorial at the back of the church, and the memorial has come to be known as the Bread Tomb.

187   Bread cupboard at Wiggenhall St Mary the Virgin, Norfolk

Stained Glass

Medieval glass once added glorious colour to the churches of England. Sadly, it suffered wholesale destruction by the despoilers of images after the Reformation, which has been described by Alec Clifton-Taylor as 'the greatest calamity that has ever befallen English art'. Nonetheless, it is surprising how much survives – even though much, of course, is fragmentary or restored. What does remain can be classified into four main groups: Romanesque and early, middle and late Gothic. So far as our village churches are concerned, little remains of the first; the finest is without doubt at Brabourne in Kent. A fair amount still remains from the thirteenth century, when *grisaille* glass was introduced: a greyish-white glass ornamented with monochrome decoration in neutral-coloured enamel used like paint and fired into the glass and so arranged that the leadwork itself made patterns, sometimes relieved with lines of colours. Fine examples of this can be seen at Chartham in Kent, Chetwode in Buckinghamshire and Stanton Harcourt in Oxfordshire. In some village churches there are beautiful roundels, as at Madley in Herefordshire and Aldermaston in Berkshire.

By the fourteenth century a wider range of colours became available, many of which had a very rich, deep tone. More realistic figurework appeared, surmounted for the first time by delicately painted canopies derived from the pinnacled stonework of the period, as at Stanford on Avon and Aldwincle St Peter, Northamptonshire.

By the fifteenth century Perpendicular windows gave the glass-painter greater scope, and it was during this period that his art was reaching its zenith. The old standard medieval pot-metals (glass which had been deeply coloured throughout) with their painted detail, were greatly enriched by the introduction of silver stain, which, when painted on to the white glass and fired, produced a variety of yellow stains, from lemon to rich orange. The glass of this period is perhaps the most beautiful, and is best seen in large areas, as at St Neot, Cornwall, with its numerous scenes showing in detail the *Creation* and the lives of Noah, St George and St Neot, as well as the Evangelists, other saints and donors. Other notable windows are at Doddiscombsleigh in Devon (the only complete example of glass showing the *Seven Sacraments*), Winscombe in Somerset and Almondbury in West Yorkshire.

As the size of the windows increased the *Tree of Jesse* became a favourite subject. There are several variations, but the recumbent figure of Jesse usually figures at the base of the window, and from him rises a vine with Kings of Israel together with prophets seated among the branches, signifying the maternal ancestry of Christ; the Virgin Mary and Our Lord are at the top of the tree. Although the finest examples are in our cathedrals and in some town churches, there are excellent examples in village churches; at Leverington in Cambridgeshire, the Jesse Tree has 61 figures, although only one half is original, while the east window at Margaretting in Essex, has a Jesse Tree of 24 figures.

In the main, medieval glass in our churches is fragmentary, or at best restricted to a few windows, so it is remarkable to find a church with a complete series of twenty-seven windows, all of late fifteenth-century date, which has been described as 'the Bible in glass'. That church is Fairford in Gloucestershire – consecrated in 1493 – and its glass is described by F.S. Eden as 'the great surviving example in the British Isles of what, in more or less varied form we might have seen in every church great and small in medieval Europe'. It is all original except for the *Last Judgement* scenes at the top of the west window, which were damaged in a storm in 1703. Why the glass here survived when so much was destroyed can only be explained by the assumption that it was removed during the religious strife of the sixteenth and early seventeenth centuries and remained hidden until after the Restoration. It was temporarily removed again during the war in 1940.

Wall-paintings

Before the Reformation almost every square foot of wall space in the church was covered by paintings – either simply decorative or illustrating legends, miracles and the doctrines of the church – which often served as a means of visual teaching in days when comparatively few people could read or write. Some idea of the way these polychromatic painted interiors looked can be obtained from the Norman church at Copford, Essex, where the restored decorations cover the whole of the original building.

All wall-paintings required was a smooth surface, and this was obtained by coating the walls with a thin layer of plaster. With rare exceptions English wall-paintings were not true frescoes – that is to say, painted on wet plaster and so incorporated into the surface as it dried – but were executed in tempera applied to dry plaster. The pigments available were limited to red and yellow ochre, lime white, lump or charcoal black, and sometimes green from copper. As E.C. Rouse points out in his pocket guide *Wall Paintings*, they were never intended to last indefinitely, and sometimes new paintings were executed on top of the original ones at a later date, as at Stoke Orchard, Gloucestershire.

True frescoes are rare in England. The finest are those that nearly fill the little Norman chancel at Kempley, Gloucestershire. They date from around the second quarter of the twelfth century and cover all the walls above the height of five feet with the Apostles and other figures, including, next to the east window, an imposing bishop. On the tunnel vault is *Christ in Majesty* with the sun, the moon, seven golden candlesticks, the Evangelists' symbols and some of the heavenly hierarchy. The paintings were rediscovered in 1872, when they were given a coat of resinous varnish in the hope it would preserve them. Unfortunately it did the opposite, but in 1955-6 Eve Baker was able to remove the varnish and restore them.

After the Reformation colourful church interiors were no longer approved of, and the Order in Council of 1547 decreed the 'obliteration and destruction of papists and superstitious images, so that the memory of them shall not remain in the churches'. The paintings were subsequently covered with whitewash, in some cases over thirty layers. Many were rediscovered in the nineteenth-century period of restoration, although many hundreds were irretrievably lost during the same period, when much of the surface plaster was torn down so that the masonry beneath could be exposed and neatly pointed. In most instances the wall-paintings that have survived are in a fragmentary condition.

By far the most numerous of the narrative subjects to have survived appears to be the Doom or *Last Judgement*. To the people of the Middle Ages sin was an ever-present reality, and the Doom was placed in the most prominent position in the church – usually above the chancel arch or on the wooden boards of its tympanic filling, so all those entering the church were constantly reminded of the rewards and punishments of the Day of Judgement.

Considerably more than a hundred examples of the Doom are known to exist, and all more or less follow a standard scheme.

Generally, this consisted of a figure of Christ in Majesty, often seated on a rainbow, showing His wounds and pronouncing the destiny of the dead, who rise from their graves to join the living. Below, on the left, angels conduct the righteous to the mansions of Paradise, and on the other side demons drive lost souls into the mouth of Hell.

The earliest Doom painting, at Patcham in East Sussex, dates from around 1180-90. It was discovered in 1880 after the removal of no less than thirty coats of whitewash. A large example of a Doom is to be found at South Leigh, Oxfordshire, where it spreads beyond the wall of the chancel arch on to the adjoining nave walls. The famous Doom at Wenhaston in Suffolk, dating from around 1480, is painted on a boarded tympanum 17' high and 18' across which once filled the chancel arch. The composition is broken up by the three blank spaces covered by the rood and the figures of St Mary and St John, which were attached to the oak boarding. At the Reformation the painting was whitewashed over, and it was not until 1892, when the church was being restored, that it was redis-covered. The tympanum was taken down and thrown out into the churchyard, and it was then that heavy rain washed off the white-wash to reveal the painting beneath. It is now back in the church in a position that allows its detail to be carefully studied.

The restoration of Penn church, Buckinghamshire, in 1938 brought to light another Doom painting on boards. The tympanum was removed, and, while it was lying in the churchyard awaiting removal as rubbish, a workman observed colouring beneath the plaster; after the removal of the plaster a fifteenth-century painting of the Doom was discovered. The work, which is not of particularly high quality, is of two different dates; the first work, of around 1400, predates the roof, and the later is a coarser late fifteenth-century repainting in crude but rather brilliant colours that replaced and simplified the original treatment. The second phase postdates the building of the present roof, which was probably the cause of the changes.

Only three other Doom paintings on boards survive – at Dauntsey in Wiltshire, Mitcheldean in Gloucestershire and St Michael's church in St Albans, Hertfordshire. In many instances the Doom was painted directly on the plastered wall above the chancel arch; good examples are to be found at Combe, North Leigh and South Leigh in Oxfordshire.

188   Chaldon, Surrey (about 1200) with important wall paintings of the ladder of salvation and the heavenward way

Closely related to the Doom is the allegorical painting of *The Ladder of Salvation and the Heavenward Way* on the west wall of the nave at Chaldon, Surrey (188). This remarkable painting of about 1200, in dark reds and yellow ochres, is 17' long and 11' high and covers the whole of the west wall of this small church. *The Ladder of Salvation* is a subject common in the Eastern Church, but this example is unique in England. The painting is divided longitudinally by a stylized band of cloud, with the salvation of souls depicted above and the torments of Hell below. A ladder passes through the middle from below to a bust of Our Lord on a cloud; on the lower part of the ladder souls are struggling or falling, but above the cloudy division their ascent is certain. On the left-hand side of the lower section gigantic demons pitchfork souls into a cauldron, and on the right is the Tree of Knowledge with the serpent hiding among the branches and, beside it, two demons shouldering a beam studded with spikes over which souls are struggling to pass; beneath the beam two demons pitchfork a soul into the flames. On the right-hand side of the upper section a large figure of Christ is harrowing Hell by trampling on Satan and releasing the souls of the righteous. On the left St Michael is weighing souls, and Satan tries to weigh down the scales; three saved souls are being led away by an angel.

After the Doom the most common narrative subjects are the *Crucifixion*, the *Resurrection* and, after the thirteenth century, episodes from the *Life of the Virgin*. There are examples at Witley in Surrey, Chalgrove in Oxfordshire and a superb *Coronation of the Virgin* of about 1300 at Sutton Bingham in Somerset.

Saints were another popular subject. One was St Michael, who usually appears weighing souls on a pair of scales, with demons trying to pull the scales down but never succeeding; examples can be seen at Swalcliffe and South Leigh in Oxfordshire and Bartlow in Cambridgeshire. By far the most popular saint – indeed the most popular single subject for wall-paintings, was St Christopher. He is represented as a huge figure wading across a river, in which there may be fish, ships or even mermaids, bearing the infant Christ on his shoulders; the Child holds an orb (representing the world) surmounted by a cross. A hermit with a lantern and his chapel is also frequently included. The subject was popular in medieval times, but more especially in the fifteenth century. Generally it was painted opposite the main entrance, so that it would be seen immediately by all who entered the church, and those setting out on a journey would be preserved from sudden death and the perils of the road. According to C.E. Keyser in 1883, no less than 186 paintings of this legend appear, in whole or in part, on the walls of our churches. Many fine examples survive in almost perfect condition; one at Little Missenden, Buckinghamshire, was uncovered on the north wall in 1932.

St Christopher was without rival until the fifteenth century, when St George replaced St Edward the Confessor as the patron saint of England. St George, confronting the dragon, captured the imagination of the English public and soon became an appropriate subject for wall-paintings. The earliest example, dating from the twelfth century, is at Hardham in West Sussex, but one of the finest is to be seen at Little Kimble in Buckinghamshire – though, strangely, in this case without the dragon.

The *Seven Deadly Sins* was another popular subject; pride was considered the root of all other sins and was usually represented as a human figure, or as a tree rising from Hell, with scrolls leading to the jaws of six dragons, on which the remaining six sins are shown: anger, envy, sloth, avarice, gluttony and lust. Examples can be seen at Padbury, Buckinghamshire, and Trotton, West Sussex. Trotton has, in addition, an example of the *Seven Corporal Works of Mercy*: feeding the hungry, giving drink to the thirsty, clothing the naked, housing the stranger, visiting the sick, comforting the prisoners and burying the dead.

Another subject, which appears to have been popular, was the *Three Living and the Three Dead*, a morality picture depicting three crowned Kings hunting in the forest being accosted by three skeleton Kings – a grim reminder of the ultimate end. The finest examples are to be found at Pickworth, Lincolnshire, where E.C. Rouse discovered a series of fourteenth century paintings, together with decorative pattern work, in 1947-8. Apart from the *Three Living and the Three Dead* on the west end of the north clerestory wall, there is a Doom above the chancel arch (sadly, partly destroyed when the roof of the nave was lowered) which also extends to part of the adjacent south wall of the nave. On the east end of the north clerestory wall is the *Ascension*, and on the spandrels of the nave arches St Michael weighs a soul, with the Virgin Mary in attendance. Opposite the south door of the nave is a large *St Christopher*. In addition to these figure subjects, there is a great deal of decorative pattern work on the walls.

Although most surviving wall-paintings are fragmentary, there are some whose remains are extensive, although the state of preservation varies considerably. The West Sussex church of Clayton is unique in England for the extent, preservation and date of its wall-paintings. They date from around 1140 and originally must have covered the north, south, east walls, and probably the west wall as well. Of slightly earlier date are those at Hardham, also in West Sussex; these are even more extensive, for all the walls of the nave and chancel are covered. Here (and at Copford in Essex) is one of the very few cases where one can get a sense of what the appearance of a painted twelfth-century church would have been like. Unfortunately, however, much has faded to no more than a confused blur of red and yellow ochre, and, except in one or two places, it is difficult to distinguish the subjects depicted. How much has been lost due to poor preservation since the paintings were discovered in 1866 is impossible to say.

High up on the north wall of the nave at Claverley, Shropshire, is another remarkable series of paintings dating from around 1200. Laid out in a band some fifty feet long and almost five feet high, it illustrates the *Battle of the Virtues and the Vices* by means of armed knights on horseback. The series, which was discovered in 1906, is one of the most important of its date in England. Below the main area, in the spandrels between the arches, are further paintings of angels and saints.

Several churches have post-Reformation paintings. The most distinguished, no doubt, are those at Passenham, Northampton-shire, which show life-size figures of prophets and evangelists standing in shell-headed niches within an architectural framework. These paintings had been whitewashed over and were in a poor condition before being restored by E.C. Rouse in 1957. They are unique in an English church and, together with the beautiful oak furnishings of the same date (1626), make the church worth a visit. Also worth seeing is the small Norman church at Little Braxted, Essex, where every inch of every wall was painted by a rector in the last century to provide hidden messages and symbols to concentrate the minds of his congregation.

Consecration Crosses

As we have seen earlier, twelve consecration crosses were marked on the external walls; internally another twelve were depicted. These were usually painted, so comparatively few survive in a good state of preservation; notable examples can be seen at Edington in Wiltshire, Crosthwaite in Cumbria, Holnest in Dorset, Carleton Rode and Bale in Norfolk, Fairstead in Essex (189), and on the east wall at Bishop's Sutton, Hampshire.

189 Painted consecration cross at Fairstead, Essex

Graffiti, Votive Crosses and Masons' Marks

Graffiti (scribbled drawings or inscriptions) are often considered to be a modern-day phenomenon, but graffiti have been scratched on the stonework of our churches since the early Middle Ages. They survive in a great many churches – on columns, doorways, towers, arches, window sills and rood-loft stairs – yet most churches have none. Some were undoubtedly lost during nineteenth-century restorations, when stonework was vigorously scraped clean; others have been lost beneath successive layers of whitewash.

The subjects scratched on the walls vary greatly. Dates, names (sometimes with dates), inscriptions (often in Latin), poignant messages, heraldic shields, weapons, Christian symbols, buildings, human faces and figures, birds, reptiles, animals and other motifs are all to be found. Many of the early inscriptions must be attributed to the priests, for nearly everyone else was illiterate. Certainly, particularly in the sixteenth century, they recorded their names on their church's walls, and in the days before parish registers references to burials and marriages were occasionally scratched on church walls.

Although many churches have them, a few are rightly renowned for their graffiti. Probably the best known is Ashwell, Hertfordshire, which is famous for its drawing of a large cruciform church with double transept and a central tower and spire. It is often thought to be a representation of old St. Paul's cathedral, but may well be Westminster Abbey, to which Ashwell was appropriated in 1223. In addition to this, another unfinished graffito on one of the piers shows a church with a tower at each end. There are also many inscriptions in Latin in various parts of the church; the one in the tower refers to the Black Death – 'The start of the plague was in 1350 minus one' and '1350 wretched fierce violent the dregs of the populace live to tell the tale. At the end of the second [pestilence] a mighty wind. This year S Maur thunders; in the heavens, 1361'. On St Maura's Day (15 January) 1361 a violent storm struck the church, and part of the nave and tower were damaged. A number of piers to the nave also carry inscriptions in Latin: 'In year of our Lord 1381 five ploughlands of the church were exchanged'; 'At my end is the piece of Heaven'; and a disparaging remark about the mason's craft, 'the corners are not joined correctly. I spit on them', shares a pier with 'Drunkenness destroys whatever wisdom touches'. In another part of the tower a list of the wages and materials devoted to its construction is scratched on the wall.

Nearly all graffiti are found inside churches, but, uniquely, two large figures are incised on the external walls of North Cerney, Gloucestershire: one is a manticore (a fabulous beast with the head and arms of a man and the body of an animal), the other a smaller manticore, or possibly a leopard, with its tail between its legs.

Little scratchings in the form of a cross are sometimes to be found on doorways and elsewhere in the church. These are votive crosses made as evidence of a vow. In pre-Reformation England marriages were solemnized in the porch rather than at the altar, and in recognition of their vows the couple would scratch a cross on the wall. Others were also scratched by crusaders or people about to make a journey, pledging themselves to make an offering to the church on their safe return, or by passing pilgrims. The dressed stone of window or door surrounds offered ample scope for these crosses. Stodmarsh and Kenardington, both in Kent, provide excellent examples on the jambs of the main doors, while on the window sill in the south wall of the chancel at Westhampnett, West Sussex, there are signs reputed to have been made by pilgrims.

Far more common than votive crosses, are mason's marks. There are two kinds of these: one indicating the position in which a stone was to be placed, and the other (the so-called bank mark) indicating which individual craftsman cut and shaped a stone. The position mark was frequently used in the construction of intricate features, such as windows filled in with tracery. Bank marks, which often included initials, were cut by the craftsmen who shaped the stones on a bench (or bank) and were used to monitor the quality of workmanship (this seems to have applied to journeyman masons whose skills were unknown to the master-mason). Masons' marks are often encountered, and notable examples appear at Rettendon and High Easter in Essex and at Northleach in Gloucestershire.

Acoustic Jars

In order to add resonance to the voices of the priest and choir, earthenware jars were frequently embedded in the church walls to act as amplifiers. They were generally inserted in the chancel walls or, less often, in the walls of the nave. A few still survive, as at

Lyddington in Rutland, Denford in Northamptonshire and Tarrant Rushton in Dorset.

Wafer Ovens

A rarity now in our churches is the wafer oven, constructed to make the wafers for Mass. It must at one time have been a common feature, but many probably disappeared during restoration in the nineteenth century. Examples still survive in a few churches: Smarden, Kent, has one in the chancel; Mundham, Norfolk, has one in the tower.

Musical Instruments

There are records dating from the tenth century indicating the use of organs in churches – although it seems that originally the term 'organ' was applied to almost every kind of musical instrument used in a church. Before the Reformation most churches, even small ones, would have had an organ situated on the rood-loft. These were very different to the large structures now in use and very much smaller, comprising a collection of pipes supplied with wind by means of a bellows at the back that was worked by an attendant and not the player. By the fifteenth century these instruments were in common use. However, in 1562, and again in 1644, such was the Puritans' objection to such things that it was ordered that 'all organs and the frames and the cases in which they stand in all churches and chapels shall be taken away and utterly defaced and none other hereafter set up in their place'. So widespread was the destruction that only one pre-Reformation organ-case is thought to survive in Britain (at Old Radnor, Powys, in Wales).

With the Restoration, many restrictions were lifted, including those on organs, and for the next fifty years some of the finest of our organs were built. Even so, the vast majority of our churches remained without one. Even in London, only twelve of the fifty-three churches built by Wren had an organ installed at the time they were built.

Throughout the seventeenth and eighteenth centuries, and even during much of the nineteenth, the average English village church could not afford an organ and would, it seems, have managed perfectly well without one. Instead, village orchestras supplied the music in most country churches, and were an important feature not only of church but also of village life. These orchestras were housed in the west gallery. Such galleries were not always very large, and at Trentishoe in Devon the double-bass needed more space than the narrow gallery provided so a hole was cut in the parapet to accommodate the bow.

The enthusiastic but not always harmonious sounds usually came from the bassoon (a reed instrument), the hautboy (the predecessor of the modern oboe), the flageolet (a small flute), the vamp-horn (a sort of giant megaphone into which the conductor or leader of the orchestra hummed to give body and harmony to the other instruments), the serpent (a bass wind instrument) and the ophicleide (a large bass trumpet). In addition there were other instruments including clarinets, bass fiddles, piccolos, flutes and violoncellos.

Where these old instruments survive they have been greatly treasured and are usually housed in a glass case. The rarest of these instruments is the serpent; Upper Beeding in West Sussex, Barking in Suffolk and Owslebury in Hampshire all have examples. Shermanbury, West Sussex, has recorders and violoncello; Old Alresford in Hampshire and Rumburgh in Suffolk, each has a clarinet; Great Milton, Oxfordshire, has a key bugle and an ophicleide. Ridlington in Rutland, still keeps its complete set of instruments (violin, flute, two clarinets and bassoon), and Yateley in Hampshire has a bassoon, piccolo and four clarinets. At Giggleswick in North Yorkshire there is a complete set of hautboy, clarinet, bass fiddle and set of drums, while at Lythe in the same county there is a pair of ophicleides. The bassoon, the most popular of Georgian church instruments, can be found at Buxted in East Sussex, Church Broughton in Derbyshire and Feering in Essex (made by W. Milhouse of Newark in 1770). The vamp-horn still survives in surprising numbers; there are examples at East Leake in Nottinghamshire (some 7'9" long), Braybrooke and Harrington in Northamptonshire, Charing in Kent (claimed to be the only one in the country that still has its wooden mouthpiece) and Willoughton in Lincolnshire. The vamp-horn at Ashhurst in West Sussex is made of sheet iron and painted green with yellow lettering: 'Praise Him upon ye strings and Pipe, 1770. Palmer fecit'. In some areas church orchestras were still performing well into the second half of the nineteenth century; at Redmire, North Yorkshire, an orchestra comprising fiddles, cornets, woodwind and euphonium was still performing in 1879.

In addition to the instruments used by the orchestra, the conductor of the choir used a pitch-pipe: a wooden pipe, blown by mouth, with a stopper that could be moved in and out to regulate the note. This was used from the seventeenth century to the first half of the nineteenth century to give the pitch of the notes for vocal music. Very few now remain; they are to be found at Ditchling in East Sussex, Matterdale in Cumbria, Morton Morrell in Warwickshire and Warblington and Crondall in Hampshire (the last dated 1783).

In the nineteenth century barrel organs – played by turning a handle, which in turn rotated a barrel, or cylinder, preset to play several tunes – began to be introduced in many rural churches that did not have enough musicians to form an orchestra. Now these delightful curiosities are few and far between, and those in full working order are even rarer. One excellent example is to be found in the beautifully kept village church at Woodrising, Norfolk; built in 1826 by Flight & Robson, it was restored in 1957, and one of its three barrels was replaced in 1960. Its repertoire of thirty hymns is now reserved for special occasions. At Wissington, Suffolk, there is another, recently repaired and still played at the occasional service. Other barrel organs still capable of playing a few hymns are at Bressingham in Norfolk, Shelland in Suffolk (made by Bryceson around 1820), Farnham in North Yorkshire (made in 1831) and Piddinghoe in East Sussex.

In Victorian times great changes took place in the musical arrangement of British churches; the choir, which had sung from the west gallery for some three hundred years, was moved to the chancel, and in many cases the organ moved with it. During the restorations of the nineteenth century many organs were introduced, and now, sadly, some of our village churches contain organs that are musically too large for their needs and often impossible to site pleasingly. Church interiors are often spoilt by an obtrusive organ – as at Ingham, Norfolk, where the organ fills two whole bays of an aisle.

Harmoniums, invented in 1840, are also to be found in some churches. They generally come from America – like that at Ford, West Sussex, which dates from around 1870 and was designed by the Chicago Cottage Organ Company.

Lighting

Generally, there was little or no artificial lighting in early medieval churches, apart from lights burnt for devotional purposes (which would have been few and far between). Cresset stones were sometimes provided near doorways and other vantage points for general lighting purposes. These were small stone slabs with cup-like depressions (some had only one, others had twelve, like that at Weston, North Yorkshire) in their upper surface that were filled with grease or oil and a floating wick. Today these stones are extremely rare, because in the past they were often discarded by those ignorant of their use.

The earliest form of general lighting would have been tapers or rushlights secured or hung in holders. The holders are now rare but an early example is at Warnham, West Sussex (190). By the

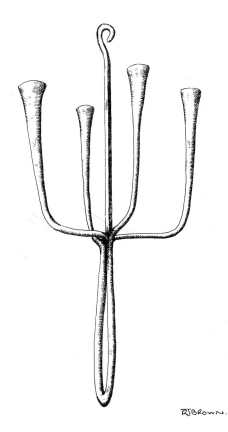

RJBROWN.

190   Rushholder at Warnham, West Sussex

thirteenth century candles were being used, either in iron brackets fixed to the wall or on prickets (spikes). These are now extremely rare, but two ornamental examples remain at Rowlstone, Herefordshire (191), with prickets and decorated with cocks; in one the tails of the cocks are up and in the other they are down. Another less decorative example is to be found at Long Stratton, Norfolk.

Coronas were also used though few of them remain today. These consisted of a circlet of wood or iron bearing a number of candles – from twelve to twenty – around its rim. These were often suspended before the rood and were frequently known as 'rowells' or 'roelles', especially in East Anglia. At the east end of the nave pulleys remain in the roof of some churches (for example Chediston, Ubbeston and Fressingfield in Suffolk) which were doubtless used for raising or lowering the rowell. Coronas were probably also used for general lighting; some (as at Monksilver, Somerset) would be a single circlet, others would consist of two or three circlets placed one above the other and diminishing in size.

Coronas were forerunners of the chandeliers that were so popular in the seventeenth and eighteenth centuries. The latter usually have two or three tiers of branched candlesticks on gracefully curved stems that spring from a central shaft with globe and pendant and top finial. The globe often bears the date and the name of the donor. The examples to be found throughout the country

191   Candle bracket at Rowlstone, Herefordshire

always enhance the appearance of the church. Nearly all are made of brass, but at Great Witcombe in Gloucestershire there is an eighteenth-century specimen made of iron.

Oil lamps generally replaced candles and are still in use in some churches – Layer Marney in Essex and Barton Turf in Norfolk, for instance. They are often quite decorative, made of brass, silver-gilt or copper and often have coloured glass shields. Many were removed when gas or electric lighting was installed, but some have been adapted for electricity. In the churches where they have survived they are now generally appreciated and preserved, even if no longer used.

Burial Furniture

It was not until the eighteenth century that coffin burials became general. Previously – and, for the poor, until the end of the eighteenth century – it had been customary for the corpse (wrapped in a shroud tied at head and foot) to be carried to the church in the parish coffin or shell, from which it was then removed to be laid in the grave and covered with earth. The shroud was usually of wool, since – for the encouragement of woollen manufacture – it was laid down by Parliament that after 25 March 1666 no corpse 'shall be buried in any shirt, shift, sheet or shroud or anything whatever made or mingled with flax, hemp, silk, hair, gold or silver or in any stuff other than what is made of sheep's wool only'. In an attempt to enforce this Act an amendment was made in 1679 requiring a properly attested certificate to be produced before any funeral took place, and imposing a penalty of five pounds on the estate of every person not buried in a woollen shroud. In the cases of those rich enough to be buried in linen, the fine imposed was shared '50 shillings to the poore and 50 shillings pd to the informer'. Many churches still retain their Woollen Registers. One of 200 certificates still remaining in the church at Hawkshead, Cumbria is on display. A copy of the 'Act for bury in woollen' is in the church safe at Gosbeck, Suffolk. The Act was not rigidly enforced after 1696, but it was not formally repealed until 1814.

A few churches still retain some items of parish burial furniture. One of the most common is the bier carried by two bearers and used to carry the parish coffin to the place of burial. It was customary for every parish to possess one, and so it is not surprising that so many have survived. Although a few are claimed to be of pre-Reformation date – for example those at Ridgewell in Essex and Dummer in Hampshire – the majority date from the seventeenth or eighteenth centuries. A few are dated; the one at Old Buckenham, Norfolk, carries a date 1666, though others are somewhat later: Purse Caundle in Dorset (1733), Methwold in Norfolk (1737), Bramley in Hampshire (1746) and Trent in Dorset (1757). Most biers have drop or extending handles, but at Kempstone in Norfolk an (undated) bier has cross bearers at each end. At Lastingham, North Yorkshire, the handles have circular holes bored in them, thought to have held a support for the pall (the cloth spread over the coffin). The finest of all, at South Wootton in Norfolk, is dated 1611; it is braced and has drop handles, but what makes it unique is the light, semi-circular removable herse on the top for supporting the pall. Unlike most, which are generally left without any form of applied decoration, the bier at South Wootton is painted with texts inscribed on it. In some of the later examples the handles were dispensed with, and the bier was mounted on a set of four wheels. Good examples can be seen at Bressingham, Norfolk, and at Wittersham, Kent. A rare example of a child's bier can be seen at Mendlesham, Suffolk.

Parish coffins have rarely survived, but a few coffin-stools, on which the coffin was placed during the service, are still extant. They date from the seventeenth and eighteenth centuries and a few are dated, like those at Nunton (1736) and Alderbury (1778), both in Wiltshire. They usually have four legs but the pair at Beddingham, East Sussex, have three. A coffin-trestle can be seen at Chenies, Buckinghamshire.

Occasionally to be found, generally in some inconspicuous place in the church, are portable wooden graveside shelters looking rather like small sentry boxes, known as hudes or hudds. They were used mainly at the graveside in the eighteenth and early part of the nineteenth centuries to provide protection from the elements for the priest officiating at the committal. Some of them are on wheels and a few (like that at Walpole St Peter, Norfolk) were carried on poles thrust through brackets on the sides, after the fashion of the sedan chair. These shelters were flimsily made with thin framing, to make them light enough to move, and were just over six feet high and two feet or so square (although the one at Dorrington, Lincolnshire, is of heptagonal plan, with two of the sides omitted to form the opening). Most were open-fronted, but the one at Silverton, Devon, has a half-door to give additional protection. Other hudds can be found in the churches of Friskney, Pinchbeck and Quadring, all in Lincolnshire, Maxey in Cambridgeshire, Wingford in Suffolk, Crondall in Hampshire, Brookland and Ivychurch in Kent (192) and Bucklebury in Berkshire.

Banner-stave Lockers

Before the Reformation processions in and around the church formed an important feature of medieval church life. All the parish guilds had their banners, which were carried in processions on festival days and other important occasions. The banners themselves would be placed in the guild's chapel, but the staves on which they were carried would be housed in specially constructed cupboards. These cupboards were tall, narrow niches, which were usually located in the wall at the west end of the nave or in the wall of the western tower (because these banners were the responsibility of the congregation, and not the priest). They were usually around seven feet high (but could be up to twelve feet), eighteen inches wide and about twelve inches deep. They were rebated and fitted for doors, and many surviving examples retain their hinge hooks (though few still have their original oak doors). These cupboards are a common feature of village churches in east Norfolk and east Suffolk but only one – that at Barnby in Suffolk (193) – retains its original pierced door. Although mainly to be found in East Anglia these recesses also survive elsewhere; Stelling in Kent and Broadwell in Oxfordshire have typical examples.

A similar cupboard is to be found in the east wall of the chancel at Castle Rising, Norfolk. It is eight feet high and has an ogee-arched head adorned with crockets and finials; its position and ornamentation suggest that it was used to store the processional cross.

192   Hudd at Ivychurch, Kent

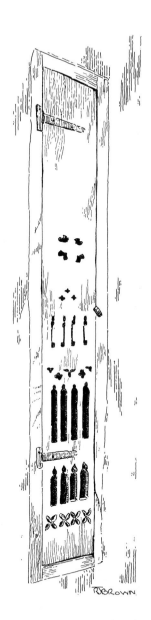

193   Banner-stave locker at Barnby, Suffolk

Sexton's Wheels

A rare survival, only to be found at Yaxley in Suffolk and at the nearby church at Long Stratton in Norfolk, is the sexton's wheel, which was used to determine the beginning of voluntary fasting days in honour of the Virgin Mary. In the fourteenth and fifteenth centuries, when veneration of the Blessed Virgin was at its height, penitents would sometimes be ordered (or would choose) to observe the Lady Fast. They would live on bread and water either for one whole year, or on one day each week for seven years. If they chose the former they would come to the sexton in order to determine which day the fasting was to begin. Six feast days in the church's calendar are set aside for the honour of Our Lady – 2 February (Purification), 25 March (Annunciation), 2 July (Visitation), 15 August (Assumption), 8 September (Birth), and 8 December (Immaculate Conception) – and six long threads were tied to the rim of the sexton's wheel, each one identifying a particular feast. It is not clear exactly how the wheel was operated, for the numerous accounts available are not only difficult to understand but differ from one another. In Thomas Kirchmeyer's poem, written in 1559, he describes how the sexton would spin the wheel and the penitent would grasp the thread at random in order to decide on which day the feasting was to commence.

Armour

From the time of Edward II each parish was compelled to furnish and equip soldiers for home or overseas service if called upon by the sovereign. In Elizabethan times the armour was held in the church for safe-keeping (often in the room above the porch, if there was one) in the charge of the churchwardens. Up to a hundred years or so ago a great many churches had such armour and accoutrements, but they have mostly now disappeared. Some items survive, however, in about twenty churches. The finest collection is housed in the chamber above the porch at Mendlesham, Suffolk, which contains armour ranging in date from 1470 to 1600. The chamber itself is lined with heavy oak boards, the door iron-banded and the windows closely boarded.

Fire-hooks and Fire-buckets

When many of the houses and cottages in the village were roofed with thatch, fire was always a constant fear. Before the introduction of fire-engines, attempts to put out these fires were made with primitive appliances. Fire-hooks (metal hooks on long handles) were used to pull burning thatch from roofs, and fire-buckets made of leather were used to fetch and carry water. These appliances were kept in the church, and a few churches still have them. In the porch of the church at Bere Regis, Dorset, there hang two fire-hooks which date from about 1600. Another pair of hooks is to be found at Halford, Warwickshire. A number of fire-buckets once hung in the porch at Haughley, Suffolk, but they have now been moved into the church for safe-keeping.

Dog-tongs and Whips

Now very rare, though once common in village churches (particularly in Wales and Scotland) are dog-tongs. It was customary in country areas for dogs to accompany their masters to church, and, since it was not uncommon for them to become unruly, an 'expellor' of disorderly dogs was appointed. Whips and dog-tongs, to grip the neck of the dogs, were the tools of his trade. It is doubtful if any dog-tongs now exist in an English church, but a set can still be seen at Clynnog Fawr, Caernarvonshire. A dog-whip can be found at Baslow, Derbyshire.

Implements of Correction

Implements of correction, such as stocks (ordered to be set up in every village in 1376) and whipping posts, were sometimes sited near the church and are still to be found in a few villages – in some cases inside the churchyard. There are stocks at Crantock in Cornwall and Marden in Kent (although those at Marden were moved from the market square, in order to preserve them, long after they were last used). A few have even found their way into the church, as at Feock in Cornwall, Chaceley in Gloucestershire and Folkingham in Lincolnshire; at Rock in Worcestershire and St

Kew in Cornwall both stocks and whipping post are in the church. Most stocks were made of timber, although a few were made entirely of stone, like those at Kirkby Malham in North Yorkshire. At Colne in Lancashire the stocks are mounted on wheels so that they could be moved.

Pillories and ducking-stools were also once to be found in church premises (a ducking-stool, last used in 1809, can be seen at Leominster in Herefordshire), but these are now rare. Another rare survival is the finger-stocks at Ashby-de-la-Zouch in Leicestershire, in which the fingers of the offender were trapped: a particularly painful punishment.

Another rarity is the gossip's bridle, used to punish women who were guilty of spreading false information about their neighbours. It consisted of an iron frame which fitted around and over the head and a 'bit' that was so placed as to keep the tongue down and thus prevent the offender from talking. The nose projected through an opening in the iron frame, and the complete frame was padlocked at the back. An example survives at Walton-on-Thames, Surrey.

Bibliography

Addison, W., *Local Styles of the English Parish Church* (Batsford, 1982)

Betjeman, J., *Collins Pocket Guide to English Parish Churches* (Collins, 1968)

Blatch, M., *Parish Churches of England in Colour* (Blandford, 1974)

Bond, F., *Fonts and Font Covers* (Frowde, 1908)

Boyle, N.E., *Old Parish Churches and How to View Them* (Skeffington, 1951)

Bradds, D., *English Country Churches* (Weidenfeld and Nicolson, 1985)

Cautley, H.M., *Suffolk Churches and Their Treasures* (Boydell and Brewer, 1982)

—— *Norfolk Churches* (Boydell and Brewer, 1980)

Chatfield, M., *Churches the Victorians Forgot* (Moorland, 1979)

Child, M., *Discovering Churchyards* (Shire, 1982)

Clarke, B. and Betjeman, J., *English Churches* (Studio Vista 1964)

Clifton-Taylor, A., *English Parish Churches as Works of Art* (Batsford, 1974)

—— *The Pattern of English Building* (Faber & Faber, 1976)

Clucas, P., *England's Churches* (Colour Library Books, 1984)

Cook, G.H., *The English Medieval Parish Church* (Phoenix, 1954)

Cox, J.C., *English Church Fittings and Furniture* (Batsford, 1923)

Cox, J.C. and Ford, C.D., *Parish Churches of England* (Batsford, 1954)

Cox, J.C. and Harvey, A., *English Church Furniture* (Methuen, 1907)

Crossley, F.H., *English Church Monuments* (Batsford, 1921)

Crossley, F.H. and Howard, F.E., *English Church Woodwork* (Batsford, 1947)

Cunnington, P., *How Old is that Church?* (Blandford, 1990)

Dunning, R., *Fifty Somerset Churches* (Somerset Books, 1996)

Green, M., *Hampshire Churches* (1967)

Hayman, R., *Church Misericords and Bench Ends* (Shire, 1989)

Howard, F.E., *Medieval Styles of the English Parish Church* (Batsford, 1936)

Hutton, G. and Smith, E., *English Parish Churches* (Thames and Hudson, 1952)

Jones, L.E., *Enjoying Historic Churches* (Baker, 1964)

—— *Observer's Book of Old English Churches* (Warne, 1969)

—— *What to See in a Country Church* (Phoenix, 1960)

—— *The Beauty of English Churches* (Constable, 1978)

Kemp, B., *English Church Monuments* (Batsford, 1981)

Kersting, A.F. and Vale, E.A., *Portrait of English Churches* (Batsford)

Needham, A., *How to Study an Old Church* (Batsford, 1944)

Nye, T.M., *Parish Church Architecture* (Batsford, 1965)

Pevsner, N., *Buildings of England* series (Penguin, 1951-89)

Platt, C., *Parish Churches of Medieval England* (Secker and Warburg, 1981)

Randall, G., *The English Parish Church* (Batsford, 1982)

—— *Church Furnishings and Decorations in England and Wales* (Batsford 1980)

Richards, R., *Old Cheshire Churches* (Batsford, 1947)

Rouse, E.C., *Medieval Wall Paintings* (Shire, 1991)

Slader, J.M., *The Churches of Devon* (1968)

Verey, D., *Cotswold Churches* (Batsford, 1976)

Vigar, J.E., *Kent Churches* (Sutton, 1995)

Wickham, A.K., *Churches of Somerset* (David & Charles, 1965)

General Index

Place Index

378

Index